"*Writing for the Screen* is perhaps the most powerful book on 'making it' in screenwriting that I've read in years. It is feverishly real, with raw truths and unabashed encouragement."

—Dr. Pieter Aquilia, Head, Screenwriting,
Australian Film Television & Radio School

"An essential book—so accessible, so beautifully written, so encouraging and realistic and specific. It covers all the bases. Anyone contemplating a career as a screenwriter MUST read this book!"

—Dr. Linda Seger, Script Consultant, Seminar Leader,
Author of *Making a Good Script Great*

"This book answers all the hard questions every aspiring writer asks and the rest of the screenwriting manuals avoid. It's astonishing that this essential addition to every screenwriting library hasn't existed before—and a cause for celebration that it finally does now."

—William Rabkin, Author of *Writing the Pilot*,
Professor of Television Writing and Producing at
Long Island University's TV Writers Studio, NY, USA

# PERFORM
## Writing for the Screen

*Writing for the Screen* is a collection of essays and interviews exploring the business of screenwriting. This highly accessible guide to working in film and television includes perspectives from industry insiders on topics such as breaking in; pitching; developing and nurturing business relationships; juggling multiple projects; and more. *Writing for the Screen* is an ideal companion to screenwriting and filmmaking classes, demystifying the industry and the role of the screenwriter with real-world narratives and little-known truths about the business. With insight from working professionals, you'll be armed with the information you need to pursue your career as a screenwriter.

- Contains essays by and interviews with screenwriting consultants, television writers, feature writers, writer-directors of independent film, producers, and professors.
- Offers expert opinions on how to get started, including preparing your elevator pitch, finding mentors, landing an internship, and moving from an internship to the next step in your career.
- Reveals details about taking meetings, what development executives are looking for in a screenwriter, how and when to approach a producer, and how to pitch.
- Explores strategies for doing creative work under pressure, finding your voice, choosing what to write, sticking with a project over the long haul, overcoming discrimination, and reinventing yourself as a writer.
- Illuminates the business of screenwriting in the United States (New York and Los Angeles) as compared to other countries around the globe, including England, Ireland, Peru, France, Australia, and Belgium.

# PERFORM: Succeeding as a Creative Professional

The PERFORM series aims to offer engaging, uplifting, and expert support for up-and-coming artists. The series explores success in the arts, how we define success in artistic professions, and how we can prepare the next generation of artists to achieve their career goals and pay their bills.

The books in this series include practical advice, narratives, and insider secrets from industry professionals. Each book will include essays by and interviews with successful working artists and other professionals who represent, hire, or collaborate with these artists.

Ultimately, the goal of this series is simple: to illuminate how to make a living—and a *life*—as an artist.

**Volumes in the series:**

*Acting for the Stage*, edited by Anna Weinstein and Chris Qualls

*Directing for the Screen*, edited by Anna Weinstein

*Writing for the Screen*, edited by Anna Weinstein

# PERFORM

Succeeding as a Creative Professional

## Writing for the Screen

EDITED BY ANNA WEINSTEIN

Routledge
Taylor & Francis Group

NEW YORK AND LONDON

First published 2017
by Routledge
711 Third Avenue, New York, NY 10017

and by Routledge
2 Park Square, Milton Park, Abingdon, Oxon OX14 4RN

*Routledge is an imprint of the Taylor & Francis Group, an informa business*

© 2017 Taylor & Francis

*Library of Congress Cataloging in Publication Data*
Names: Weinstein, Anna, 1972- editor.Title: Writing for the screen /
edited by Anna Weinstein.
Description: New York : Routledge/ Taylor and Francis Group, 2017. |
Series: Perform | Includes bibliographical references and index.
Identifiers: LCCN 2016033786| ISBN 9781138945111 (hardback) |
ISBN 9781138945128 (pbk.) | ISBN 9781315671574 (e-book)
Subjects: LCSH: Motion picture authorship. | Motion picture
authorship—Vocational guidance.
Classification: LCC PN1996 .W745 2017 | DDC 808.2/3—dc23
LC record available at https://lccn.loc.gov/2016033786

ISBN: 978-1-138-94511-1 (hbk)
ISBN: 978-1-138-94512-8 (pbk)
ISBN: 978-1-315-67157-4 (ebk)

Typeset in Adobe Garamond and Avenir
by Keystroke, Neville Lodge, Tettenhall, Wolverhampton

For my children, Abraham and Gabriel

# CONTENTS

# ACKNOWLEDGMENTS

I owe many thank-yous for this book. First, I am deeply grateful to the contributors who jumped on board to participate. It was a true pleasure to reconnect with old friends, make new friends and colleagues, and spend time with some of the film and television professionals I most admire. They took time out of their busy schedules to share their perspective and expertise, which is among the most generous of gifts. I must also acknowledge the many photographers who graciously allowed us to include their work in this book. Thank you also to Orli Auslander for contributing the extraordinary original illustrations to Chapter 5.

Thank you to my friends, colleagues, and mentors who supported or influenced this project from the outset and onward. University of California Riverside-Palm Desert faculty members Kate Anger, Joshua Malkin, Bill Rabkin, and Deanne Stillman are not only all-round good humans, but they've consistently gone above and beyond more times than I can count. Several additional people came in early to read the proposal for this book and series, as well as early proposals for other projects; their feedback was priceless. Thank you to Trai Cartwright, Lisa Channer, Lee Michael Cohn, Chuck Erven, Sarah Huffman, Jim Jennewein, Kevin Jones, Brian Lipson, and Chad Parsons. Thanks also to Celia Burger, Glenda Freeman, Mark Futterman, Wendy Peterson, Allison Phillips, Cindy Reed, Andrea Stewart, and Carol Whatley for hiring me, inspiring me, or any combination of the two. Thank you to Bobby Mitas and Andy Ziskin for an incredible opportunity. To Jay Paul Deratany, Connie Haneline, Mindy Seidman, Claire Wilson, Jeff Wood, and Hilary Wyss for indulging me more than my fair share of coffee and cocktail time to discuss this project as it unfolded.

To my students at Auburn University, thank you for providing perspective, inspiration, and laughter. To AU's Media Studies faculty members George Plasketes and Hollie Lavenstein, thank you for the support in the early stages of this project.

Two interviews in this book are reprinted from the "Diva Directors" series in Intellect's *Film International*: in the second chapter, "Anne Fontaine: The Art of Discipline and Persistence" and in Chapter 4, "Claudia Llosa: Writing From Personal Experience." I must also thank my past and present editors at *Film International*, Daniel Lindvall and Matthew Sorrento, who often wait long stretches without pressure or complaint.

I am indebted to my editors Emily McCloskey and Stacey Walker at Focal Press | Routledge. They initially saw the possibility in this series and advocated for it from the beginning. Elliana Arons supported the early stages of development, and Meredith Darnell and John Makowski expertly shepherded the manuscripts through development. I am grateful to Helen Evans for her expertise in taking the book through the production process and to Sarah Cheeseman for copyediting. Thank you also to Nicci Leamon, who has been transcribing interviews for years now, to Susan Cochran for her last-minute transcriptions, and to Ande Nichols, Jill Nusbaum, and Geneva Willis for their truly excellent editorial support.

Above all, I am grateful for my family. Thanks to my parents for encouraging me to pursue the arts, and to my siblings for applauding me along the way. Thank you, girl, always. And of course, this book wouldn't exist without my husband's willingness to take this journey with me. Chris Qualls, this has been incredibly fun, but it would be meaningless without you and the kids.

Finally, thanks to my children, who have been so patient these past few years and have also offered unique insight at crucial moments during the making of this book and series. You're my inspiration, boys. I hope you will continue to pursue your dreams with tenacity, enthusiasm, and confidence.

# INTRODUCTION

How can you break in as a writer's assistant? When is it appropriate to give your script to a friend or colleague in the business? What does a producer expect in collaborating with a screenwriter? What is the process of writing independent films as compared to studio films? What does a pitch look like in the room? How can you break into writing for children's television? What is the day-in-the-life of a successful indie writer-director?

Unless you're already working as a screenwriter, chances are, you don't know the answers to these questions. But you will soon enough. After reading about the experiences of dozens of seasoned professionals in this book, you'll have answers to your questions about the business of screenwriting, as well as details and little-known truths that you've never heard before. You'll be challenged to face the reality of the profession of screenwriting and ask yourself tough questions about how hard you're willing to fight for a career in the business.

If you've skimmed the chapter titles of this book, you've likely surmised the cyclical nature of a screenwriting career: We get started on our journey. We keep sticking it out. We succeed. We try to get ahead. We find ourselves beginning again.

This doesn't imply that the cycle begins in your twenties and ends when you've reached a ripe age of wisdom. Sure, that's one way to look at it. But more realistically, the cycle can happen every few months or every few years—or in even shorter time spans. You finish a screenplay; you start a new one. You bomb a meeting; you take another. You have a bad writing day; you try again tomorrow.

Nobody said this career would be easy or fair or profitable—or would even make a lot of sense. Who succeeds and why can be a bit of a mystery. How to make a living in an industry with seemingly closed doors can also be mysterious. Why Oscar-winning writers are rewritten by other Oscar-winning writers? Also mysterious.

Whether you already know a lot about the industry and how it works, or you're just beginning your exploration, you'll find in this book insight that will help to shape your understanding of how a screenwriting career can play out—and exactly how you can take control of your career.

# How to Use This Book

This book is about the *business* of screenwriting. There are other books about *craft* that reinforce the tasks associated with developing your skills and talents. But this book is specifically about the work involved with becoming a working screenwriter.

You don't have to read it cover to cover. It won't benefit you necessarily to read the essays and interviews in order—although there's certainly nothing wrong with that approach. The book is structured so that you can pick and choose what to read when, at the pace that works best for you. Flip through the pages and browse the interviewee introductions and contributor bios. These will give you insight into the personalities, successes, and individual perspectives on what it takes to succeed as a screenwriter.

What is it like to intern as a production assistant (PA)? What is it like to be a working television writer? Or a working feature writer? What is it like to have written one of the most iconic films in movie history?

You'll hear from a range of writers, directors, and producers in this book. You'll read stories about writers who had no intention of going into the business, and writers who worked their way very intentionally from local TV to showrunning.

You'll read about starting as a playwright, and as a secretary, and as a writer's assistant. You'll read about the relevance of mentorship and getting feedback from the masters. You'll read stories of persisting despite depression and hardship. You'll read about overcoming setbacks and balancing multiple projects as a means of self-protection and necessity. You'll learn how independent film can satisfy a deep need to share a story and further a cause. You'll read about the challenges of marginalized groups and how screenwriting can support your efforts to achieve a greater good.

You'll get perspectives from screenwriters in Australia, Peru, France, and Belgium. From writers and producers in New York and Los Angeles. From writers of sitcoms, one-hour dramas, feature films, independent films, documentary films, and films from the 1970s, 1980s, 1990s, and 2000s.

The range of advice, wisdom, and stories you'll read in this book is meant to give you perspective. The essays and interviews are grouped thematically, exploring the overarching ideas of Getting Started, Sticking It Out, Finding Success, Getting Ahead, and Starting Again. But these groupings don't indicate that you'll find a sequential rendering of how-to advice in each chapter. You won't!

Some interviews include topical questions and responses about how to approach specific goals and situations as a screenwriter, and others take a broader exploratory approach, with the interviewees sharing personal narratives or opinions about some of the more intangible aspects of the career. The same is true of the essays. You'll find a range of scope, from direct advice to first-person stories to analytical discussions of genre and the types of stories that sell in the marketplace.

The key is this: Don't look for advice alone. Look for insights. Look for new ways of approaching challenging aspects of the career. Look for information about the realities of the business. Above all else, look for a deeper understanding of how to celebrate the *pursuit of* success as well as the *result of* success.

# CHAPTER 1

# GETTING STARTED

"You want to be a writer? A writer is someone who writes every day, so start writing. You don't have a job? Get one. Any job. Don't sit at home waiting for the magical opportunity."

Shonda Rhimes

**W**riters are used to the blank page—the Herculean task of putting fingers to the keyboard despite the glaring empty screen in front of them. But the task of taking the first steps toward building a career as a writer can often be even more overwhelming than the writing itself, particularly when it's an industry and career track with nebulous rules, apparently involving a move to either Los Angeles or New York.

Where do you begin?

If you want to work as a doctor, you know exactly what you need to do to get started. You can't become a physician without a license to practice medicine, and to get that license, there's schooling involved, as well as passing a series of exams.

These are facts. Rules.

But if you want to become a screenwriter, you don't need licensing. There's no formal exam to pass, and no rules you must follow to succeed.

## Who Knew?

Did you know that Barry Morrow (*Rain Man*) was discovered after writing about his experiences befriending and becoming the guardian of a mentally impaired man twice his age? (And this was before he met the man who would inspire Dustin Hoffman's character in *Rain Man*.) Did you know that Michael Arndt (*Little Miss Sunshine*, *Toy Story 3*) quit his job as personal assistant to Matthew Broderick so he could pursue screenwriting full-time? And did you know that he wrote *Little Miss Sunshine* in three days and then proceeded to do more than 100 revisions on the script before it made it to the screen?[1]

Although there are no explicit rules for how to become a working screenwriter, there *are* guidelines, and you can begin to compile your own list of guidelines as you gather insight from the pros.

Here's what you'll find out about in this first chapter:

- Breaking in as an intern, secretary, production assistant (PA), or writer's assistant
- Working with film development executives—what they're looking for in a writer, as well as their expectations for the initial meeting or series of interactions
- Etiquette for how and when to give your colleagues or supervisor your writing samples
- Qualities you need to have to succeed in the early career support positions
- Steps you can take so you're prepared when an opportunity presents itself
- What a television producer is looking for in a writer and why
- What it takes to work your way up in television, from intern to showrunner
- Strategies for career prep, beginning before you finish school

Let's start there. You're about to graduate from school . . . now what?

# EXIT STRATEGIES

## Preparing to Leave School and Begin Your Screenwriting Career

▶ By Gabrielle Kelly

To succeed in the competitive job market these days, you need not so much "strategy" singular as "strategies" plural. Think of these strategies as an ongoing process of building your skills, contacts, and experience. You'll be making many "exits" over time in your work, so your strategy has to always be in play—and the better prepared you are, the more likely success will follow.

As a screenwriter, your work will be primarily freelancing. This isn't specific to screenwriting, of course. Anyone who trains in arts and aspires to making a living in the arts realizes that they're unlikely to find themselves working 9 to 5 in a cubicle with lunch breaks and benefits. And my guess is, most artists don't want that.

It's not easy to make a living as a screenwriter, which is why they say of the film and television business, "you can make a killing, but often can't make a living." It can be feast or famine, and it takes a constant balancing of art and business skills to stay in the game. This reality has certain implications. One such implication is that the marketing and management of your work become increasingly important, and this marketing and management often transcend talent. In other words, talent is great, but relationships get you hired.

So let's assume you're in the final stretch of school, and you're preparing to embark on your career. You might not know whether you plan to move to Los Angeles or New York, or whether you'll stay put and save money first. Or will you relocate abroad? Or will you buy some time by getting a writer's residency somewhere in upstate New York or in a lakeside castle in Switzerland?

Not sure yet? First things first . . . let's look at some strategies to bear in mind as you embark on your career.

# Updating Your Résumé and Portfolio

Updating your résumé and portfolio is a constant process. Create what I call a "Me File." This is where you keep the accolades, recommendations, photos, and thank-you emails that you've received from friends, professors, mentors, colleagues, or bosses. Anything that sells you goes in this file. Be sure to get letters while you're still in school or in your internship, and ask for emails or recommendations that you can add to your website or on your LinkedIn page.

Compose a general résumé that you can fine-tune according to the specific needs of jobs and internships. Think of your résumé as your own personal press release. This isn't a time to be modest. And if you're worried that you don't have the official screenwriting jobs and credentials to flesh out your résumé, don't be. It's difficult to get paid work writing a feature script, TV script, or Web series. For your first scripts, you'll "hire yourself," writing on spec for no money just to prove you can do it. On your résumé, list your internships, jobs, and experiences that show writing as part of what you did, and be sure to list the different types of writing in your skill set.

As you transition from college to work, you have to realize that your success is directly tied to what you can do for the people who hire you. Résumés that itemize what you hope to get from a job—as in "Seek a job where I will grow in my skills"—will fall flat. Your employer is hiring you to make the company succeed, not to oversee your up-skilling, except as it benefits them. Your professional development is up to you, and it's your creativity and smarts that will propel you to other opportunities. Professors are paid to draw out from you what you know, don't know, and are learning. It's their job. But when you work, that's *your* job. Quite simply, it's the reverse of all you've experienced in college. So keep this in mind as you craft the language of your résumé.

Also in your Me File, create a portfolio of work samples. Your screenplay samples, certainly—but this should also include other forms of writing that you've created for yourself, for school projects, or for employers. As your portfolio grows, swap out samples you created for school so your work portfolio becomes entirely professional. You might label these samples "Sample Press Release," "Sample Feature Story," "Sample Social Media Marketing," or "Sample Comedy Routine."

Update your professional social media profile regularly, and keep copies of all cover letters in your Me File so you can find and repurpose them for other applications. Make sure they are typo free and grammar perfect!

And remember, digital platforms are more forgiving of online-speak, and texting is a language in and of itself, but none of that is appropriate for business interactions. Behind the scenes, show business is all business. Be showy and artistic in your art, but businesslike in your work.

## Your Online Portfolio

Many schools today encourage students to build websites that demonstrate who they are and their range of experiences. This is a great way to provide prospective employers with a quick link to a beautifully designed site that houses your résumé, writing samples, and letters of recommendation. Don't mistake this for your Me File, though. You want to keep the extras in a private file to which you control access and exposure.

There are many easy-to-use, free websites where you can build your online portfolio. Check out the latest, as they're improving all the time. And make sure to reserve a custom URL (yourname.com) versus a generic URL for your website—this helps with your personal branding. Set up your social media profile handles, and ensure that you're updating these pages regularly and interacting with relevant profiles.

## Continuing Your Education

You're graduating from school, and now your real-world education begins! No matter where you live, you can subscribe to every screenwriting podcast, blog, and newsletter. If you live in a metropolitan area, you can go to talks and seminars with working writers. Join a writer's group, whether online (via Skype) or face-to-face. You're looking to create a situation where you'll get the kind of feedback and support that you have with your college writing workshops. By joining a group of committed screenwriters, not only will you get good notes, you'll also get the encouragement to simply *keep writing*.

Do you need to move to Hollywood or New York to continue your education and set yourself up for working in the industry? It's true there are many more opportunities there, but that's a big and expensive commitment, so it's important to have a plan before moving. The film and television industry isn't for the faint of heart. It's not predictable, safe, or reliable. In fact, quite the opposite is true. So think it through before you make the move.

- Are you committed to working in the industry?
- Are you committed to the endless writing and rewriting necessary to succeed?
- Are you willing to work in whatever job you initially land just to get in the door and get some exposure?
- Are you willing and able to live frugally so you can "pay your dues"?

As you transition from school to work, the goal is to continue your education in whatever you're doing. Quentin Tarantino got his film education working in a video rental store, and Lena Dunham pooled money with friends from babysitting and art-assistant gigs to write and make the Web series that first got her noticed.[2]

As someone who aims to be a screenwriter, you want to find work that relates to your goal. Very few go directly from college to working as a writer's assistant, where you work with the writing staff on a TV show. Its equivalent in film would be a screenwriter's assistant or researcher. Landing such a job is a privilege, and you'll usually work your way into this position starting out as an intern, a secretary, or a production assistant.

Early in my career, I had the opportunity to work in several jobs as an assistant, and I savored every moment of researching scripts and stories, typing and retyping screenplays, transcribing tapes of dialogue, oral histories, and the like. One of the great benefits of these jobs was being forced to deliver writing under pressure—not waiting for the muse to find me, but instead scouring every corner for the muse just to keep my job!

The point being, even on the job, I was continuing my education. But the most common route to landing a job like that is to begin with an internship.

# Getting an Internship

Internships related to screenwriting can help set you up for success in the industry. Be sure to talk to your internship coordinator or career advisor in your school program to find out what's available to apply for and when. It's much easier to get an internship while you're in school, so make the most of this opportunity. Once you land your internship, your goal is to shine so people on the job will notice you.

Paid internships can be especially difficult to get, but don't give up. Always try to turn an internship into a paid situation, even if the pay is low. This can boost your shot at a job once the internship is over.

The other benefit of an internship is that you'll discover more about you. You'll find out how you do and don't like to spend your time, your strengths and weaknesses, your natural talents, and what skills are easily honed. You may not be writing screenplays in your internship, but you could find, for example, that you have a knack for writing marketing copy or for blogging. Or perhaps you'll discover that you're particularly good at sound, or that you enjoy working in the camera department or in an entirely unrelated job.

Still too, don't write off a paid internship that allows you time to write your spec screenplays. It's unlikely someone will pay you a lot to write starting out, but you need writing samples to get work. So get writing. Build your writing portfolio as you intern.

## Just Luck?

It's easy to dismiss someone's success as merely good luck, especially when we're certain that person lacks talent. First, remember this: You aren't the final judge on talent. And neither is the person reading your screenplay at this very moment. Or is the next person. Or the next! Talent is subjective.

Here's what we do know about luck: You create it. Luck is where opportunity meets good timing, so you should devote time to making your own luck. The strategy for your exit from school to work, from internship to job, and from one job to the next should be about envisioning and planning your next move while being ready to take unexpected opportunities that arise along the way.

# Landing Your First Job

Strive to find a job where you can practice writing. Writing is a skill that is needed in a wide variety of jobs, so make an effort to find a job where you get paid to sharpen your writing skills and craft. Ideally it would be in a screenplay-friendly environment, but good writing is good writing, and many screenwriters come from other disciplines. One successful screenwriter I know started out typing legal briefs, an arduous summer job that nonetheless got his typing up to warp speed and exposed him to some good stories. Make your work count so that you're always improving your skills.

Much of the current job economy resembles what used to be true *only* for arts graduates: temporary, project-driven employment, relationship-based hiring, and the need for flexibility, teamwork, and collaboration.[3]

So as an arts graduate, you're already ahead of the game. A friend of mine who owns a temp agency loves hiring arts graduates. She finds them flexible, quick on their feet, and good at reacting to change and fast-paced environments, because this mirrors so much of work in the arts sector.

To make a film demands a team of possibly hundreds of people who combine efforts to create a work that is both artistic and commercial. Delegation, teamwork, and adherence to budgets are crucial—and more than anything else, relationships and communication are key. These are the exact skills needed in today's workplace, where the office is often a tablet or smartphone and the distinction between home and office is increasingly blurred. It's about meeting goals on a deadline and under pressure. How and where you meet those goals has undergone vast change and will continue to do so. Your individual goal, however, is to be remembered for doing your job well. If you strive to do every job to the very best of your ability, it forms good habits for your work and creative life, and this is also how you get recommendations from your supervisors.

When you're just starting out, there are no bad jobs. But jobs done badly won't get you ahead, regardless of how much you feel you should be doing something more creative, for more money, working for someone who appreciates your ideas and skills. It's often not clear that a low-level job can lead to something better, but it can. To thrive in this demanding world of constant change, entrepreneurism is required above all else. You must constantly sell and upgrade your skills.

And green light yourself! Industry folks will take you more seriously if you show that you're passionate and can actually deliver rather than just talking about what you *could* deliver given the chance. Give yourself the chance.

Keep sharpening the sword of your skills and creating work. Fine-tune the description of what you're doing so you can explain it succinctly and with confidence. Many professional jobs today require presentation skills, so if you have expertise in this area, you'll have an edge in the workplace. A newbie writer I know was very good at this and offered to write presentations for co-workers, which led to her speedy promotion. Take a public speaking class, or join Toastmasters. As a screenwriter, you always have to pitch your ideas, but as much as you're pitching ideas, you're always pitching yourself. Your idea may not sell, but your skills as a storyteller, researcher, editor, or content generator will come across even if your script idea doesn't fit the company's needs.

In the end, people mostly hire people they like hanging out with. Connectivity is paramount—a sense that you're easy to work with, proactive in your thinking, and can turn around any form of writing quickly and without fuss and complaining.

Also, remember that we're in a global economy. It's worth looking outside your home country for internships and jobs. Storytelling for media content creation is now a global business, and you may be able to work as a translator or screenwriter for those developing markets. You could very well skip three or four rungs of the career ladder by taking work outside your home country. Also, that experience overseas can boost your appeal back home, wherever that may be.

## Money talk . . .

In a world of freelance and portfolio-driven careers, there are ups and downs over the years. The key to surviving happily is to live like a pauper as you dream like a king or queen. Spend as little as possible on daily living. This isn't easy in bigger cities where there's more networking and more expenses, but it's crucial to keep your overheads low so your dreams can soar.

Basic budgeting is something that will serve you well in life and in work. The bottom line is always: How much does it cost?

Finally, remember that of the 300+ credits at the end of a movie, most people only know the job of director, actor, and possibly writer. These are the jobs most people want to do, but it's statistically more likely that you'll be doing one of the other 297 jobs—and one you may like even better. You have a very good chance of doing a job that you don't even know exists, so keep an open mind. Remember this as you expand your horizons! Keep your options open, and lay the preparation for luck to be on your side.

---

**GABRIELLE KELLY** has taught screenwriting at NYU Tisch School of Arts, Asia, USC, UCLA, Chapman, and London's PAL LABS, and she has mentored in screenwriting for the Middle East Sundance Lab in Jordan. She has led global storytelling seminars in Russia, India, and China, and is the recipient of two Fulbright Awards. In 2014, she co-edited the bestselling book on women directors around the world, *Celluloid Ceiling: Women Film Directors Breaking Through* (Aurora Metro Press). She has worked with renowned filmmakers Sidney Lumet and Jay Presson Allen on films such as *Daniel*, *Prince of the City*, *Deathtrap*, and *The Verdict*. She developed projects with Andy Warhol's Factory on an audio-animatronic show, *From A to Z and Back Again*, the musical *La Cage aux Folles* with Mike Nichols, and scripts for music

Gabrielle Kelly

maven Malcolm McLaren and CBS Theatrical Films. Head of producer Robert Evans' company at Paramount Studios, she worked in development and production on a slate of diverse projects, and she was an executive and producer with companies such as HBO, Fields Hellman, CBS Films, Eddie Murphy Productions, and Warner Bros. She now writes and produces for the global marketplace and is a world authority on Media Labs.

# TEN ACTIONS YOU CAN TAKE

## To Be an Active Hero in Your Career

▸ By Jen Grisanti

For over twenty years, I've been working in the business of teaching and mentoring screenwriters on "story" from the studio executive perspective. In all those years, one thing is clear: The difference between the writers who make it and the writers who don't comes down to the decisive actions they take to make their dreams a reality. Here are the top ten actions you can take—beginning right now—to actively pursue your goal of becoming a working screenwriter.

## Understand Your "Why"

Why do you want to write? What is the emotional fuel behind your journey?

When I teach or guide, my intention is to take the storyteller to a deeper place of understanding the why. Focusing on the why leads to transformation. Here are three whys that have significance in this process:

Why do you want to write the story?

Why are you the perfect writer for the story?

Why does the central character want what he/she wants? Or, why does this character want to achieve the goal?

For example, if the reason you want to write your story has to do with a personal life experience that inspired a strong message and you want to articulate and send out this message to the world, then we understand your why—why you want to write the story and why you're the perfect writer to write it. When you come from a worldview based on personal experience, you add an authentic layer to the story.

To better understand your why, write in a journal or notepad. Be an observer and absorber of your life. Know what's going on in your mind and your heart. Think about why you see things the way you see them. Know what is going on in the world. Understanding yourself and your whys will add emotional fuel to the stories you tell and will help to pave your path to success.

# Do the Emotional Work

When the rug is pulled out from under you and your world is thrown out of balance, what do you do to bring it back into balance? This is the hero's journey. To understand how to write this journey, you need to do the emotional work in your own life. What do you do after hitting your "all is lost" moment? How do you bring your story back into balance?

Write down three to five of your "all is lost" moments. Think about the sequence of decisions and events that led up to them. Think about what you did after they occurred to recover. Did you take the time to heal and understand your loss? Was there a specific action you took that contributed to your growth and allowed you to move through it? If so, what was this action?

In my own life, after losing a job mid-pursuit as a vice president to running a studio, I had to take a step back, breathe, and take inventory. I had to pull apart the moment that led to my contract not being renewed. I had to understand my own part in the outcome. I had to do the emotional work to bring my life back into balance. I had to heal. This "all is lost" moment was actually the trigger incident for my new story. Without it, I wouldn't be an author and a story/career consultant for writers, a calling that I love.

Fear of failure holds us back, but when we do the emotional work after we go through failure we become stronger and often move in a more positive direction. We alleviate the weight of failure by using it as a learning opportunity. When you learn in life that you can *fail forward*, your world will open up in a whole new way. Your story will always be evolving. By doing your emotional work, you become an active hero in your own story and the author of your life.

# Write

Write, write, write. The biggest action you can take toward your goal is to write. Dive into your creative process. Learn what this means for you. Build your writing portfolio. Write with intention. Write with a strategy in mind. Keep writing.

What is your writing routine? You need to figure out when is the best time for you to write. It helps to think about when your brain operates at maximum capacity. I learned that 4:00 a.m. is my magic hour. It's when I'm coming out of dream state, and I can feel thoughts coming through me. Set a time to write, and commit to the time.

Where do you want to go with your writing career? What material do you need to write to help you to reach that destination? Are you building your writing portfolio strategically? Are the scripts that you're writing the right ones to lead you to a sale or to land you on the staff of your dream show? If not, think about how you can start building in a direction that will support your desired outcome.

Every time I gave Aaron Spelling—my mentor of twelve years—a set of development notes or a card, he would say to me, "You should write. You should write. You should write." I was on the executive path at the time. My fear of failing got in my way back then. It took my "all is lost" moment to push me in the direction of being an author. The action I had to take to realize this dream—the one Aaron already saw—was to write.

Writers can write their way into any job. So the only thing between you and your destiny is the blank page. The more you write, the better you get. Trust this journey. Do the work. Commit to the process of writing.

# Become Educated and Work With a Consultant or Coach

Make sure that you're always taking classes and reading books to elevate your craft. We learn by educating ourselves. I'm constantly reading and taking classes. I'm a teacher for a moment and a student for life. You have to put in the time to get what you want. When you take action to educate yourself, you'll see that knowledge is power. Education leads to desired outcomes. When you're open to learning how to do things better, you'll always be improving.

I highly recommend that you work with a consultant or a coach to get your scripts to the strongest place possible before you submit your work. With consulting and coaching, you'll get a professional sounding board in a safe space. You'll receive a direct response about what is and isn't working with your story. If you do your research and hire someone with strong credentials, you'll have a guide who is working in alignment with you to get the outcome you desire. I've been giving notes for over twenty years. When I was an executive I saw my notes executed on up to five shows a week. I saw what worked and what didn't with story. I learned how to elevate story. This was my job. Many consultants have background experience that will be particularly beneficial to you and the specific story you're telling. I recommend that you meet with three to four consultants and see who gets you the most. I also recommend that you look at their credentials and past client testimonials. Hiring a coach or consultant is a very strong action you can take that will lead you toward your destiny.

# Enter Writing Competitions and Network Writing Programs

The intention behind entering competitions and writing programs is to create the recognition you need to capture the attention of industry professionals. You can include these successes in your creative bio, and they will add to your marketability in the business. To succeed in this business, it's all about creating heat around your name and work. People like to know that talent has been recognized, and then they want to jump on board. One way to create heat is by placing in or winning a reputable writing competition or getting into a strong writing program.

## Top Ten Writing Competitions and Programs

The Nicholl Fellowship
Final Draft
The Austin Film Festival
TrackingB
ScreenCraft
The Page International Screenwriting Awards
Writers On the Verge at NBC
Disney/ABC Writing Fellowship
WB Writers' Workshop

CBS Diversity's Writers Mentoring Program
Sundance Screenwriter's Lab
Sundance Episodic Lab
HBOAccess Writing Fellowship

# Write a Creative Bio and One Sheet

Write a creative bio. This should go through your marketing points and reveal your voice. It should give us a glimpse into your personal story and the world-view that resulted from it, and it should list your accomplishments, like placing in writing competitions, writing programs, and any Internet presence that you have. Your fan base is key.

Write a one sheet. List log lines for your top four scripts. If you have ten scripts in your portfolio, only list the top four that you think are the most viable. Agents and managers get nervous when they hear you've written ten to fifteen scripts and nothing has happened. By listing your top four, you alleviate this.

If you're pursuing a career in TV, the one sheet with four scripts should ideally have a spec script of a current, existing show (no more than two years old), two original pilot scripts, and a feature, play, short story, or one act.

If you're pursuing a feature career, there are different schools of thought. You could have four scripts that are unified through your brand, genre, or theme. Or you could have four scripts in different genres. Some people think that as a feature writer you don't need to fall into a specific brand until you have your first hit. Then, you should write scripts that fall under the same brand.

# Network

Go to panels all over town. You can do this through the Writers Guild Foundation, PaleyFest, and The Nerdist, to list a few. Network up and down. You never know where you'll cross paths with someone again—that PA may one day be an executive you're sitting across from during a pitch! Think long term.

Learn how to build and nurture relationships in the business. When you go to a panel, engage with the panelists. Ask a question. Go up to them afterward and tell them how much you loved what they had to say. Then, the next day, send them a request on LinkedIn.

Another action that I learned from working with Aaron Spelling is to write letters. If you love someone's work, write to them and tell them how much you loved it. This could be by snail mail or by email. At the time I started at Spelling, people wrote old-fashioned letters with pen and paper. What I learned from seeing his joy when he received these letters was that no matter how big we become in the business, we all love to hear that our work is resonating and making an impact.

# Build Your Brand

If you have a clear understanding of what type of writer you are and you know your personal story, this will help you understand what fuels the scripts you write.

You might write sci-fi or female-driven procedurals. You might have humor that is outside the box. You might write conspiracy stories with a twist or psychological dramas. You might write dark comedy. Be aware of what your brand is. This should be the thread that unifies your writing portfolio.

A question I often ask writers is, "What is your wound?" I had one writer answer this by telling me that her wound was emotional abandonment. This came from a personal life experience. While we were talking about it, she suddenly realized that without intending it all of her scripts had an arc with emotional abandonment. This is how you understand your brand and write from a place that clearly establishes for decision makers why you're the perfect writer for the story.

Part of understanding your brand is having clarity on what you want to say with the stories that you tell. When you know what you want to say with your stories, pitching becomes easier.

# Believe, Meditate, and Visualize

Believe that you can be a working writer. Meditate on the type of career you want. Visualize yourself in exactly the place you want to be. See it. Believe it. Make it happen.

In my experience as a story/career consultant, when a writer truly believes that success is within his or her grasp, magic happens. Belief is the key ingredient that will determine whether you make it.

By identifying what you want and seeing yourself in this place of being, you'll be amazed how the term "ask and you shall receive" takes on a new meaning.

# Tell and Sell Your Story

Learning how to tell and sell your story is a huge action you can take. There are three things to think about with this: 1) Tell a story they can't ignore; 2) Develop a strong personal narrative; and 3) Sell with passion.

## Tell a Story that They Can't Ignore

**Concept**: Have a concept that's original and comes from a worldview that's different from what we've seen before.

**Execution**: Think of the terms trigger, dilemma, and pursuit when telling your story.

**Emotional truth**: What is your truth in telling this story? If the core emotional truth is there, it will ring true to the people you're pitching to.

## Develop a Strong Personal Narrative

**Inspiration**: What inspired you to tell and sell this story? That's important. Share it!

**Setting up your *why***: You did this work already, so now, explain it. Why do you want to tell this story? And why *now*?

**Anecdotes**: Do you have any anecdotes that illustrate the well you can draw from with this concept? This will help sell the idea that *you* should be the one to do the telling.

## Sell With Passion

**Enthusiasm**: What excites you about this story?

**Market**: Why is the market ready for this story?

**Strong close**: Close with as much passion as you start with. Leave them with the idea that no one else can tell this story the way that you can.

By taking these ten actions, you will be an active hero in your own story. When you are an active hero in your own story and clearly know what you want, anything is possible. It all starts with a dream and a plan. The actions you take can turn your dream into a reality.

---

International speaker **JEN GRISANTI** is an acclaimed story and career consultant with her own firm, Jen Grisanti Consultancy, Inc., and a writing instructor for Writers on the Verge at NBC. She spent twelve years as a studio executive, including working as Head of Current Programming at Spelling Television and Vice President of Current Programming at CBS/Paramount. Jen also blogs for *The Huffington Post* and is the author of *Story Line: Finding Gold in Your Life Story*, *TV Writing Tool Kit: How to Write a Script that Sells*, and her new book, *Change Your Story, Change Your Life: A Path to Your Success*. Grisanti has taught classes for the TV Writers Summit (in Los Angeles, London, and Israel), the TV Writers Studio (in Australia), Story Expo, The Big Island Film Festival, Chicago Screenwriters Network, Scriptwriters Network, Screenwriting Expo, and the Great American Pitchfest.

Jen Grisanti

Photo by Michael Hiller

# IMPRESSING THE DEVELOPMENT EXECUTIVE

▸ By Trai Cartwright

Joining the ranks of paid screenwriters involves more than just mastering your craft. Familiarity and preparation for being involved in the film business are also crucial. There are methods to help you find the people who are looking for you—presenting yourself professionally in the marketplace and delivering a spectacular script that all of your new bosses can get excited about. Okay, maybe not *all* of them, but at least the majority.

Development executives are our own rare breed, not quite content creators and not quite producers. We are frontline media workers who need to know a bit of everything about the industry—storytelling, team leading, filmmaking, finance, marketing, and above all else, how to develop a project across all of these fronts. How else are we going to sell our bosses on a project unless we can answer their questions and take away any concerns?

What does this mean to the writer? Everything. The better you understand what development executives are looking for, the better you'll be able to address those issues in your script and in your meetings.

The development team you might encounter could be any of the following personnel: the assistant to a producer, actor, or director with their own shingle; a creative executive who's climbed the ranks from script reading; a development executive or even a vice president of development. The primary difference between them is this: the power to green-light a purchase.

The one thing they have in common is their thirst to get a project made. And that thirst works to your advantage if you know the target they're aiming for.

## The Script

I served in nearly all of the capacities I've just described for a range of companies—Paramount Pictures, Universal Pictures, New Line Cinema, HBO, and private production companies like Prelude Pictures. In that decade, I learned a lot about picking a winner. Let's start with the query, because before there's a script, there's always a query.

## What About a Query Makes Me Request the Script?

One word: *professionalism*. Addressed to me and not the person in the next bungalow. No typos, no grammatical errors. This might surprise you, the power of punctuation, but the fact is, we need to believe that you know what you're doing. Writers need to know how to write. If you can't write a correct sentence, we will not for a moment believe you can write a coherent script.

We do want to get a sense of who the writer is, but your letter can't be about you or about how the death of your dog made you realize that life is short and it was time to pursue this crazy dream. Keep focused on the telling of your story. If you're funny on the page, but you're trying to get me to read a thriller, there's a disconnect. If you're fiery and lyrical in your text but want me to read a car chase flick, I'm worried about overwriting.

In general, let your movie do the talking. A clear, concise, exciting logline and well-written, focused query will open many doors.

But there is a caveat on that dazzling letter. Your movie needs to be "right" for my company. If we specialize in supernatural teen action-ers, and this is a rural coming-of-age comedy, this tells me you didn't do your homework to find the people who would be excited to hear from you.

And finally, I'm looking for any professional accomplishments. Win any awards? Get into the semi- or quarterfinals of the big six contests? You're in. Sell something prior? Are you making a Web series? You're in. Published in the fiction realm . . . well, honestly, less interesting, but at least it tells me you're competent in other realms.

To review:

- Error-free copy
- A bit of your personality
- A banging logline
- A story that's right for my company
- Professional accomplishments related to writing, or expertise that makes you the perfect person to write about the subject matter

# What Do I Look for in a Script?

I look for what everyone else looks for in a script . . . a story that thrills me. Some of the best advice I ever got was this: Don't confuse. Don't bore.

I love clean, modern screenwriting prose, which is a format unto itself. If the narrative is dancing on the page in bursts of energetic glee, I know I'm in the hands of a powerful storyteller. I relax immediately in the presence of a pro and let the story flow over me rather than feel a constant need to edit. Do your homework by reading produced scripts in your genre to see what the narrative is meant to look like.

I love voice on the page. Some genres don't support this, sure, and some development executives despise any breaking of the fourth wall, but when a writer can do this well, I will read everything he's ever written. Why? Because it tells me that he knows the craft well enough that he can level up his storytelling with an infusion of his own excitement. Shane Black, anyone?

If in reading your own script you tend to skip over a scene, guess what? We will, too. If you're boring yourself, you're boring us. We can easily spot an unnecessary, underdeveloped scene, so don't try to get away with a couple weak links. They can sink the whole enterprise.

There are two dead zones in every movie. One happens right around the time the romantic interest is trotted on screen, and the other is after the false resolution when everyone's got to catch their breath and talk through all the craziness we just experienced. There's never any new information, and the tone flatlines, so this is where readers get distracted and put down the script. If you can write these sections in a way that keeps me turning the pages, you win points.

As we're all well versed in structure (there was a time when structure wasn't something people talked about—dark, meandering days), please make sure you're hitting your beats. And then go one step further: Don't be obvious about it. My favorite movies are the ones that are structurally sound but are so inventive in their plotting that I stop ticking off the beats in my head.

Who doesn't love sparkling movie banter dialogue? This is the movies, after all. A flair for dialogue will forgive other errors or omissions.

And finally, the characters. I'm looking for the same things actors are looking for—something to play. Texturized, well-built characters. Have you explored the protagonist's central internal struggle in every single scene?

Movies are short. They can't afford to step off theme for even an instant. If your script missteps, you've just spun your entire crew into a catastrophic cinematic smash-up, what with everyone interpreting things their own way. Let literary fiction writers leave the theme to the audience. Movies are entirely theme-driven. What's your script saying?

Oh, and under ten typos. If you're no good with self-editing (and who is?), hire an editor.

## Why Do I Meet With a Writer?

Three reasons: First, because her query letter assured me she is a professional and not psychotic in any way. Second, because she's got a great script we either want to make or at least makes us want to be in business with her at some point. Third, her follow-up emails and calls are, again, non-psychotic.

If you are unkind to me or my staff, I will not meet you. If you are overaggressive or pouty when I have to bow out of our meeting a couple of times, I will not reschedule for the third. If your agent is any of these things, I might not bother either. Working with you is working with your representation, and if they are jerks, it can seriously impact your career. If you're a jerk, you will struggle mightily to have one at all.

# The Meeting

Once you've written a terrific script, you can expect to go on the "Arrowhead Tour." Making the rounds meeting everyone who loved your writing is hugely important, as this is how you build relationships. That script might not sell, but if you've done your job and met a bunch of folks, you'll have a whole network waiting for your next project and keeping you "in mind" for in-house writing jobs. (An in-house writing job is when the production company has an idea and needs writers to come in and pitch their take. The best take wins the job.)

So let's assume I've asked you to come in. The first thing you'll need to understand is what kind of meeting we'll be having. Sometimes it's just an informational meeting (a "meet and greet"). This is where I'm wildly effusive about your script even as I lament not buying it. The other kind of meeting is the one where I try to talk you into addressing issues in the script so that it might better align with my company's requirements and expectations. Very rarely does a script get bought outright (and then it's often because of a "weekend read" that results in an auction). More often, you spend time getting to know the development team and addressing their concerns (these are revisions that, despite the Writers Guild of America's [WGA] campaigning against the practice, you may well do for free). Your goal here is to get the development team so invested (called "getting them pregnant") that they will finally buy your script.

So how do you get from "Love your script" to "We want to make an offer"?

## Look Nice

Nobody wants to hear this, but appearance matters. So let's hit the basics.

Shower, please. Wash your hair, and look like you made an effort. This meeting is important. What to wear . . .? For men it's easy. Jeans, a cool T-shirt reflecting some aspect of how you interface with pop culture (concert Ts, movie or comics Ts, witty quotes, ironic philosophical musings), and you might consider a button-down shirt left open. Patterns and colors are okay—just try not to clash. Money doesn't matter here, but appearing that you have some sense of style is important (unfortunately). If you want to keep it very simple, just try to emulate the casual styles you see in celebrity magazines.

Women. Well, this is an entirely different story. There's a double standard here, but it's a mistake to pretend it doesn't exist. If you come in dressed like the men, you'll appear sloppy. If you come in wearing a dress or typical office wear, you might remind us of our assistants (and then we can't imagine partnering with you). Think trendy, but aim to look polished and be as put-together as possible.

Here's the bottom line for both genders: Dress to feel confident. This means if you aren't a tie guy, don't bust out your barely remembered Windsor knot now. Ladies, if you don't usually show a little cleavage or strap yourself into Spanx, it'll throw off your game if you start today. Definitely don't blow your paycheck on a new wardrobe. Instead, live it up *a little*. Invest in (or borrow!) a few key pieces. I've seen a great watch or necklace get the conversation started. Shoes are a subject both genders can bond over. (Who knew?) Be thoughtful, be comfortable, be your best yourself.

## Take the Water

This is why it's called the Arrowhead Tour—everyone in town seems to buy their bottled water from Arrowhead, and when the assistant offers you a bottle, say *yes please*. Saying no is unnecessary, and some may even consider it rude. Even if you don't drink it, take the water.

## Be Good in the Room

We're forming a relationship here—we're trying to decide if we like you enough to work with you for two years. Here are some tips:

- Small talk: Expect some. If you're uncomfortable with small talk, go online and research some nice softball comments to make. In Los Angeles, talking about traffic is always a bonding moment. There's no weather to speak of, so skip that. I often asked what part of town writers lived in (different neighborhoods attract a different personality, so it told me something about them), and often we'd get to talking about our favorite secret backstreets. (Tipping off an exec to Washington as an amazing crosstown alternative to the 10 is serious points in your favor.)
- Do your homework. You *must* be a fanboy or girl in this meeting. Know the execs' histories and résumés, and have smart questions to ask. Know who has the power in the room and be sure to address them the most—but don't forget the others if you get the whole development staff in there. It's nice to include the "underlings" in the room, but there are politics going on you can't possibly understand, and you don't want to accidentally align with the person on his or her way out. Stick to addressing the person who invited you and the person with the ability to take your script to the next level.
- Be able to talk about yourself. Invariably, you'll get an impossible question like, "So, tell us about yourself." Have an answer. Make it concise. They don't want your life story—they're just looking for commonality. Do you love the same kinds of movies? Do you know the same people? Did you go to the same schools? Prepare and practice a bullet-point guide to what's most interesting about you and how it might relate to them.
- Come in with other scripts to talk about. You'll most likely be turned down in the room, but if you're there, it's because they like your writing. They'll always ask, "What else do you have?" Pitch the other projects you're working on. Especially the ones tied to other companies. Even if no money has changed hands, it will assure them that you've been vetted and are "in play."

- Take notes. Obviously. And don't do it on your phone. Bring a piece of paper and pen so you don't disengage from the conversation. Trying to type into a phone instantly breaks all human contact.
- Say "Yes" or "That's interesting, I'll have to play with that" to all of their suggestions. Work out what actually makes sense later. This isn't a negotiation or a debate or the time for you to explain in detail the thematic underpinnings that they obviously aren't getting. This is a conversation about how the two of you might continue down the path to getting your film made. If the development executive is worth her salt, she's read and taken notes on your script (or at least has read the notes from her script reader), and she'll have intelligent, helpful things to say. The best scenario is for the two of you to have a creative meeting of the minds, where you bounce ideas off each other and realize you both see the film the same way. The worst-case scenario (and this happens all the time) is that they make it obvious they're only barely familiar with your script and throw out such generalized and clichéd ideas that you shudder at the prospect of working with them. In this case, be glad they tipped their hand and now you can walk away knowing you dodged a bullet. While they're judging you, remember that you're judging them, too.
- As Mamet reminded us in *Glengarry Glen Ross*, always be closing. Go into the meeting with something you want, and don't leave until you get it. Get them to agree to read something else of yours, or let you pitch for an open job, or put your name on that list of available writers they keep for open assignments. Even if you've pitched everything you've got and it's a pass on all of them, at the very least get the development exec to agree to read something else down the line.

## What You *Shouldn't* Say

"There's been a lot of interest." Either name names who are genuinely interested, or say nothing. You can't bait these people. "So-and-so was attached." And now they've passed. Oops. "It's a really funny / unique / touching / thrilling script." Saying it doesn't make it so. "And then chaos ensues." This tells me nothing except that you blew a chance to show me what a good storyteller you are. "It's the next *Harry Potter*." No, it's not. "I really think Will Ferrell would be great for this." He's great in everything, which is why his asking price is something we can't afford, and besides, he's booked for two years, or didn't you know that before you pitched him? "I'm really nervous." I know. I'll try to help if I can, but please don't make me feel like I have to play shrink to you. I'm just trying to buy a script here.

## After the Meeting

Call your agent/manager immediately, and tell them the meeting was awesome—unless it really, *really* wasn't. Now is not the time to discuss petty complaints, recite the exchange moment by moment (unless asked), or angst over story-related suggestions. Now is the time to help your rep keep your script and *you* alive. Unless you seriously hated whomever you met, or it was the sort of disaster everyone is better off just walking away from, the feedback is that you're excited to move forward with this team. The agent will then call and assure the development executive that she's loved and all her ideas are stellar. Now she's even more likely to want to work with you, knowing you are a positive and cooperative team player.

> ## By the way . . .
>
> If you don't have an agent or manager yet—and if you're just starting out, you likely don't—this is when you call the person who referred you or got you the meeting and do everything I've just described. Did your teacher hook you up? Your neighbor? Your cousin? Get on the phone! Thank them! Profusely.

If you were *not* loved in the room, the development person will do one of three things:

- Say, "We're not buying right now, but we'll keep you in mind." This will either be a lie or it won't be.
- Say, "You don't really write what we're looking for, but thanks anyway." This is a polite way of saying that what you write (and therefore you) aren't at the level they need you to be to hire you.
- Not say anything at all. In other words, they won't return your or your agent's call. This is a "soft pass." Don't take it personally. They just weren't that into you.

In your life as a writer, you'll do hundreds of these meetings. Learn to love them, or at least get good at hiding your nerves or boredom. You'll meet with people at all levels, and many of these meetings will be total wastes of your time. Some of them, though, will be magic—and those will be the pathway to a sell. Your goal is always to impress, cajole, befriend, and mind-meld with the development executives. We may very well be the ones who make the biggest difference in advancing your career.

As a fifteen-year Hollywood development executive, **TRAI CARTWRIGHT** has consulted on thousands of screenplays for HBO, Fox, Paramount, Universal, and New Line. She has produced three independent films and is currently producing her first Colorado-based indie. She has also optioned her own screenplays to Academy- and Emmy-award winning producers, and she was assistant director of Leonardo DiCaprio's online ventures, the Hollywood liaison for a multiplayer online role-playing game company, and made really bad cell phone content for 20th Century Fox. She currently teaches the art of story development to writers of all mediums at the Colorado Film School and the University of Northern Colorado. She also works one-on-one with novelists and screenwriters across the nation. Trai can be found at www.craftwrite.com.

Trai Cartwright

# WRITING FOR TELEVISION
## What It Takes
▶ An Interview With Fern Field Brooks

Fern Field Brooks' career in the entertainment industry began in 1975 on Norman Lear's television series *Maude*, starring Bea Arthur. Most recently, she served as co-executive producer on *Monk*, starring Tony Shalhoub. She was nominated for an Oscar for her short film *A Different Approach*, which she made to encourage the employment and accurate portrayal of persons with disabilities. During the course of her forty-year career, she received a Distinguished Service Award from President Ronald Reagan, won a primetime Emmy, two George Foster Peabody awards, two Humanitas awards, and the NAACP Image award. As an author, her first nonfiction book,

Fern Field Brooks

*Letters to My Husband*, was published in Canada, the United States, and Japan, and she recently launched her second book—a "meowmoir" titled *They Call Me Destiny*.

**I'd love to hear from your perspective what a producer is looking for in a writer.**

How well they write. It's really that simple, because what we do is read scripts. We're not going to sit down with a writer just because we like them and say, okay, write this script for me. Basically, you look at the body of work and you go from there. So you have to see samples. If somebody's a good writer, then you want to work with them.

**When you were working for the Lear companies, how did you find writers for your shows?**

Well, in those days, for comedy writers, they came up from vaudeville, from radio, from early television. There were many training grounds that they were graduates of, these writers. They'd done radio or *I Love Lucy*. They didn't come without credits to Lear's stable.

One day a script came over the threshold, and it turned out to be a brilliant *Maude*, where she goes to the psychiatrist, and it's a twenty-two-minute monologue. That script came in unsolicited from Jay Folb, who then was hired to be a staff writer. But he wasn't a beginner—he was experienced at the time.

**What was the rewriting like during *Maude*? Did the staff rewrite each other? Did the actors improv?**

The writers would listen to story ideas and go off and write, and then everything was rewritten in-house. One of the things you learned when you went to work for the Lear companies—a writer needed to have a really strong ego or just not care, because everything was rewritten ad nauseam. And sometimes it got better, and sometimes it just was the same but different, and sometimes it didn't improve. But it was very collaborative.

**Would you say that's pretty typical in television?**

Well, we were like a family in the early days, and the writers and producers—everybody worked together. And we did it in front of a live audience and gauged the audience. If the audience didn't react well during the dress taping, the show was rewritten between dress and air. We had Hal Cooper, who was an amazing director, but we also had some directors who couldn't shift gears that quickly to reblock. So it was hard, intensive work.

**What would you say to the aspiring screenwriter who is bothered by the idea of rewriting or being rewritten?**

He should become a playwright. In the theater, it's still very much a writer's medium. Or maybe he should become a producer. This is why a lot of writers become producers—so they have more control over their material. And sometimes that's a good idea, and sometimes it's not such a good idea, because not every writer is a good producer.

The thing is, if you get a note from somebody, it means that whatever is in your head didn't make it to the page, and people are having a problem with it—

whether it's an actor or a producer or the audience. So you have to look and see why you're getting the note. And sometimes the note is ridiculous.

There's a book with all the network notes in the days of *Mork & Mindy*— *A Martian Wouldn't Say That*. It's a brilliant book. Some network notes are ludicrous, and you really get into a problem when network executives, instead of simply saying, "It's not working for me," they try to fix it.

But your first draft isn't written in granite, and if you think it is, you shouldn't be in this business.

> "One of the things you learned when you went to work for the Lear companies—a writer needed to have a really strong ego or just not care, because everything was rewritten ad nauseam. And sometimes it got better, and sometimes it just was the same but different, and sometimes it didn't improve. But it was very collaborative."

**How often do producers or executives do the rewriting?**
Well, nowadays—and again, my references are television—nowadays almost all the showrunners are writers. And like I said, sometimes that's wonderful.

**Can you explain what a showrunner is?**
It didn't used to exist, that title, but what they started doing in television was giving producer credits to writers instead of raises. What they found was that if a writer can get what producing is all about, that will improve the show. In fact, they have a class through the WGA now, teaching writers how to be producers. But a showrunner is the writer—or sometimes director—who's producing the show.

**You mentioned that the TV writers used to come up from vaudeville or radio. How do you think comedy writing has changed today? Any advice for aspiring comedy writers?**
You have to be able to gauge what works and what doesn't, and that changes all

the time. Comedies are treated very differently these days than when I was doing it. We used to use a laugh track only to smooth over the transitions between the dress taping and the air taping, because you would sometimes take a scene from one and edit it into another. Now, the laugh tracks are incredibly intrusive. I can't watch studio comedies anymore with laugh tracks, because when somebody comes in and says, "Hello, how are you?" I'm sorry, but that's not funny. I don't care who's saying it, and I don't need to hear a laugh there.

Perhaps what's happening is that a lot of the younger executives, they're running scared. They don't trust the material, and they don't trust the audience. Go to any taping, and I'll guarantee you that when you see that show on the air, all those laughs have been enhanced. It's ridiculous—it's intrusive. I can't watch it.

**So the alternative to the laugh tracks would be trusting the scripts? Trusting the audience? Rewriting if necessary?**
Right, they have to trust the material. If we had any network objections to anything, Norman would say, "Let's see how it plays." And if it got the wrong response from the dress taping audience, it was rewritten. Sometimes we rewrote a whole show between dress and air. But we never tried to put in a laugh where the audience didn't think something was funny. We might have tried to smooth a cut or something like that, but look at those shows now—you're lucky that you hear the dialogue there's so much laugh track.

**What year did you begin producing *Monk*?**
2002.

**The staff was in New Jersey on *Monk*, right? How did that work?**
Well, it took me a couple of seasons to make sure we got a writer on the set— because things happen on the set. Like in season one, we're in Toronto, the writers are in New Jersey, and we're shooting at midnight, and there are two bodies on the floor, and suddenly Tony says, "I'm supposed to be the smartest detective in the world, I'm obsessing about this one body, but I'm ignoring the other body. Why is that? Does anybody have an answer to that?" Well, you can't call the writers at midnight. They probably wouldn't even answer the phone. So I don't remember how we solved that one, but that's when the producer will sometimes step in to help.

**_Monk_ is pretty unusual in that there was a staff in New Jersey, right?**
It's pretty unusual, but it doesn't matter because a seamless show works. When I supervised *La Femme Nikita* for USA and Joel Surnow was our executive producer/

writer, they were shooting in Toronto, and sometimes he was writing from LA, but he'd put together a team who understood what the show was about, and it was a well-oiled machine. We could never tell when Joel was there or not there. And he's a brilliant producer and had a good writing staff.

> "I don't think it's helpful for writers to worry too much that they'll end up working with a director or producer who doesn't appreciate the writing. We see it. And we realize, too, that we need a writer on the set— just in case an actor misinterprets."

**Writing for television as compared to film—what do the opportunities look like?**

There's a lot of opportunity in TV, especially these days. The biggest handicap an aspiring writer has is that they lack the experience. Sometimes they're one-shots, because they'll do a brilliant script and then they can't do it anymore, because they haven't had the time to hone their talent.

It's a problem today. Because the writers I worked with most of my life had been writing over and over again. They had experience. Real experience. So I would suggest that aspiring writers today get the practice before they put themselves out there. You have to be able to deliver.

**Could you address the ups and downs, how you have handled the highs and lows? For instance, the down times when you're waiting for *Monk* to come along?**

One thing that's important for a writer is to be current. On a couple of the shows, I would say, "This feels like the seventies, guys, and I'm the oldest person here." For me, there came a time after *Monk* when I didn't look for another job. I thought, it's time to move over and let the three generations coming up behind me take over. A lot of the comedy that works these days isn't my cup of tea, so you have to recognize that you're either in sync with what's going on or not.

But for the young writers, they have to remember—and this is true whether you're a writer, a producer, a director, or a grip—it's the old adage "it's who you know." People like to work with people they're familiar with. If an actor has done a good job for you, you're going to call him again to do a good job on another show. The same is true with a writer.

You can't isolate yourself. You have to network and get out there. You have to stay in touch with people that you work with on a show, because then they'll be doing another show. It's about maintaining relationships—that's really important. Keep the relationships. And also, be a brilliant writer. That takes the cake over everything.

## A Different Approach . . .

*Sometimes, when you take a chance, it pays off in a big way. When the shows Fern was producing at the Lear companies went off the air, she went on to produce her Oscar-winning film,* A Different Approach *. . .*

It was totally by accident. We had produced an episode on *Maude* where she goes to a college reunion, and her best friend has had a stroke. The episode made an impact on everybody. So one day after he'd had a meeting with Lear, Rod Parker asked me to find a factory with an assembly line with disabled people working on it. My research put me in touch with a committee in the South Bay who said they wanted a short film that would be a conversation-breaker when they called on corporate execs to encourage them to hire people with disabilities.

I remember a meeting at the Governor's Committee in Sacramento when this very sexy guy in a wheelchair said to me, "You guys from the entertainment industry are always coming and exploiting us." And I'll never forget this phrase, he said, "And then when you're done, you leave and we disappear into the back bedrooms of America."

And that was it. I was hooked. In fact, through my company, Brookfield Productions, we did three award-winning films on the subject—employing people with disabilities. I remember we did a screening in New York at Coler Memorial Hospital, which is basically a facility for people who are severely disabled, and we showed the films (*A Different Approach*, *It's a New Day*, and *Just the Way You Are*), and afterward, a gentleman in a wheelchair came over to me crying, tears were streaming down his face. And he wanted to say something, and finally all he could do was take my hand. And he said, "Thank you."

# WHERE DO YOU BEGIN?

## Notes From the Screenwriting Guru

▶ An Interview With Erik Bork

Erik Bork is a screenwriter best known for his work on the HBO miniseries *Band of Brothers* and *From the Earth to the Moon*. He has sold pitches and written pilots for NBC and FOX, and he's worked on the writing staff for two primetime dramas. He's written features on assignment for Universal, HBO, and TNT, among others. In 2014, he was listed as one of the "Top 10 Most

Erik Bork

Photo by Lisa Robinson

Influential Screenwriting Bloggers" by former MGM exec Stephanie Palmer. Bork's blog and consulting service is called the *Flying Wrestler*.

## By the way . . .

The title of Bork's blog is homage to his favorite movie, *The World According to Garp*, adapted by Steve Tesich from the John Irving novel, and directed by George Roy Hill. As Bork says, "This was a film about an aspiring (and eventually successful) writer, who is also a wrestler. T.S. Garp (played by Robin Williams) dreams of flying, like his father—who he never met." Also, Bork says, it's a metaphor for screenwriting. You're wrestling with story and ideas and the business—but sometimes, when the hard work pays off and everything lines up right, there's a transcendent quality to it, like flying.

**I know you got your start with Tom Hanks. Can you tell me what your breaking-in story looked like? How did you get your spec scripts to him?**
I moved to LA from Ohio, where I got my Bachelor's in film production, with

the intention of initially working as an assistant and writing on the side—this is what one often does, get a secretarial position at one of the studios. So that was the plan, and I started temping, which is what I still recommend to people today. So I was just a secretary and eventually got assigned to Tom Hanks' production company as a temp, and that turned into a full-time assistant position. And then I eventually took a class at UCLA extension in sitcom writing and became interested in trying to write television. I wrote a spec *Frasier* script that got me my first agent.

So I was still working as an assistant, but I had this agent, and she was coaching me in writing sitcom specs. I wrote two others and eventually, after working for Tom for two years (four years total as an assistant), his senior assistant suggested I show him one of my scripts, and so I did, and he liked it. And that led to him eventually suggesting this incredible promotion, which turned into me helping to ultimately write and produce the miniseries *From the Earth to the Moon* for HBO.

**Four years in. And who was your agent at the time? Is this the same agency where you are now?**

No, my original agent was at the Candace Lake Agency. It was a small agency and an agent who had just recently become an agent. At the time, she functioned a lot like managers do now, where she gave me a lot of hands-on time with reading these scripts, gave me lots of feedback, and I did a lot of rewrites for her before she would send them out anywhere. But then eventually I switched over to CAA [Creative Artists Agency] after she left the business. I'd started getting to know a lot of CAA people during my work on *From the Earth to the Moon*, as they were involved with the project and represented Tom Hanks and other people I was working with.

**You said that you would still suggest people get temp jobs. So if you want to be a writer and you're from Arkansas, is moving out to Los Angeles what you would recommend?**

It's always better to live here if you can. It's not necessary, because writing is writing and you can do writing anywhere—and theoretically you can learn about writing anywhere, and you can send your writing to the right people and get noticed from anywhere. But the most serious screenwriters are doing it for years, script after script, and moving here is part of that commitment. But it's expensive to move here, and you don't just do it on a whim. You have to have a plan. And not everybody is cut out to do secretarial work—but if you are, for an aspiring writer, it's a very good day job.

**What if you want to write for TV and not film? Still secretarial work?**

The classic job for an aspiring writer interested in television is to work on a TV show as what they call a *writer's assistant*. This is where you assist the writing staff. I did that also before I worked for Tom Hanks. I did that on a show called *Picket Fences* for one season, a David E. Kelley drama that won the Emmy that year for best drama. It's a great job because you're really around writing all day.

**How did you get that job?**

Well, I got the job when it was still just a pilot that had been picked up to go to series, which is the time when you get jobs as an assistant. I was working at the studio in the temp pool, getting assigned to all these different places around the studio, and I had my ear to the ground about shows that were going to be based at 20th Century Fox studios—shows that were going to be on the air and were going to be hiring writer's assistants. So I figured out where to send a résumé, and then I got interviewed and got hired. For some people, that's really a way in (being a writer's assistant), because they eventually get an opportunity to write an episode of the show they're an assistant on.

> "You have to not be overtly trying to service your own ambitions to do something bigger than that job of secretary."

**When you say you figured out where to send your résumé, where was that and how did you figure that out?**

If you're working at a studio as a temp, the trades are around every day, because every office you temp in, they'll get the trades delivered daily. So you can read them, and it just becomes part of your arsenal of knowledge and tools. It wasn't online back then, but now, Deadline.com, *Hollywood Reporter*, *Variety*, I think they might all still publish these lists of the shows on the air and the production companies, their address and phone number—so you could scour that. But basically, you want to send your résumé to the production office for the show that they're staffing up.

**So you just sent in a résumé and got the job?**

For that one, I also got a recommendation, I think, because I temped for somebody who was at the 20th Century Fox television business affairs department.

She liked me, and *Picket Fences* was staffing up, and I think she might have put in a good word to somebody for me, or maybe she told me who I should apply to or who was going to be hiring, something like that.

**You mentioned earlier that not everybody's cut out to do secretarial work. What does that work involve? What qualities does a person need to have to succeed in that kind of position?**

First, you have to not be overtly trying to service your own ambitions to do something bigger than that job of secretary—which, of course, everybody has those ambitions. But you just need to look and behave professionally in an office environment: You're cool-headed and resourceful, and you're good on the phone. You're answering the phone a lot, so that's a big one. You're doing a lot of scheduling, just doing the grunt work of getting coffee and lunches—whatever the boss needs you to do. Manning the desk outside their office, being their guardian, their channel to the outside world. People come through, you to talk to them, and the boss goes through you to interact with the larger world to some extent, and you're just there to serve that. So you have to be reliable and trustworthy, a good communicator, organized and detail-oriented—just all the things someone would want in an office employee.

**I have this perception that you're a secretary or an assistant, but you're not supposed to raise your hand and say, "I'm a screenwriter, too, actually!" So when do you know that's an okay thing to say?**

That's never an okay thing to say, if you're saying it to try to get others to help you further your ambition and they haven't asked what you really want to do. Tom Hanks told people years later—and it came back to me—that he was impressed that I never did that with him. Of course, there was a part of me that wanted to, and my agent was even pushing me—maybe you should ask him if he can get your work to someone who can hire you to write for a show, etc. But I never did.

**So how does it work then? How do you get your script to Tom Hanks?**

You have to let your writing do the work for you. I was in the right place at the right time, but at the end of the day, I think the reason most people teach the craft, including myself, and don't talk much about the business side is because 99 percent of the business challenge for the writer lies in the craft. Because if the craft isn't there—and for most writers it isn't, because it's not easy to write something that will break through the noise and launch a writer—none of the other stuff matters. If the writing is there, it will find its way out there. I really don't believe there are these brilliant screenplays that just aren't getting there because the doors of Hollywood are too closed. I don't believe that's true at all. It's not about closed doors—it's about writing something that will impress the professionals when they read it, which 99.9 percent of writers probably aren't doing. And I'm not saying that mine was so special, but for whatever reason my *Friends* and *Frasier* spec scripts were good enough to impress an agent and good enough to impress Tom Hanks. If they weren't, it wouldn't matter what contacts I had. So it's really not that writers should or shouldn't be doing certain things to market their work. It's that writers should be *writing*. Yes, there are things you can do—but not very many, and most of them won't work at all unless your writing backs it up.

> "I really don't believe there are these brilliant screenplays that just aren't getting there because the doors of Hollywood are too closed. I don't believe that's true at all. It's not about closed doors— it's about writing something that will impress the professionals when they read it, which 99.9 percent of writers probably aren't doing."

**Let's assume that the aspiring writers reading this book are that .0001 percent. So your friend who got the script to Tom Hanks . . .**
She was a fellow assistant. Actually, she was above me in the hierarchy. She was his first assistant, and I was the second assistant who reported to her. And eventually, I'd paid my dues. I worked there for two years, and I guess she liked me enough to think it wasn't a big deal to ask Tom to read a *Friends* script. It'd be bigger to ask him to read a feature—much bigger, because it's longer and more difficult to read a feature, and then you have to tell the writer what you think about it diplomatically. But with a *Friends* script, we all know the characters, it's a funny show—the worst that can happen is it'll not be a great *Friends* episode. But it takes a half-hour to read, so I think that was part of it, probably.

**So when did this assistant first read your writing, and under what circumstances?**
I don't think she'd even read it. I think somehow she just got to know me and knew that the latest thing I was doing was writing spec TV comedy scripts. She

might even have known I'd signed with an agent. I can't remember. She just said, oh, we should show Tom your little script there, that kind of thing. It was very casual, as I recall.

**So when you're teaching somebody or working with a client, is there a next step once the script gets good enough to put out into the world?**
Yeah, sometimes a script that I work on with someone over a long period of time—multiple drafts, lots of sets of notes—sometimes the script will get to a place where it's really coming together. Usually, it's that the writer will be impatient to get it out, as opposed to me saying it's time, young man. But a point comes sometimes where it's time to send it out, and then there are some things I recommend. I can tell you what they are, but there's no magic secret.

**I would love to know.**
It's always better if you have some personal connections, of course. But most people I'm dealing with don't work in the industry, don't have access to someone who knows someone or anything like that. So you can do queries. You've written a script, you want people to read it, so you can send an email with a short—and I mean *short*—synopsis. The best people to send those to are managers, because nowadays it's very hard to get an agent without already having a manager. Managers are the first hurdle, and once you have a manager, the manager will often eventually try to help you find an agent. That's the common way it works these days.

**Any tips for figuring out which managers are worth querying?**
You only want to bother with the ones who are actually legitimate, because there are plenty of people saying they're managers who aren't really tapped in and can't help you. But there are websites that will tell you every spec script that's sold in a given month or year, who the manager was, the agent, the producer, the logline. There's this guy I know—Jason Scoggins—who compiles all this in what's called the *Scoggins Report*. A bunch of people subscribe to it. Or you can also get that information on his Spec Scout website, where he offers a coverage service that I also like. But this is an easy way to make your own list of managers. I don't know if there are other places to get this without having to do the work yourself to figure out who the legit managers are. But the ones on Scoggins' list, these managers are definitely legitimate. If their client has sold a script to a big enough company that he got on the list—just go back two or three years, and you'll have a list of 100 legit management companies.

**What about emailing producers? Yes? No?**

For mainstream Hollywood, you're generally trying to get a manager. People always want to go straight to producers, but most producers don't take unsolicited material. They take it from agents and some managers they respect, so there's a reason why writers have to first go through these various hurdles. And again, 99.9 percent of the scripts that those producers would read if they came straight from the writers, they'd feel they wasted their time if they read them. So they have systems in place to make sure they're reading potentially viable material. It's a huge stack of scripts to read, but they're scripts that have been vetted by agents and managers, so it's all there for a reason. It's annoying when you're trying to break in, though, trying to get something past those people.

> Tip . . .
> Bork has an excellent blog post about breaking in. Look in the archives on his website for a post called "The Keys to Industry Access."

**If you're a screenwriter and you've been sending out query letters, and you haven't gotten a manager to agree to read the script, what's wrong at that point? Your logline?**

That's difficult. If they haven't wanted to read the script, yeah, it probably means your logline didn't impress them. But more likely, it's the actual story that they think sounds flawed in ways you can't fix by just changing the logline. The reality is that the vast majority of ideas for movies that screenwriters write would have been shot down at the idea stage if the managers had a chance to do so. In fact, once you have a manager, that's what they'll do. They'll have you pitch your ideas *before* you spend the time writing them. They don't want you to waste the time writing them, as they would say—so they'll shoot down most of your ideas.

You can also work with a consultant, instead of a manager—or *before* a manager. When people come to me, if they come in with ideas, I'll do that same thing. I'll help them figure out which of their ideas has the best chance and is maybe most worth writing. And this is almost the most important part of the whole process— identifying a story idea that you *could* synopsize in a logline and managers would really want to read it. That's where people make the mistakes that they can never get past, no matter how good the writing is.

**When you email someone your logline, and they ask for a treatment, what's that about?**

It just means that they don't want to commit to reading the whole script. They want something longer than the logline but not a whole script. A treatment gives them more detail about your story essentially.

**How long should the treatment be?**

I don't think anyone wants to see a forty-page treatment in that situation. They might want to see four pages—I would say between four and twelve pages is probably what they have in mind. It's hard to know without asking them specifically, though. I think most people would just want the script, but there are some that would ask for a treatment.

**If you say most people would want the script, then what is the point of the treatment?**

Generally a treatment is just something writers use for their own process—to plan out the structure and scenes before they start writing. If you're writing a script for a studio—they've hired you, you've pitched it, and they're paying you to write the script—then you have to turn in a treatment or outline as part of your deal with them. Before you write the script, they're going to approve the outline. They'll give notes, make you rewrite it—so that's just part of the steps you have to take as a professional writer. But when you're writing on spec, there's really no point in having a treatment for anyone else's purpose, because no one else usually wants to read a full-on treatment. Usually you just have a short, under one-page synopsis, and then the script.

**Any last comments about the nature of the business and what writers need to understand?**

It's always an uphill climb to get anything sold or made, no matter what it is. The odds are against you at every point, no matter how good your stuff is. It's always something of a miracle when anything breaks through—when a movie gets made or a script gets sold. It's not every day for anyone. Even people that have been doing this professionally for a long time, it's a big deal to have either of those things happen. A lot of professionals are writing their scripts on spec and not selling most of them. Or they have their agents not want to send them out, because they don't think they can do anything with them. It's not all just about breaking in in this business—it's sustaining it, too. And that's challenging.

# FROM WRITER'S ASSISTANT TO SHOWRUNNER

## Interning, Knocking on Doors, and Making Connections

▶ An Interview With Stacy A. Littlejohn

Stacy A. Littlejohn has been working steadily in television since the mid-1990s, and she is one of a select few African American women to bear the title of Showrunner. She has written for shows such as *The Hughleys* (1998–2000), *One on One* (2001–2002), *Cedric the Entertainer Presents* (2002–2003), *Barbershop* (2005), *All of Us* (2004–2007), *The Wanda Sykes Show* (2009–2010), *Single Ladies* (2011–2014), *Mistresses* (2015), and *American Crime* (2015–2016). Littlejohn has producer credits on many of these shows, most notably *Single Ladies*, *Mistresses*, and *American Crime*.

In 2011, Littlejohn created the hit series *Single Ladies* for VH1 in partnership with Queen Latifah's company, Flavor Unit Entertainment. The series shot in Atlanta, and Littlejohn served as showrunner for the first two seasons. She has worked closely with Will Smith, Jada Pinkett Smith, and Oscar-winning screenwriter John Ridley (*12 Years a Slave*). She is currently a writer and co-executive producer on Ridley's *American Crime* for ABC.

Stacy A. Littlejohn

Amanda Edwards/WireImage/
Getty Images

**Did you always know you wanted to write for television?**
Not at all. I was convinced I was going to be a criminal defense lawyer, but during my senior year I realized that I could possibly be defending people who

were guilty. I don't know why that never occurred to me before. I guess I was thinking I'd be the hero and defend people who'd been wrongfully accused. So I panicked, because I was three years into college. I was working, putting myself through Berkeley, and I was supposed to be figuring out what law school I wanted to go to.

**Where were you working?**
I had four jobs throughout college at the same time. I was a preschool teacher Monday, Wednesday, Friday; I was a bank teller at Wells Fargo Tuesdays and Thursdays; I did concert security at night for Bill Graham Presents; and I was the chief of staff to the student body president.

**So you've always been accustomed to hard work.**
I guess so. I'm sick of it now. I've proven that I can do it. Now I'd like my very rich husband to come along and sweep me off my feet and let me just be home to raise my baby boy.

**How old is your baby?**
He's 2 now. I'm the center of his universe, I've got to tell you. This boy is so happy when he sees me, and the feeling is mutual. But anyway, those were my jobs throughout school. So I took a semester off, not wanting to waste money doing something I didn't want to do, and I sat around my house while my roommates all went to class. And while I was sitting there, I was watching an episode of one of the early black sitcoms, maybe it was *Good Times*, and I remember getting offended hearing the voices, thinking they weren't genuine or authentic. I'm not saying that you have to be black to write for a black person or you have to be white to write for a white person, but this was so off that it was really making me angry. I was getting all self-righteous, but thinking, if you're not out there trying to make a difference, you don't really have a right to complain about it. So in that moment, it clicked for me—maybe I could help contribute to the voices on television.

## By the way . . .

Littlejohn created her own major at Berkeley, Gender and Ethnicity in Mass Media, and she ended up writing a thesis paper on images of black women in film from the 1970s to the 1990s.

**What was your first job in the business?**
My first job in television was in 1992 at Channel 2 News in Oakland. It was an internship, and my job was to bring the copy to the talent. There was a teleprompter back then, but the news anchors needed copy just in case something went wrong with it. So they would write the news, they'd hand me that piece of paper, and I'd hand it to the anchorperson in the studio. They told me, "Don't talk to the talent. Just put the paper on the desk and walk away." Now, the minute someone tells me not to do something, I'm like, why not? So I would go up and say, "Here you go"—just being the little snarky 21-year-old I was.

One of the reporters, Faith Fancher, she got a kick out of me and invited me out on her journalistic adventures. I got to see how she interviewed people, how she cut it together, what she wrote. She's passed away now, but she was a huge newsperson in the Bay area for many years. She was in everyone's living room for twenty-something years on television. So at that time, this was a big deal. She ended up being an important mentor for me. She helped me believe in myself and see that I could have a job that I enjoy that also makes a difference in the world.

**You were still in school at the time?**
Still taking classes at Berkeley, and then I did an exchange program with Howard University in DC where you could do all the hands-on stuff. And while I was in DC, I worked at BET, because that was important to me. That's what got me into it to begin with.

**Channel 2 News, BET, and then you interned at Nickelodeon?**
Yeah, there was a communications job fair at Howard where you could get an interview with the major networks. MTV networks were there, and I was thinking I wanted to do documentaries. Remember how MTV used to have the rockumentaries? So I thought that could be a fun way into documentaries. So they looked at my résumé and said, "You've been teaching preschool for four years, and you said you want to do programming for children?" and I'm like, "Yeah, I do, but now I'm interested in rockumentaries." I was a little all over the place.

I kept trying to steer the conversation back to the rockumentaries, but they were focused on what my application said, and they told me they'd consider me for Nickelodeon. So I ended up having to apply and then interview for the internship, which is a whole other story, just getting down to Florida for the interview. But when I got there, they asked, "What are your opinions about Nickelodeon?" And I said, "Well, I don't want to offend you, but I feel like you don't have enough people of color on your channel, so it's hard for me to relate to anything on there." It had been a long trip down, and I think I was just exhausted, but I thought, oh, Lord, why did I say that? There goes my job. But turns out that comment got me the internship.

**What was the show? And what were you doing as an intern?**
It was a show called *My Brother and Me*, and when I started, they told me I'd be making copies and getting the writers coffee, but the executive producer, Calvin Brown, Jr., he asked me what I wanted to do in the business. I told him I wanted to write, and he said, "Well, if you want to write, then you're going to come in the writers' room with us and you'll pitch and see what happens."

Now, at the time, I didn't know how huge that was. I was able to pitch jokes that went into the script, and I wrote teasers and tags. In my twenty-something years of television, now I know that this just doesn't happen. I had to beg my friend to help me with the plane ticket, I almost missed my connecting flight, I had to walk I don't know how many blocks in my high heels to get to that interview in the full sun, and I was supposed to be making copies . . .

> "I do believe that if your energy is pointed in a direction, it's going to happen for you. It's just a matter of how you get it. But you have to be steering that train."

**Seems like everything lined up for Nickelodeon to happen for you.**
Everything lined up, but it was also my will to do it, because I do believe that if your energy is pointed in a direction, it's going to happen for you. It's just a matter of how you get it. But you have to be steering that train. I couldn't just wait for people to give it to me. I think things were falling in line for me because I was so focused. I had my eyes on the prize.

**I'd love to unravel this with you, because you were also open-minded enough to recognize a different prize when you saw it. You wanted to work for MTV doing the rockumentaries, but they saw you writing for kids instead, and you didn't dismiss that. You changed your pursuit.**
You're right, and I could have dismissed it. You do have to be open. I guess because I'd had my eyes on the criminal defense lawyer prize for so long and

that ended up not happening, I learned not to be so married to something. I remember thinking, a year and a half ago I didn't even know I'd be this into TV and suddenly I'm pursuing a career in television. So maybe documentaries aren't where I'll start, but it's important to just start.

**I like that—it's important just to start.**
Yup, all I wanted was experience in the business. When that Nickelodeon experience ended that summer, they said, "You should call us after you graduate. We might be working somewhere and could give you a job as a PA." So when I moved to LA and looked them up, they were all working on *Moesha*, but at the time, they'd already done their hiring. I'd taken some time off for a few months after school, and I didn't realize that you had to come in at a certain point in the season to get work for the upcoming season, so I'd missed the window to get hired.

So I was told I should get a job as a PA—that this was the easiest way to get in and work your way up. I had this list, and every morning I would call the shows and studios and ask if they were hiring PAs. I did this every morning for about two months, until one day, I think I bugged the hell out of people, because they were like, oh my God, can you stop calling? But I knew how competitive it was. I knew that I had to be the one who stands out in people's minds. So I finally got the PA job.

**What was the show?**
It was a show called *The Last Frontier* on Fox. They didn't invite me into the writers' room like the other showrunner had. Believe me, I was making the copies and getting lunch for the writers. So that's when I knew I'd had a unique experience with Nickelodeon. But I did that for thirteen episodes on *The Last Frontier*, and then I was like, okay, it's time to be a writer's assistant. How do I get into a writers' room?

Well, all the other PAs were trying to be writer's assistants, too, and they were like, "Uh-uh, you've got to pay your dues." And I'm going, I just paid them! Didn't I just pay them? How many more dues do I have to pay? But I kept digging, and I would go to parties, always making people laugh. And these writers I was hanging with, they knew I wanted to write, so I got invited to punch-up sessions for pilots.

### What's a punch-up session?

People want to sell their pilot, but they need the jokes to be sharper, so they invite a bunch of writers to come in. It's like your audition as a writer. If you get jokes in the script, they'll remember you. So I started getting known for doing this punch-up work around town.

### And it was through the punch-ups that you got to be a writer's assistant?

Somewhere along the way I met up with Mara Brock Akil. She went on to create *Girlfriends*, *The Game*, and *Being Mary Jane*, but at the time she was just an assistant. She had just gotten her first writing job on *Moesha*, and she hooked me up with her old boss who needed a writer's assistant for a show he'd created on Fox called *The Show*. It was short-lived, but through that I got to meet John Ridley, and I got to pitch jokes to the executive producers, Matt Wickline and John Bowman. Now, you've got to remember these names, Matt and John, because they're important—they're going to come up again.

Now, at that time, John Ridley had written and was going to direct his first film produced by Oliver Stone, and asked me to be his assistant. I was like, hell yeah. So I assisted him for that film, and when it ended, those folks I knew from Nickelodeon, they were still on *Moesha*, and they called me in to be a writer's assistant. So now I'm at *Moesha*, and I'm in the second season doing that, and I'm sitting at my desk and my phone rings. It's Matt Wickline from *The Show*. And he says, "Hey, I'm creating a show for D.L. Hughley. I think you have his voice. Do you want to come write on the show?" So I left *Moesha* and thanked God for Matt Wickline and John Bowman. That was in 1998, and from that point forward I've been working my way up ever since.

> "All the other PAs were trying to be writer's assistants, too, and they were like, 'Uh-uh, you've got to pay your dues.' And I'm going, I just paid them! Didn't I just pay them? How many more dues do I have to pay?"

**So do you think you could pinpoint the reason why you got that initial gig with Matt and John?**

All of this happened because of relationships I built when I first got to Los Angeles. And by the way, John Ridley has hired me three or four times on different shows that he's had along the way. But just to clarify, these were genuine relationships, not born out of wanting to use anyone to get ahead. It was interesting, though, now that I think about it, because I barely had time to keep up these relationships. I hadn't talked to Matt in two years because I was so busy. You're easily working eighty-/ninety-hour weeks. You want to keep in touch, but when you finally get off work, you're lucky if you sleep five hours, and then it's off to work again. My paychecks were so high when I was a writer's assistant because I was in overtime, then gold time. There'd be times where you come to work at 10:00 a.m. and you wouldn't get off work until 2:00 a.m. the next morning and have to be right back in eight hours to be there at 10:00 a.m. again. And as a writer's assistant, you're not on salary, so they've got to pay you.

**Could you describe what a writer's assistant does on a sitcom?**

You sit in the room with the writing staff, and as they come up with the words and actions in the script, you're typing it. The script is up on a screen, and they're all looking at this script as they talk, and they're making changes like, "No-no, we don't want him to say that—have him say this." And you have to type what he said. "Okay, now we want him to walk across the room and slam the door." So you type that. You're literally typing all their words and creating the actual script that will go out to the actors, studio, network execs, and the entire production.

**And getting tons of experience in the writers' room obviously, hearing how the writers do it.**

Exactly, and that's what I wanted, because everyone had said, if you want to be a writer, get in that room and see how it's done. So once all the writers go home at maybe 11:00 or 12:00 at night, as the writer's assistant, you have to stay, because now you have to edit the script. And then once you have a clean draft, the showrunners take it back into their office to read. And you've got to sit there and wait. You've been at work ten or eleven hours already, and now you're waiting for them to change stuff again, which easily adds another few hours to your day. And then you put in those changes and make sure the script is ready to go out that night to get delivered to the actors' homes and the networks and the studio tomorrow. Everyone's got to get that script so that when we come back in the morning, everyone is ready. This routine happens every day, and at the end of the week we film that episode. That's how it works, week in and week out, at least in sitcom world.

**During this period when you were a writer's assistant, did you believe that you were going to somehow get the respect to move on from there? Were you writing your own scripts?**

I was still doing punch-up at this time, so people on the outside knew that at least I could tell jokes. But I didn't have time to write my own scripts. When Matt Wickline called me that day at *Moesha*, my heart started pumping because I didn't have a script. To get hired, you need at least one spec script to show people that you can create a full story, but I was so busy working that I didn't have time to even think about anything else. So when I met D.L., and he put his stamp of approval on me, that's when Matt said, "Okay, now the network and the studio need to read your spec script. What have you got?" I told him I didn't have one, and he said, "Well, you better come up with one, because if you don't have a script in a month, there's nothing we can do. They have to see some evidence that you're a writer."

I'd actually already written a *Roseanne* spec script before I got to LA, but *Roseanne* had gotten canceled three months after I arrived and I was told that people wouldn't bother reading a spec for a show that was no longer on the air. So I ended up writing a *Frasier* spec, because I thought, I'm a young black girl, they wouldn't expect me to write that. So I wrote that script in a month, and it almost killed me, because I was doing those crazy hours at *Moesha*. So it was really intense, but I thought, I can't be this close to victory and let it go.

> "I was always one of two women in a writers' room, because in comedy, guys typically don't think girls are funny. It's better nowadays, but that's how it was— you're literally one of two women."

**_Single Ladies_. What was the impetus for that show?**

I created *Single Ladies* during the strike. I'd been working on a sitcom called *All of Us* that was just getting canceled, and usually when a show ends, writers have time to create original material while looking for their next gig. So I did what we call the "couch and water tour." You literally take all these meetings and sit on people's couches in their offices, and they offer you water and you talk for an hour—and then boom, you have another contact that could potentially lead to another writing job.

Maggie Malina had responded to one of my spec scripts over at VH1, so I got a meeting with her. Turns out VH1 was teamed up with Flavor Unit, which is Queen Latifah's company, and they were looking for a show that appealed to black women. They didn't know what that show was yet, only that they wanted two female leads that had two different outlooks on love and relationships. So they asked me to think of some ideas and come back and pitch to them.

This is how it works when you're not coming in to sell a specific idea of your own. Writers come in, and the studio or the network tells you what they're looking for. You go back home and think of a world where these things could happen, and you come back and pitch it to them. And they either say, thank you but no thank you, or we love it. And in my case, they said, we love it.

**Which is how rare?**
It's a miracle that it happened. I've been in so many meetings where they tell you they love it, but then you never go back. So when they bought it, I was like, "What? Did I hear this right?" I was blessed that I had the winning idea of all the writers they met with. I was just blessed—and was lucky enough to have my finger on the pulse of what they wanted. Sometimes they don't know what they want until they hear it. It's so random and so subjective it still amazes me when shows get sold.

**So you went home to work on it, and what did you come back to them with in your pitch?**
I came back with characters. I pitched them who I thought these women were and what the world might be, what their ideas of love were, what a pilot episode could be, and if I were to do a season, where the season might go and how it would end. I also talked about ideas beyond season one, because it's important to show them that there are years worth of interesting stories to tell. I memorized this pitch and did it verbally at first—it was a quick pitch. And then later I gave it to them in writing.

**I'm so curious to hear why you left the show. You were showrunning, shooting in Atlanta, but you left after two years?**
When I told you about those grueling hours on *Moesha*, those seventy- to ninety-hour weeks, you have to imagine even longer hours as a showrunner. Those first two seasons of *Single Ladies*—this is not an exaggeration—I worked eighteen hours a day. For about two years, I took three-hour naps at night, because that

was all I had. So at the end of two years, I thought, life is just too short. I hadn't seen my friends or family for any significant amount of time because I was working weekends, too. As showrunner, I could only hire two writers, when normally an hour-long show will have six to ten writers. And the second season was even more intense. So when I heard we were being picked up for a third season, I was like, oh no-no-no. Bless you and God be with you so you can keep it going and I can keep getting checks, but I will not be here.

**When was your son born in the midst of all this?**
Well, that's right. I'd been planning to have this baby basically when the show first began. I was trying to figure out when would be a good time to get pregnant, and it was obviously not going to be during the first season, because the show was my baby. So once the second season started and it was even more intense than the first, I was like, okay, I'm going to go get pregnant and do nothing for a year. And in fact, when I left, that's when it happened—I didn't take a meeting, I didn't read a script, I didn't pitch an idea. I didn't want to do anything but have a peaceful pregnancy. I had my baby when I was 42.

The thing was, as I was growing up in the business, I was seeing all these women without families. By the way, I was always one of two women in a writers' room, because in comedy, guys typically don't think girls are funny. It's better nowadays, but that's how it was—you're literally one of two women. And I was always the youngest person in the room. The women were in their late 30s, early 40s, and they were all single, or if they weren't single, none of them had babies. That was a sad reality that really stuck in my mind.

**Single ladies . . .**
Right? And by the way, I'm a single lady, a single mom, now. Not by design—it's just how it worked out. But I looked up to these women. They'd all reached a level of success that I was aspiring to, but barely any of them had families, which made sense because you're literally married to the business. So I was like, no-no, this can't happen to me. That's a part of history I didn't want to repeat.

So here I am in my 40s, and I've been blessed with my career, and I have a healthy baby. I'll keep the career going, but I'm in a weird stage where I'm trying to figure out how to divide my time and be a mom and a writer, because truly I love both. But honestly, being a mom trumps everything.

# Notes

1 Austin Film Festival, Q&A, October 2011.
2 Jada Yuan, "Almost Famous," *New York Magazine*, August 16, 2009, accessed April 27, 2016, http://nymag.com/arts/art/features/58305/
3 Max Mihelich, "Special Report: Staffing Still Soaring," *Workforce*, October 1, 2014, accessed April 27, 2016, www.workforce.com/2014/10/01/special-report-staffing-still-soaring

# CHAPTER 2

# STICKING IT OUT

> "There's no such thing as talent;
> you just have to work hard enough."
> David Mamet

**No matter what career path you choose**, there will be ups and downs. It's never a straight line up to ringing bells and a crowd cheering with delight at your finally having achieved success. That sweet smell people talk about is actually the smell of blood, sweat, and tears.

As a screenwriter, though, the path to success can be even more jagged and less predictable than in other fields. The highs are higher and the lows lower. You're hot one day, and the next day you're not. You think you're "in" only to discover you're way in the outfield. You write and rewrite for two years only to find out that someone else has written your exact story and it's now in production with huge stars.

The stories of what it takes to stick it out and succeed as a screenwriter are simultaneously inspiring and overwhelming. Do you have the drive? Are you so committed to your future career that you're willing to weather the highs and lows on the road to success? Are you emotionally capable of it?

Melissa Rosenberg, writer of the *Twilight* film series and executive producer of *Dexter* and *Jessica Jones*, once said that the determining factor in a screenwriter's success is how quickly she can pick herself up off the floor when she falls.[1] The successful screenwriter will be fired. The successful screenwriter will be ignored. She'll bomb in a pitch meeting. He'll lose a producer's interest. Her movie will tank at the box office. He'll be rewritten by a master—or by his former assistant.

Again, there are no rules in this career.

## Who Knew?

David Magee did a staggering 170 rewrites on *Life of Pi* before it went into production.[2] What if he stopped on the 150th rewrite? Sticking it out as a screenwriter doesn't mean six months, or even five years. Allan Loeb, writer of *Things We Lost in the Fire*, *21*, *Wall Street: Money Never Sleeps*, *The Switch*, and *Just Go With It*, was a struggling writer for close to a decade before selling his first screenplay.[3]

In this chapter, you'll read about:

- What it takes to succeed in a pitch meeting, what these meetings look like, and how you can prepare
- A veteran film producer's experiences getting started in independent film and what you can learn from the evolution of a script from the first draft to the last
- Tips for staying productive and inspired before you get your big break
- What a showrunner is looking for in a writer in responding to feedback
- Three writers' programs for new voices at CBS, Humanitas, and the Writers Guild of America
- Working with a screenwriting coach in preparation to take meetings with industry executives
- An award-winning writer-director's take on working on multiple projects simultaneously to avoid the inevitable downfall that happens when a project comes to an end
- How to take lessons from your protagonist's journey and avoid and overcome obstacles in your screenwriting career

That's a good place to begin. What if you were the protagonist in your screenplay and you could write your own journey?

# THE SCREENWRITER'S JOURNEY

▸ By Pat Verducci

One thing they never tell you in film school is that while you're figuring out the structure for your screenplay—where the hero must step into the cave, kill the monster, appear to die once more at the end, but seize the sword and miraculously transform—is that you, the writer, will have to undergo your own hero's journey as you work toward becoming a professional screenwriter.

You may not have to enter an actual cave. It may just be your apartment that becomes dark and scary, filled with pizza boxes and dirty clothes that you're too depressed to launder. You may not have to lift an actual sword, but you might have to come up with a shiny idea that has a sharp edge to save your butt in the writers' room. You probably won't have to answer a classic "riddle" to gain entrance to a labyrinth, but you may have to decipher what's code for "passing" on your project, or figure out what to do next when someone says they "love" your script but never calls you back.

Thank you Joseph Campbell, for studying all those myths and fairy tales and discovering that they are all the same story. Thank you for breaking it down into the twelve phases of *The Hero's Journey* so we can better understand the heroes in our narratives.

And thank you for creating the perfect metaphor for the writer's experience so that we, as humble film scribes, can use it to actively pursue and survive our careers.

So here it is—*The Screenwriter's Journey*. I'll give you two versions of the story. The first is the most common version, the journey you *don't* want to emulate. And the second is the one you *must* embrace if you hope to succeed . . .

# The Screenwriter's Journey, Version 1

## Ordinary World

We find you, the hero, sitting in a college chemistry classroom. Your father is a doctor who makes great money, takes fantastic vacations, and seems pretty happy. What's good enough for him is good enough for you, right? The class is hard, though. I mean "moles," really? It's kind of a nightmare, and your heart really isn't in it. Your roommate asks you to go to the movies. Desperate to escape your chemistry textbook, you agree.

## Call to Adventure

You're in a darkened movie theater. You can't really afford to buy popcorn—you're a poor college student after all, so you bring your own. Damn, it's hard to fit that Pop Secret bag inside your backpack. The lights dim. You shouldn't be here. Movies are your Kryptonite. You're helpless against them. And this one is really good. You're on the edge of your seat. You feel alive. You feel exactly the opposite of how you feel when you're sitting in front of your chemistry professor. What the hell are you doing with your life? Why are you settling for fulfilling other people's expectations? You've always wanted to be a screenwriter. Why are you giving up on yourself already?

The next day, terrified, you walk over to the film department and talk to a professor there. She's amazing. She has crazy hair and wears hipster clothes and talks about the semiotics of Quentin Tarantino, and you feel almost like you're high on drugs.

You walk back to your dorm and decide to tell your parents that you're switching departments and becoming a film major. To bolster your argument, you go online to gather success stories to share with them.

## Refusal to the Call

Instead of success stories, the Web is filled with cautionary tales. You're afraid now. Very afraid. There's no way you can be a film major.

## Meeting With the Mentor

But that night, you sneak out to see that movie again. This time, by yourself, and without popcorn. Your heart still pounds. Again, you feel alive. There's no way to escape the film's cellular pull on you. Forget being a doctor. No way you're going to play it "safe." Damn the statistics. You'll be the exception!

## Crossing the Threshold

You have a long, complicated conversation with your parents, where they try to be supportive but express their fears with you. You listen, but then blow them off. They are old. They don't know what they're talking about. You'll invite them to your blockbuster premiere, and they'll be puffed up with pride! You declare your major. You work on your friends' films and pull apart the script for *Citizen Kane* 400 times. You learn about three-act structure, and yes, The Hero's Journey. You explore how to motivate your characters. You watch a million movies. You knew you would be special, and you are. You win the screenwriting competition at your college. You're on top of the world! You've got your feature comedy script tucked under one arm and your one-hour TV pilot tucked under the other.

You graduate, pack your meager belongings, and head to Hollywood!

## Tests, Allies, and Enemies

You move in with some people you met on Craigslist. Some are actors, and you imagine the hilarious stories you'll tell twenty years from now about living together in this crappy apartment on Hayworth Avenue (trust me, at some point, you *will* end up on Hayworth Avenue. F. Scott Fitzgerald did, and so will you).

You get a job as a temp and start sending out your scripts to the list of agents you've compiled. Each morning, you get up and crank out four pages. You become friends with the people at work (wow, is *everyone* in Los Angeles an aspiring actor or writer?). You send your finished scripts out to contests and get no traction.

You start attending "networking" events and screenings. You send impassioned letters to your favorite filmmakers. You never hear back.

You've been rejected by every agent you've approached.

Maybe you weren't meant to be a writer after all?

## Approach to the Inmost Cave

The company you're temping for goes belly up. You can't find another day job. You check your bank account. It's looking bad. *Very* bad.

## Ordeal

You keep looking for work and stop working on your pages. You start replaying that phone conversation you had with your parents where they expressed their concern and you blew them off. You start living on Top Ramen. You feel light-headed all the time. You tell your roommate you might be short on rent this month. She isn't happy and says you better get the money or else you're out. You don't want to call your parents, but you have to. You tell them everything's great, you made the semifinals in the Podunk Valley Screenwriting Contest and you *know* you'll make the finals, but right now you need a loan. Of course, they give you the money, but your mother starts to worry.

You keep waiting for those agents to get back to you. None of them does. They must really hate your writing.

All of your friends ask how your writing is going. You say it's going great, but the truth is you haven't sat down to write in weeks. You are frozen in fear. You have no ideas. How are you supposed to be creative when you're totally stressed out?

You get another temp job. Everyone there is an aspiring actor or writer, too. You start to understand all those horror stories you read on the Internet. You become cynical. There's no way to make it. There's just no way.

One of your friends from film school gets signed by CAA. Whaaat? He's a total hack! You start to believe that your moment has passed you by. You're a failure.

It's confirmed when you get the rejection letter from the Podunk Valley Screenwriting contest.

You can't go to the movies anymore. It's just too painful. You spend a lot of time in your room with the blinds drawn thinking about F. Scott Fitzgerald.

## Seizing the Sword

You go home for a family wedding. You listen to your father talk about this amazing case he's been working on. He was able to save the patient's life using a new titanium screw that allows paralyzed people to breathe. He's actually doing important work in the world. Okay, so chemistry wasn't your strong suit, but you were good in Bio. Maybe it's time to let go of the dream?

## The Road Back

You talk to your parents about moving back home and going to med school. They are awesome. They never say, "I told you so," but your mom's no longer lighting candles at Our Lady of Angels. You get a job working at the same hospital where your dad's on staff and study for the MCAT. You do really well. You apply. You get into your second choice. You accept.

You dive into med school with a vengeance. Yeah, the people are a little science nerdy, and they have no idea who Godard is, but that's okay.

## Resurrection

You're at the end of your first year. You're exhausted from studying. Who knew there were so many freaking body parts? A friend asks you to go to the movies. You're wary, but just to get away from your books, you accept.

It's the *same movie*. The one that changed your life. The one that made you feel alive and understand your purpose. You watch it with your teeth clenched. You grip your popcorn.

You decide to let it go. It wasn't meant to be. You weren't special enough. It wasn't the right fit.

## Return With the Elixir

You go back to your apartment. You crack open your biology book. You don't hate it. You don't love it. You become a doctor. But in the back of your mind, for the rest of your life, you wonder . . .

*What if?*

All right. Sorry to put you through that, but it's better just to read this story than to actually live it. (By the way, if you turned this tale in to your screenwriting professor, you'd get a B minus and a bunch of notes about how your protagonist is too "passive" and has a weak goal.)

Now, here's the version you *must* live to create a screenwriting career.

# The Screenwriter's Journey, Version 2

Let's just fast-forward from the Ordinary World through Crossing the Threshold. You'll probably be inspired in much the same way . . .

*TO RECAP: School bores you, you go to a movie with a friend, suddenly realize what you're meant to do with your life, meet the funky-ass film professor, read the scary cautionary tales online, almost buckle in fear, pull yourself together, try to win your parents over to your new life plan, tell them off in your head, and move to Los Angeles. SMASH CUT TO:*

## Tests, Allies, and Enemies

You move in with some people you met on Craigslist. You understand this is a long game—so yeah, you focus on getting the scripts you wrote in film school out there, but you also sign on for projects that make you happy, for free. While you're temping, you work on a Web series with some friends, and you write another TV comedy. You go to networking events, but instead of trying to meet Steven Spielberg, who's on the panel, you hang out in the bar with the other writers who are there for the same reason. You get to know each other, you read each other's scripts, create a support system. Together, you work on projects that you write, shoot, and edit yourself. You're not waiting to "break in" to a business that exists outside of you, but instead, you're making "your own" show business.

None of the agents or managers responds to your scripts. Still, you keep writing. You're working on creating a body of work. The more projects you have under your belt, the better.

You start writing a blog about how tough it is. It's funny and sassy, and you make jokes about what a crappy doctor you would have been. Some producer reads your blog and thinks it's funny. She calls you up. Hey, she's doing a weird

TV show on cable for 18 cents. Are you interested? You bring a bunch of ideas to her. She decides you're too green, but she likes you. She asks if you'll be a PA.

You say, "Hell yeah." You live on Top Ramen and craft services until the thought of eating one more piece of Red Vine licorice literally activates your gag reflex.

You finish your new TV pilot. The producer comes by and asks how you're doing. You say, "Great!" She's starting to walk away, and you feel like you're going to throw up, but you open your mouth, and you hear yourself *asking if she'll read your pilot*. (This is key—you reach out to the people you've created relationships with and get them engaged in helping you succeed.) She says yes, and she loves it. She sends it out.

Amazon says they want to make your show.

## Approach to the Inmost Cave

You do multiple rewrites, tell all your friends, and they are supportive of you. Drinks! On the house! Still, some of your new friends have also gotten close with projects that never happened. So you don't sit on your butt, wallowing in possible future glory. While you wait for Amazon to give the official green light, you start writing another project. The producer calls you. Amazon has decided not to make your pilot. You get depressed, but just for a couple of days. You start sending out the script and your new project to agents and managers. A young manager likes it. He says you need to write some more scripts.

You return to your temp job, and you do write more scripts. No one buys them.

## Ordeal

You've now been in Los Angeles for two years, and you're right where you started. You have a manager, sure, but nothing's happened. You're basically dressed in rags and driving a crappy car that barely runs. You start to wonder if this is all worth it.

You close the drapes in your apartment. You start to eat pizza every night. You stop seeing your other writer friends. But one of them is a huge pain in the butt. Her name is Katrina, and she's from Germany. She's constantly bringing you chocolates. You've gotten fat but no longer care. She pounds on your door. That chocolate is damn good. You open up.

Katrina's depressed too. But she has a great idea: a comedy about two depressives. It makes you smile.

## Seizing the Sword

You decide to work on it together. You eat lots of chocolate and start to have fun again.

## The Road Back

It's a tough comedy concept (depression—ha-ha-ha!), and it's the first time you've worked with someone else, but you know there's gold in there somewhere. You set a schedule and write at the same time every day: nine until noon, Monday through Saturday. You treat it like a real job, with a paycheck. You continue to work at your temp job in the afternoon and reassure your parents that everything is fine.

You stop eating chocolate. You take up jogging, because you can't afford a gym but want to feel good so you write better and more efficiently. You argue with Katrina about which jokes are funny. You write new scenes, cut others, and fine-tune until you're both bleary-eyed and fading.

Finally, you open up the drapes. You think you see the ghost of F. Scott walking past, but realize it's just an out-of-work actor you know.

## Resurrection

You call your manager (whom you haven't heard from in months) and say you have something new. You send it.

One week. Two weeks. He doesn't return your call. You keep trying until a month has passed. Katrina is starting to lose heart, and so are you. You feel like you've been here before. A million times. Why won't anyone give you a chance?

You're tempted to buy some chocolate, but instead you go see that movie that inspired you. It's a comedy, but you're crying. You go home and ask yourself, "What would I do if I were fearless?"

You send an email the next day to your manager and fire him.

You go to El Coyote to commiserate with your friends. Six giant margaritas in, one of your buddies has an announcement. She's gone to the dark side and become a junior executive at Sony. You and Katrina look at each other and immediately start pitching her your depression comedy.

Your Sony friend reads the script, loves it, and shows it to her new boss, who thinks it's *A-mazing*. They buy it.

Suddenly, your manager is calling you off the hook, but you've moved on and found another manager who's really willing to work for you. The pilot gets green-lit, but you and Katrina find out they're hiring a new writer to "fix it." For a moment (again) you feel horrible. All the bad feelings come back about being worthless, but this time you've learned the lessons of the journey. You and Katrina are already preparing a series of pitches together and strike while the iron is hot. No one buys your pitches, but one of the producers likes you and Katrina and has another project that needs a rewrite. She takes you to the studio. You get the job.

## Return With the Elixir

Your ordinary world is now one of a working screenwriter. By the way, they fired that other writer who rewrote your script, and you and Katrina are back on the project! The elixir, or the wisdom you've gained on your quest, is threefold: 1) You must always be actively writing; 2) You cannot wait for others to give you a job; and 3) You must be part of a community of like-minded artists. You will support them, they will support you, and they (not your manager or agent) will often be the ones who create your next opportunity.

Your comedy pilot about depression ends up being a huge hit and even saves lives. Your parents are proud.

*FADE TO BLACK.*

The really tough thing I need to tell you is that this is only Act 1 of the many hero's journeys you will undertake in your life as a screenwriter. You will go through terrible lulls, some of them existential, where you will have to re-tap into that feeling you had back in that college movie theater. You will need to be flexible, embrace your stick-to-itness, and use discipline as weapons. You must be a good person and make friends. In supporting others, you will be supported.

By the way, every successful screenwriter you admire has been through some form of this journey. And sometimes, each project can be its own hero's journey.

Just like the characters in your screenplay, you must be active. The dragons and labyrinths are many. They will be both internal and external. You will have to go to the land of the dead multiple times. But the elixir is amazing. You get to make stuff up.

What better life could there be?

For every hero living the screenwriter's journey, the story will be different in its particulars. But at its core, the narrative will always be the same . . .

*It'll be about facing your fear, embracing it, and continuing to walk forward, fingers on the keyboard.*

---

**PAT VERDUCCI** is a writing coach and story consultant who works with *New York Times* bestselling authors, experienced screenwriters, and beginners of all stripes on their novels, memoirs, and screenplays. She has worked as a story consultant for Disney/Pixar and has written screenplays for Touchstone Pictures, Witt-Thomas Productions, and Disney's animation division. She wrote and directed the feature film *True Crime*, and her writing credits also include documentary films. Pat has written and directed featurettes for HBO and Showtime, and she co-produced the award-winning documentary *Somewhere Between*. Pat is a member of the Writers Guild of America, teaches screenwriting in UCLA Extension's Writing Program, and has been a mentor at the Meryl Streep/IRIS Writing Lab for Women. She has also served as a volunteer teacher for InsideOUT Writers, a non-profit that facilitates writing workshops for incarcerated youth inside Los Angeles County's juvenile halls. You can sign up for her weekly blog on writing at *patverducci.com*.

Pat Verducci

Photo by Amy Shertzer

# WHAT IS A PITCH . . .?

## And Why and How Do You Do It?

▶ By Joshua Malkin

Strangely, I was fairly far along in my screenwriting pursuits before becoming fully aware of a disappointing wrinkle. In order to make a living in Hollywood, I wasn't just expected to write. A screenwriting career would be accompanied by the unsavory prospect of presenting film stories aloud, face-to-face, and sometimes face-to-*several*-faces-at-once.

This ran counter to what I appreciated about writing in the first place—the opportunity to groom every thought and phrase prior to presentation. I'd long regarded the written word as a shield, assuming that "me on paper" was much stronger than "me in a room with strangers." I'm shy, and the prospect of public speaking made my palms sweat days in advance. I didn't understand why pitching was necessary and didn't grasp what was involved. Now I do. But before we get into that, let's nail down a basic definition.

## *WHAT* Is a Pitch?

A *pitch* is the presentation of the basic elements that define a cinematic story. In film, the word *pitch* almost always refers to a verbal presentation, not a written one. And here's something to keep in mind, something that might be obvious but is often overlooked:

*Screenwriters are always pitching.*

When someone inquires what you're working on . . .? Your answer is a pitch.

I say this not to make you feel self-conscious about casually discussing your work. Instead, I say it to 1) hopefully demystify the process a little, and 2) highlight the underlying importance of the skill. Being confident and conversant in the mechanics of story—*your* story in particular—is an undeniable essential.

Moreover, the "screen trade" is phenomenally saturated. Numerous writers vie for relatively few jobs and eyes on their material. Rest assured, there's always room for new talent, but the process is fiercely competitive. This isn't wildly different from other businesses, of course—it just puts "creative types" in the position of having to confront an at times uncomfortable reality:

*Screenwriting involves a lot of salesmanship.*

In fact, "sales" is exactly what a pitch is. I'll detail the essential ingredients of a pitch over the next few pages, but to summarize, you're essentially selling three things simultaneously:

1. That your story will make a good film. That it will appeal to an audience and that it will offer an *emotionally engaging experience.*
2. That you are the best person to write this story. Heck, that you just might be the *only* person to write it. That you have a unique insight or driving passion for the subject matter.
3. Your voice, personality, and attitude.

## Personality and Attitude

Before we move on, let's pause to talk about a few components of number 3 on that list—personality and attitude. A writing contract is a lengthy collaboration, ranging from a month to a year. The people hiring you are evaluating more than just story. They're determining what working with you might be like. Do you think quickly on your feet? Do you respond well to feedback? Are you stubborn or, conversely, someone who agrees reflexively to every suggestion? People who hire look for evidence that the frequently fraught creative process will be as fruitful as possible. Personal chemistry is a slippery subject to define or evaluate, but in general, no one wants to work with a know-it-all, a recluse, a "yes man," or a jerk. Instead, people are looking for someone who is honest and engaged, driven and open-minded, and someone who can examine his or her own story objectively.

So now that you know *what* you're selling, let's look at the *why* and *how* . . .

# WHY Do I Have to Pitch?

There are essentially three marketplace paradigms. Each largely involves the same participants, but they function a bit differently. And guess what? Pitching is a key element of every one of them.

## Spec Market

*Spec* is short for *speculative*, and it's the term we use to describe material that wasn't commissioned—in other words, material that no one paid the writer to write. The hope, of course, is that someone *will* buy it—be that someone a producer, production company, or studio.

Why then, you might legitimately ask, would I ever need to pitch something that I've already written? Wouldn't it be easier to just hand someone a screenplay? The answer is, frustratingly, yes *and* no.

Getting people—especially very busy, very important people—to read anything can be a very frustrating challenge for the emerging and professional screenwriter alike. This is one of the principal jobs of agents and managers. But few emerging writers have representation at their disposal, and moreover, most professional screenwriters know well what I'm about to say:

> *No one will be a better, more driven, more passionate advocate for your writing than you.*

While breaking in, most screenwriters are dependent on the query letter. But for those just beginning to meet people—whether via school, through friends, in mixers, or at expos—arming yourself with *short* pitches of your projects is one of the most strategically advantageous things you can do. In most meetings I take, if and when appropriate, I try to pitch one of my unsold screenplays. Which one depends on what I perceive to be the appetites and interests of the person I'm meeting with.

## Assignment Market

The assignment market is how a large number of screenwriters—myself included—make a living. There are two basic types of assignments. The first is what's commonly known as an *open-writing assignment*, or OWA. Here, a company, studio, or producer has a piece of material and invites writers to offer their version, or "take," on the story. The project might be based on a book, a magazine article, a completed movie from a foreign market, or even an existing screenplay that they'd like to rewrite. Gaining access to these jobs can be tricky, often involving the diligent work of a representative and a pre-existing body of work. I've pitched on OWAs dozens of times and can confidently report that it's tough to predict people's tastes. Sometimes producers only know what they're looking for (or what they're *not* looking for) once they hear it. That said, confidence, clarity, and impeccable presentation go a long way toward building relationships that last.

## Pitch Sale

The pitch sale is less common but more coveted. Here, screenwriters pitch stories they'd like to write—*their own ideas*—and if the company purchases a pitch, they're essentially paying the screenwriter to develop the screenplay and attaching themselves as a producer.

To procure an OWA or to sell an idea, you'll be asked for a *story pitch*, a ten- to fifteen-minute detailed presentation of the essential characters and narrative sequences of your story. This type of pitch presupposes several things: You have a meeting scheduled, you (most likely) have representation, and someone read something of yours and really liked it. Generally speaking, if you're pitching on a science fiction project, romantic comedy, horror, or thriller, they'll want to read something along similar lines. There are exceptions, though. If they love your writing, your characters, or your world-building skills enough, they might be enthused for your take on pretty much anything.

As I said, you're a screenwriter, so you're always pitching. What you've been pitching so far, most likely, is a variation of the *teaser* pitch. This is—far and away—the form that most pitches ultimately take. A teaser lasts two minutes at the most. The primary objective is to get people to read a screenplay that you already wrote, or to hook them into listening to a longer version of the pitch.

Story pitch or teaser pitch, the basic building blocks are the same, no matter that the lengths are quite different. Which brings us to . . .

# *HOW* Do I Pitch?

You have the basic gist of the story down, know the all-important beginning, middle, and end . . . so you're ready to pitch, right? Wrong. What about even in a short form—one minute that covers the basics? Nope.

We're well within the sphere of opinion here, but it's my essay, so here's mine.

Designing a pitch involves compressing the story down to the basics, sure, but the more you know, the easier the story is to summarize and the more prepared you are to present it. Before I pitch any story, I've outlined every major scene and each significant backstory. In the room, I hopefully seem intimately familiar with every facet . . . *because I am*.

And then I practice. I practice so much it's absurd. In the room, I never read from a paper and instead try to make the presentation sound fluid and unrehearsed. Some people are natural performers and excel at that, but this alone took me lots of practice. This command of the pitch—long or short—keeps me from stumbling over my words or scouring for the next story beat on the fly.

Every bit as important as the pitch itself is the part afterward in which (hopefully) the listener *gets to ask questions*. Suddenly, your story is the subject of a *conversation*. "How long were the characters married?" "I'm confused, what does the villain want?" Again, your command of the story is a big part of the audition. The less thought-through the story seems, the less appealing it's bound to be. This is the part of the meeting where the listener gets a glimpse at *you*, your process, and your facility with new ideas.

> ## Tip . . .
>
> Remember my claim that I never read from a sheet of paper? That's true, because *eye contact is important*. But it isn't inappropriate to have notes with you. One advantage of a clipboard or notebook—and I discovered this early on—is it gives you something to do with your hands other than fidget or shake. The very act of holding your notes, whether you need them or not, might offer comfort.

# Critical Components of a Pitch

Every pitch is different, reflecting the style of the writer and the story itself. Some will emphasize character, some will emphasize action, and others a unique or foreign story world. Nonetheless, the primary objective of *all* stories is to elicit emotion. This, frankly, is the hardest thing to do in a pitch.

Writers often want to walk the listener through every beat, but most successful pitches only hit upon the crucial aspects of the story: the reveals, turning points, highs, and lows. Intricate details bring about a protracted and painful death. By focusing on the following elements and with awareness of the emotional engine(s) of the narrative, it'll be easier to capture the "essence" of your story.

## Who Is Your Hero?

It might sound strange, but the "star" of your story has to be a character. It isn't a setting or a circumstance. I've heard several pitches that lead with: "This is a story about Earth in the aftermath of an alien war (or apocalypse, or zombie outbreak, or fill-in-the-blank)." Nope, it isn't. It's the story of the *people* navigating that world.

A critical component of getting a listener to root for your hero is clearly defining why we *empathize* with him. Is he in jeopardy of some kind, be it physical or emotional? Is he the victim of some deserved or undeserved misfortune? Is he likeable . . . or unlikeable, but questing redemption? Or perhaps he's just funny as hell? Maybe he's incredibly talented or supremely powerful?

## Where Is Your Hero When You First Introduce Him?

We want to understand who and where your hero is before the story actually "happens" to him, again, with a clear emphasis on emotion.

*40-Year-Old-Virgin*: (ISOLATION) An electronics store employee is secretly . . . well, a 40-year-old virgin. His life is lonely and filled with late-night-TV fueled fantasies and a massive, vintage action figure collection.

*The Incredibles*: (FRUSTRATION) An entire family of former superheroes struggles to ignore their own gifts and adjust to a banal suburban life.

## What Opportunity *Is Presented to Your Hero?*

The opportunity is usually apparent in any description of your story. The opportunity is what interrupts the "status quo" of your hero's introduction and sets things in motion.

*The Ring*: Rachel learns of a mysterious videotape linked to her niece's death.

Many stories change the location right after the opportunity, so the hero begins both a literal and psychological journey. If so, this can be very useful to economizing your pitch.

*About Schmidt*: After the death of his wife, Schmidt embarks on a cross-country trek to visit his estranged daughter.

## What Is Your Hero's Outer Motivation?

In most films, the hero's *desire* establishes a finish line that we're rooting for the hero to cross. There are lots of valid motivations that you can support along this spine—desires for self-worth, acceptance, fulfillment, for instance—but these are largely internal and therefore difficult to succinctly pitch. A cinematic goal is almost always *external*: to get the girl, to win the game, to stop the criminal, to escape the prison, to retrieve the elixir, to exact revenge, and so on.

## What Is the Conflict?

Desire drives the story forward, but the obstacles your hero faces are what generate the *greatest emotional impact*. Further, it's the obstacles that, more often than not, define your story as truly unique. This usually involves placing emphasis on the *antagonist* that stands in your hero's way. *Villains can be a lot of fun.*

Simply put, your pitch might focus on why it's virtually impossible for your hero to succeed.

## How Does It End?

Some suggest leaving the conclusion vague, somewhat like a movie trailer, seducing the listener into hearing (or reading) more. I'd passionately disagree. A solid ending is one of the most critical elements of any story and demonstrates that you've engineered a satisfying resolution. Coupled with a clear introduction and opportunity, the ending can also illuminate *character arc*. How has your hero changed in pursuit of her goals? What growth or compromises are revealed?

Character arc is one of those things you should know but not necessarily articulate. If you've done your job well, it should be reasonably easy to infer.

> Most movies bought and sold on the basis of a pitch have one principal requirement: to entertain. This is true of your pitch, too. So what can stop a pitch from being entertaining?
>
> - Too many characters: A listener can track only a handful of names over a ten-minute pitch, far fewer in two minutes. But you can often label supporting characters using just their function—mother, father, best friend, neighbor— which can keep your listeners from getting confused.
> - Too much research: You learned all there is to know about WWII submarines, and that's awesome. But the pitch isn't the time to share. As a general rule, if the information isn't integral, jettison it.
> - Elaborate choreography: It's easy to burn through a ton of time with specifics, and it can be hard to make the information engaging. If you're writing an action movie, a listener will absolutely want to hear about the amazing set pieces, but keep details spare, clear, and visual.
> - Too much interiority: If you find yourself repeatedly tempted to describe the characters' feelings and thinking, you might be in trouble. Remember, film characters are defined by their choices and behavior. External, not internal.

All right, so now you know your story intimately and have compressed it into an easy-to-digest format. But there's one last hurdle to consider and conquer . . .

## Where to Start a Pitch

Very often, the hardest thing to do is to simply start talking. It feels artificial. Finding a natural "in" can be a challenge. Let's look at a few options.

### Make It Personal

Making the presentation personal is often remarkably effective and can be an honest, candid, and engaging way to begin:

*"I think the best way to tell you about my story is to share how I came up with the idea."*

And then you do just that. This puts the emphasis on your passion. Good for the listener to hear, and—for nervous pitchers like me—it's a way to help channel your enthusiasm. It also anchors a crucial element I mentioned right up top: persuading the listener that *you're ideally suited to tell this story*.

## Emphasize Audience

Another way to go is to emphasize *audience*, especially if it isn't 100 percent clear in the first couple sentences of the story itself. As writers, we tend to assume that tone, genre, and audience are achingly obvious. "Of *course* it's a horror movie. There's a monster!" "Of *course* it's for teens. It's set in a high school!" But for a listener, these crucial elements often don't clarify until the presentation is well underway, which is a problem. Your listeners' job is to find stories that they can *market*. It's the difference between "I'm working on a children's movie" and "I wanted to write the type of movie I remember from my own childhood, the kind that brought my entire family together."

One of the many brilliant aspects of the film *Toy Story* is that its authors clearly set out to appeal to both kids and parents. Imagine how different a movie it might have been had it only appealed to one or the other. Ideally, behind just identifying the target audience, you're including yourself among them. "I know this audience's appetites really well because these are the types of movies I've always loved."

## Open With Antecedents

You could also potentially open with *antecedents*. An antecedent is a reference to another piece of material (typically another film) to clarify the tone, genre, and audience of your story. But citing antecedents has become something of a long-standing joke in recent years, due primarily to too many inexperienced pitchers conjuring attempts that make little sense ("My movie is *Elf* meets *Saw*."). Because of this, I honestly feel that you're sometimes better off just describing the tone outright.

That said, antecedents can be useful, efficient, and effective. But here's the deal: No matter whether you elect to include antecedents, you should have a few prepared just in case you're asked. What you don't want is the listener providing the antecedent for you . . . and for it to be *wrong*.

How can you make antecedent referencing actually work? First consider what the antecedents have in common with your story that sets them apart from other stories in the genre. Then figure out what sets your story apart from the antecedents themselves.

"I've always loved movies like *The Thing* and *The Blob* that present unique and unusual monsters, but I've longed for a tale told from the *monster's* point of view."

## Use a Visual Aid

Speaking of monsters, if you're working on such a story . . . what might your creature look like? Very little makes a writer look more prepared than a *visual aid*. Granted, these are more appropriate for formal pitches (it's hard to walk around with such things).

Visual aids can take myriad forms. Sometimes, sure, they're illustrations of monsters, whether fantastical or horrific. I've seen intricate maps of imaginary kingdoms, handmade photo books that explore the "feel" of a specific neighborhood or time period, and even automated PowerPoint presentations that track the entire narrative. A friend working on a NASCAR story brought dozens of detailed scale models. Personally, I tend to show slides that highlight pivotal beats. Like this one:

A slide from a horror film project pitch, illustrating the Break into 2

Illustration by Jasper Grey

Know that visual aids can (and *should*) be instrumental in establishing the tone of the story. Even more than an antecedent, a well-chosen visual aid can help the listener access the narrative in *exactly the way you imagine it*.

It's hard to talk about pitching without remembering some of my earliest experiences, in all their embarrassing glory. One pitch in particular stands out, partially because it led to my very first sale, but also because I miraculously met the rare executive who really wanted to help. She stopped me a few sentences in, and I was certain I was done for. "Joshua," she sighed, "I'm going to give you two notes before you say another word, and I hope you can take them to heart." This is what she offered:

- Slow down. You're talking too fast. *Relax.* The faster you go, the harder the story is to follow and the more I suspect you merely want this over with.
- You've got a good story. Don't apologize for it. Don't look so insecure or uncertain. If you believe in what you've got, I'll be twice as likely to as well.

Remember, pitching is—for most of us—a learned skill, not an innate one. It requires considerable practice and preparation. But learning to pitch well ultimately makes us more confident and focused storytellers. Good luck!

---

The son of puppeteers and theater professors, **JOSHUA MALKIN**'s childhood in California's Central Coast was shaped by the visual and performing arts. After graduating from the Directing program at the American Film Institute, his short film *Dust* won many awards including a Student Emmy. Since then, Joshua has completed just shy of twenty screenplays and has been fortunate enough to work for many major companies, including Universal Pictures, Lionsgate, and 20th Century Fox, as well as extraordinary directors, producers, actors, and artists of all types. He has also written and produced three documentaries—two about the art of puppetry, and the other about underground comics. He is part of the core faculty at UCR Palm Desert's Low Residency MFA in Creative Writing & Writing for the Performing Arts.

Joshua Malkin

Photo by Scott Kevan

# BUILDING A SCREENWRITING CAREER

## Advice From the Entertainment Career Coach

▶ An Interview With Carole Kirschner

Carole Kirschner runs three prominent programs in Los Angeles for screenwriters: the CBS Diversity Writer's Mentoring Program, the Writers Guild of America Showrunner Training Program, and the HUMANITAS New Voices Program. She is a sought-after speaker on the topics of the US television business, the show-runner model, and pitching, and she works one-on-one with writers looking to break into the business or take their career to the next level. Her book *Hollywood Game Plan: How to Land a Job in Film, TV and Digital Entertainment* (Michael Wiese Productions) is widely used in university class-rooms across the country.

Carole Kirschner
Photo by Lesley Bohm Photography

**Can you describe your one-on-one work with screenwriting clients?**
Sure, I work with clients on three pillars: their material, self-marketing, and industry savvy. I'm not a script analyst, but I read their material to see if it's industry ready. And then a lot of my work is in self-marketing, which is a huge part, as you know, for creative professionals who don't like to sell themselves. So I work with clients on connecting. I hate the word *networking*, but *connecting* is truthful—how you expand your community of connections and how important that is. And then what I call *industry savvy*, which is to make sure my clients are as educated about the business as they possibly can be.

**You also help clients with pitching?**
I do. I was an executive for eighteen years in television and comedy development, so I heard a lot of pitches. I heard probably more than 3,000 pitches and was involved in hundreds of scripts and dozens of television series over the years, both at CBS and also when I was vice president of Stephen Spielberg's Amblin Television.

**Can you explain what *comedy development* means in this context?**
It means listening to pitches for new television shows, essentially. We ordered the scripts, gave notes on the scripts, ordered the pilots, gave notes on the pilots. We were heavily involved, although the big cheese was far more involved in deciding which pilots got picked up to series.

**And who was the big cheese?**
That was the president of CBS. These days it's the CEO and the president. Those are the people who have the final say about who's going to get $30 million to create a television series.

By the way . . .

In her role at CBS, Kirschner helped to develop the television shows *Murphy Brown* and *Designing Women*.

**What does it take for a writer to get a pitch meeting? Do you need a manager or agent? Is there a way around that?**
In order to get a pitch meeting you generally need an agent or a manager, yes, unless you have a deal at the studio and the networks, and the studios are in the same company these days. ABC and ABC Disney and ABC Studios, for instance, it's the same company. CBS and CBS Studios are the same company. I work at CBS now with the writer's program, so if a writer has a deal with CBS Studios, then they go in with the studio on the pitch meeting. But if they don't have a deal, then their agent or manager has to set up the meeting.

**If a writer doesn't have an agent or manager and really wants to break into television . . .?**
The thing that will get a writer into television is what I call a blazing hot script. A script that is undeniable, so good that people want to be in business with them. I was just talking to a client today, and I said to her, just being good isn't enough.

> "The way to deal with anxiety and nerves is to practice so much that you know your material backward and forward. Not so much that you're doing it memorized. You should know it like it's memorized, but you should talk about it in a conversational way."

It's got to be the kind of script that everybody who reads it, or 90 percent of the people who read it want to meet you, an agent wants to sign you. That's how you know it's blazing hot. The other thing you can do is a Web series. But regardless, you have to have contemporary material that can reach a younger audience. That's what will get a network's attention, an agent's attention.

**So you finally get an agent or manager, get your first pitch meeting, and you're nervous, obviously. Any advice?**

When I work with clients, when I do workshops, what I do is encourage people to center themselves before meetings, get really quiet, close their eyes, and picture themselves having a great meeting. What I want them to do is picture what it feels like to be pitching and people are enthusiastically responding to it, and then at the end of the meeting the people they're pitching to say, "That was great. We would love to buy it!" And then you see yourself walking out of the meeting thinking, "Wow, I just nailed that."

**Do you do this visualization the night before or while you're in the waiting room immediately before you go in?**

Yes, both. I think you practice it many times before you do it in the waiting room, and then you do it in the waiting room as well. Here's what I really believe, as I'm sure you do, too: The way to deal with anxiety and nerves is to practice so much that you know your material backward and forward. Not so much that you're doing it memorized. You should know it like it's memorized, but you should talk about it in a conversational way.

**If your typical pitch in this type of scenario is going into CBS or a network, how many people are in the room?**

It can be a lot. Here's who it will be on the network side: It'll be a manager-level person, a director-level person, and a vice president. You might also have a senior vice president in the room. Then, if you have a studio executive, if you deal with a studio, it could be a studio vice president. And then your agent and manager could be there as well. You could have a lot of people in the meeting, or it might just be you and two or three people from the network.

**What's the setup of the room—at a conference table? Is the writer standing or sitting?**
No, everybody's sitting. If the writer wants to stand up, they can, but usually they're sitting. And depending on how many people there are, it's probably in a conference room. If there's just a few people, it could be in the most senior-level executive office at the network. There'll be a couch, there'll be two chairs, maybe three chairs, and then a desk, and the senior-level person sits behind the desk.

**The CBS Diversity Program, could you tell me how that got started and how successful it's been in terms of bringing in new writers?**
We're in year eleven, and I co-created that with a colleague at CBS. In the eleven years we've done it, we've helped launch the careers of forty writers of color, and there are a number of them who are now high up on staff. So it works.

**Can you tell me about the program?**
It's very competitive to get in. We probably bring in five or six people each year. It's a nine-month program. The first four months, they write a script under the supervision of a CBS network or studio executive. Then, starting in January for four months, I do weekly workshops, and those weekly workshops are an opportunity for them to learn how to market themselves and make connections. We have speakers every week: agents, managers, executives, and showrunners. And they do showrunner practice meetings. They do mock showrunner meetings, because in television the person, as you know, who can hire you to be on a series is the showrunner. So we have about eight or nine different showrunners that come in, and they practice having a meeting with them so that by the time they have to do it in real life it's a little less nerve-wracking.

**Has it ever happened where a showrunner became interested in one of the writers in the program?**
Yes, we've had that. And a really good part of the program is that the people in it generally get representation during the agent/manager night.

**That's terrific! How many people apply every year?**
It's about seven or eight hundred people for five slots.

**Who's reading those scripts?**
The first round are professional readers—and the people who come out on the top of that, my colleague and I read them. My colleague, who's a current executive at the network, and I read the finalists.

**Can you explain what "taking meetings" means for the writer? This is a term we hear a lot but might not know exactly what that looks like, how it works.**
It's a matter of expanding your connections and then using your connections. I know people who have done it on Facebook or using LinkedIn. But obviously, the best is when you have some kind of personal connection. And if you're clear about what you want, then you say to your network of people, "Look, I'm really interested in doing digital marketing. If you know anybody who knows anybody, I would love to talk to them, just for information."

> "Part of not feeling so nervous or desperate is having your successes that are quantifiable and being able to describe them to people, which is that marketing piece. And the other part is, you just fake it. For writers, I say imagine you're writing this character, this character who is that confident. You sometimes have to fake it a little."

**It's fascinating that you're in career strategies as well. I think people can get so nervous that even if they're relatively badass, level-headed people, getting a chance to participate is so important to them that they can go from nervous to almost desperate. Do you see that happen?**
That was my client from yesterday. She was a badass, but she's been out of it long enough that she's feeling desperate. So I said to her, are you going to lose your house? Do you have enough money to get by for the next three to six months? And she said, yes. And I said, then you don't need to be desperate. Part of not

feeling so nervous or desperate is having your successes that are quantifiable and being able to describe them to people, which is that marketing piece. And the other part is, you just fake it. For writers, I say imagine you're writing this character, this character who is that confident. You sometimes have to fake it a little.

**And having the language prepared so it's second nature to talk about who you are and what you do so you're not fumbling around, I'm sure that helps.**
It does. And you can talk about your successes, big or small, when you meet somebody at a cocktail party. Once you're talking about your successes—and I do these things with my clients called a *personal logline* and a *personal A story*—once you have that down, people respond to you differently, so you feel more confident.

**People can go overboard with that confidence, though, right? Any advice for how writers can effectively talk about their successes in a way that gets people interested instead of wanting to walk away?**
There's a fine line there, between confidence and arrogance. Writers need a strategy so they can get the word out about their work and feel comfortable that it's okay to get the word out. Sometimes you just need some phrases to say that take the cooties off when you talk about your successes. Like, you might say, "I've been incredibly fortunate," or "I've been so surprised," or "It was thrilling to . . .," or "This is the first time I've done this," or "I'm being shamelessly self-promoting," that's a good one, too.

**Tell me about your services. If somebody wanted to do a one-on-one consultation with you, do you typically have a once-a-week meeting, or how does it work?**
It really depends. I have free twenty-minute strategy sessions, and that's really just for me to talk to them to see if I can help. Most of the time, I don't take the new clients, because I don't take people's money if I can't help them, and there are a lot of people I can't help. But if I think I can help, I have three levels of packages—always an in-person session for the first one, and then depending on the package there are a certain number of phone calls, and I may read a script or look at a résumé, and we can do a cover letter. And then the next level up is more personal one-on-one time. So it can be weekly or every two weeks—it just depends what the client needs.

**What if someone wants to work with you but doesn't live in LA?**
The first session would be via Skype, because honestly, I want to get a good sense of who they are, and that's very hard to do over the phone. And also, I want to see

how they carry themselves—how they talk, whether they're able to be assertive without being arrogant. And when I work with somebody, I need to see where they are in that spectrum—totally confident, not confident at all—so we know where to focus the work. It's important in this business.

**Final words of advice to aspiring writers?**
Keep writing. Just don't stop writing. And also, get the support you need. You might not be where you need to be yet, but there are people out there who are looking to shape new talent and other people who are looking to find it, so keep at it.

# Carole's Ten Surefire Ways to Kill a Pitch

1. Recite your perfectly memorized pitch without any personality.
2. Look at your notes or the floor, never at people.
3. Only describe unimportant details of your story.
4. Be racist or sexist.
5. Don't give away the major plot points.
6. If someone seems bored, keep talking.
7. As the pitch goes on, talk faster and faster.
8. Keep saying your idea is the best ever, but don't explain why.
9. Give a lot of boring facts.
10. Speak as if you're presenting a formal academic paper.

# A SCRIPT READER'S PERSPECTIVE

## How to Love What You Do When You Can't Do What You Love

▶ By James Napoli

Anyone who has made the leap into a creative field has at some point heard the advice, "Follow your dream." Have you ever tried to follow a dream? First you're running, then you're flying, and the next thing you know there's your second-grade teacher with the body of a human and the head of a Thomson's gazelle.

Dreams are the wrong template for the writer's journey. They're phantoms. And chasing phantoms is crazy making. Dreams have no continuity, but your choice of profession does. The choices you make along the way build one upon the other to shape the artist you become.

If you want to endure in this business, you need to uncover the many ways your creativity can manifest while you wait for your big break, the things you can do to keep yourself vital and engaged as a creative person. *That* is the continuity of your life in action—the reality, not the dream.

First, you absolutely must amass a library of work. Should your first spec script be lucky enough to interest agents or managers, their first question will be, "What else have you got?" Screenwriter Katherine Fugate (*Valentine's Day, New Year's Eve, Army Wives*) says it this way: "You need to show range and instill confidence into your agent that you have more than one screenplay in you. That you're in it for the long haul."[4]

Yes, the long haul. And the best way to be ready for it is to have cool things to do while you're hauling. If not, all too soon you'll begin to see your career as a waiting game. Being in that headspace, constantly awaiting validation and then bottoming out when you don't get it, can be a soul-crushing experience.

Do not give your emotional power to the gatekeepers, the arbitrary tastemakers in the industry. It's not up to them when you're happy and when you aren't. How can you take back your control?

Stay creative and active.

# Ten Ways to Stay Creative and Active

## Read Screenplays

There are zillions of them online. *Watching* a movie isn't the same as *reading* a script. A movie can teach you how an army of people realize the words on a page, but it can't enlighten you as to why the words on the page inspired that army of people to crawl on their bellies to bring them to life. What made them want to read every word? What made the dialogue snap? How did the writer connect everything into a unified whole? Most of this is almost indefinable, but by revisiting the craft, past and present, over and over again, you gain an innate sensitivity to what's working.

I've read thousands of screenplays in my career as a story analyst, and the answer to the question everyone asks is: Yes. I *can* tell if a screenplay is any good on page one. The language of script reading—like the language of movie going—is now part of my DNA, as it should be with yours.

## Know the History of Your Medium

You'll be sharing your time in the entertainment business with other people who live, breathe, and eat cinema. Many of these cineastes will end up at a lunch or in a pitch meeting with you and will want to talk shop and spitball about your craft. So when an agent says your comedy reminds him of Preston Sturges, and you can only return a blank stare . . . not a place you want to live. Or if the development executive asks if you can work some Robert Towne grit into your presentation, and you can only nod and smile . . . you've lost an ally.

Terry Rossio (*Aladdin*, *Pirates of the Caribbean*, *Shrek*, the *National Treasure* franchise) said it clearly:

> One does not face this task [of screenwriting] alone. I have on my side Heinlein and Bradbury and Poe. Ellison, Shakespeare and Chandler. Serling, Asimov and Christie. Twain, Bach and Tolkien. Sturges, Simon and Vonnegut. King, Sturgeon and Chayefksy. Gaiman, Ashman and Matheson . . . You have to come at this job with a background in popular works of fiction, from all media.[5]

And if any of the above names are unfamiliar to you? Get Googling, writer!

## Take an Acting Class

It's up to actors to interpret and actualize your screenplay. It's through the actor's craft that your work will live or die on screen. So getting to know that process will make you a better writer. For instance, actors need to understand their motivation in each scene. They want to know their goal or objective, what they're fighting for. You should be asking those questions, too. You should be able to articulate to yourself what your characters want and how they're trying to get it. And diving into the acting space—the place where actors develop and hone their craft—will help you see your pages through their eyes.

Besides, acting is a great way to network with other creative people, especially for notoriously solitary and introverted writers. Rather than isolating yourself and waiting for an agent or manager to return your emails, why not start mixing with the very people who could be part of the movie you could one day make?

## Learn to Improvise!

Don't stop at an acting class. Take an improv class, too. Work with performers who are building a scene out of nothing. After all, isn't that what you have to do when you're staring at a blank page? Audiences go to movies because they want to see people doing extraordinary things. One of the basic tenets of improv is "don't deny"—meaning two people in a scene should keep it moving forward by always saying "yes" to whatever the other throws at them. How does this apply to screenwriting? It's a practice that can lead to scenes on the page that crackle with possibilities, allowing readers to go to those extraordinary places with the characters.

## Put Up Your Work as a Play

Every time you write a scene in your screenplay, you're recalling the entire history of enacted storytelling. And chances are, your community has a theater full of actors who are just waiting to do some enacting. Plus, it's a lot cheaper than making a film. And if you can't afford to mount a full production, have your new actor friends (you met them in class, remember?) do a staged reading so you can hear your words read aloud. Watching your work come to life can feel nothing short of a miracle. When before you just imagined your film in your head, suddenly actors are interpreting it for you.

And if you don't have a stage play in your arsenal, write one. Or find ways to adapt one of your screenplays into something theater-ready. That in itself is a great lesson, because there's something you can't do on stage that you do every few moments in film: cut. Your scenes will have to work within a form that's driven largely by dialogue and not visuals. Adapting your work to succeed across the two mediums can help show you where it sings the most and where it hits false notes—in both incarnations.

*New York Times* theater critic Charles Isherwood said this about theater as an art form: "It tests a writer's mettle as television and movies do not. Structure, dialogue, theme and plot are all in your hands, not parceled out among a dozen writers and script supervisors and subject to executive meddling."[6]

And speaking of testing a writer's mettle, many theater companies develop and rework plays with the writer before adding the work to their repertoire. This development process mirrors that of the film business, and it's an incredible opportunity to evolve and grow your work—and to develop a thick skin for receiving criticism. You'll need this in the entertainment business, where eleven different executives will have eleven different ideas for the ways you should approach your rewrite.

## Make a Short Film or Web Series

Yes, high-ranking Hollywood folks have been known to spend time searching the Internet in hopes of finding new talent. This is true for actors, writers, directors, comedians . . . just about any kind of talent you can imagine.

Should you shoot a from-the-hip project fueled by the certainty that it'll immediately get record-breaking hits on YouTube and rocket you to stardom? No. Remember, we're talking about loving what you do. The primary reason you should pursue any creative endeavor as you wait for your big break is because you enjoy it—and because it's another opportunity to see your work realized in some form.

Plus, there's another bonus: No matter how small it might be, you need a crew to help make a short film or Web series. You need people to hold the microphones and rig a few lights. Network with your actor and writer friends, and see if they know someone looking for experience behind the camera. This assembly of hard-working artists could very well become the nucleus of a machine that brings your work to life over the course of your entire career.

## Start a Podcast or Movie Blog

If you and your friends spend countless hours ranting about the merits or demerits of the latest blockbuster, or if you geek out on your favorite subgenres or cult filmmakers, don't just talk amongst yourselves—write about it, or talk about it in a podcast. Story analysis makes you a better writer. When you spar with a colleague at a microphone dissecting the finer details of great movies, or when you post an appreciative blog about your favorite grindhouse director, you're delving into the unnamable stuff behind what makes movie storytelling so powerful. Not only that, you're exercising your writing muscles and expanding them into other areas.

### Ouch, My Ego!

Here's a little nugget you need to be ready for: What happens when your colleague gets discovered and you don't? Maybe the biggest threat to maintaining your ongoing commitment to the creative life is that punch in the gut that occurs when someone you know gets what you can only assume (in your ego-addled haze) is the perfect embodiment of everything you have been striving for.

One approach to coping is to assume this friend or acquaintance will bring you along on his or her coattails. But the business is such that those who break in can't always usher in their buddies. (Newly discovered talents have a lot of delicate industry relationships to navigate before they're in a position to open the gates for their BFFs.) Another approach is to wallow in bitterness, secretly hate your old friend forever, and live with the certainty that the universe has it in for you. A third approach is to simply let it go. Oh, and get back to work.

## Enter Screenplay Contests

You can't always get your work in front of agents and producers, but you might be able to force them to notice you by placing in a screenplay contest. At this writing, in the last several months, three screenplays that came across my desk were contest winners. And only one of them represented the granddaddy, the Nicholl Fellowship, administered through the Academy of Motion Picture Arts and Sciences. The others were from smaller film festivals that sponsor their own screenwriting competition arms. The fact that these scripts did come across my desk means they scored some agency or management representation based on their success in competitions.

But there's another, more esoteric reason to enter screenplay competitions. Whenever we're asked to collect a representation of ourselves on paper—whether it's for a job application, a formal CV, or a piece of writing—we fill in various blanks about our history, qualifications, and life's mission statement. Preparing a screenplay for a contest—especially one that involves trying for a fellowship or future industry mentoring—sometimes involves writing creative summaries of your story, describing what made you want to tell the story and the road you took to get to where you are. Reviewing this arc of your life can be very empowering. It helps you look back on what you've accomplished so far and say, "I'm a pretty cool person, and I've done a fair amount of stuff." In some of the toughest periods of slogging through the struggling-writer trenches, simply being asked to explain why you *rock* can be just the boost you need.

It might be one year or five years from now, or it might have already happened—but at some point, you'll feel the exhilarating certainty that you'll be on this path for the rest of your life. What do you do with that frightening decision? Keep writing. Keep working out what it is to be alive and hanging around a bunch of other people who are trying to work out the same thing.

You may break through. You may get the financial rewards that can come with success in the entertainment business. I wish that for you, because it would be awesome. Mostly, though, I wish you the happiness that comes from never forgetting why you do what you do in the first place.

---

**JAMES NAPOLI** is a writer, filmmaker, and story analyst who has read and provided development notes for thousands of screenplays. He is an Assistant Professor in National University's MFA in Professional Screenwriting Program and an adjunct Assistant Professor of Script Analysis and Motion Picture History at Columbia College, Hollywood. He is also the author of *The Official Dictionary of Sarcasm* (Sterling Innovation, 2010).

James Napoli

Photo by Mindi White

# THE ART OF DISCIPLINE AND PERSISTENCE

## Moving Toward Creative Success

▶ An Interview With Anne Fontaine

French filmmaker Anne Fontaine has written and directed fourteen films since her debut in 1993. Her films *Dry Cleaning* (1997), *How I Killed My Father* (2001), and *Coco Before Chanel* (2009) brought her international attention as a writer-director, and her film *Nathalie* (2003) was adapted into Atom Egoyan's widely released *Chloe* (2009), starring Julianne Moore, Amanda Seyfried, and Liam Neeson. Her film *Adore* (2013), which she adapted from Doris Lessing's novella, *The Grandmothers*, starred Naomi Watts and Robin Wright and premiered at Sundance under the title *Two Mothers*.

Anne Fontaine

Photo by Marcel Hartmann

Fontaine is familiar with the concept of sticking with it under challenging circumstances. She began her career while still in her teens, and she was flexible enough to tweak her goals along the way as she followed a winding road to success.[7]

**How did you get your start as a director?**
I was acting in a film, working for a director—this was after I was dancing—and my director suggested that I had an ear for dialogue. That was the start of my writing then. I wrote a script, very personal to me, and he gave me the encouragement that I could be the person to direct the film as well.

**What was the timing on that? How much time from when you first started writing to when you started shooting?**

Oh, it was a long time—I think three or four years. I don't remember exactly, because I had to work to make money, to live, you know—so I think it was three years before I was able to make the film. It seems like a long time to me now.

> "It helps me to have that mindset, not to stop, not to say, now I quit. Because of course you meet people who say you aren't able to do it, it's too difficult, you don't have the money, you don't have what it takes. And you have to say to yourself, maybe this person doesn't believe in me, but I *will* be able to do it."

**Where do you think your drive came from—your discipline to stick with the project for so long?**

From my dancing, I would say. Every day you have to make this effort, more and more each day. But for me it was a personal story as well, the script—more or less, of course. And I thought it was the only way I could . . . not save myself, but it was something really important. It was my life inside of me. I was always thinking about the characters and the situations. The script was another life, a life that I preferred to my actual life, and I think I knew I was better off to imagine things, to create things, than to live day by day.

**So that desire to continue living in the world of your story, it allowed you to keep persisting, to not give up?**

It helps me to have that mindset, not to stop, not to say, now I quit. Because of course you meet people who say you aren't able to do it, it's too difficult, you don't have the money, you don't have what it takes. And you have to say to yourself, maybe this person doesn't believe in me, but I *will* be able to do it. I think someone's determination, it's very personal. For me, I was alone in Paris at 16 years old, without a family, so determination is a part of me.

**What brought you to Paris?**

It was a complicated story. A need to be away from my family and also a thought that I had to move away from Portugal. But also because I wanted to do modern ballet, and in Portugal it was more classical. It was to have a new life in Paris. But I was alone at the time.

**That's very young, 16. Did you have siblings?**

Yes, they stayed in Portugal. But I am the oldest. I felt that I had to move. At 13, 14, I felt I had to be in France, to be in another world, to dream in another way. If things become too difficult, you are used to this difficulty. It's a good training to do film.

**Do you find that stories are a safe place to explore subject matter that you're grappling with on a personal level?**

Yes, I always felt that for me to do a movie it has to be connected by something personal. I couldn't direct a movie if I didn't feel something. It doesn't mean it's entirely true to my life, but yes, it's true to a feeling of something fitting in that moment. Why I decide to say yes to a story or to imagine a story completely, it's my way to work with the characters, maybe to help them, I don't know.

**As a woman, do you feel any responsibility for how you portray your female characters?**

No, I think to be intelligent, with ability, exploring something about the human condition, but I don't feel because I am a woman that I'm more responsible for women characters. Not at all for me. What's important for me is to have the dimension of character, the opacity, the mystery, the things you can't explain but can feel—a complicated, complex character. That interests me, because it's a human being.

For me, this is true of every character I put in front of the camera. Of course, I've made movies with very strong female characters—Coco Chanel, Doris Lessing's *Perfect Mothers*—but what attracted me to these women is that they aren't conventional. They aren't operating with morals in mind. They aren't immoral either, but they're operating from their point of view. I don't like it when there's a moral point of view in a film. I like to explore a moment in time when the character isn't used to that moment and how that can change the way she lives, the way she feels. I always like to work with characters that try to *advance* their life, not to *follow* their life. That's something very interesting in a movie to me—for characters not to follow the program of their life, because everybody has that kind of program.

**Your films often seem to circle discussions of gender and sexuality. Is that a conversation you like to have, about the blurred lines between masculinity and femininity?**

Yes, because to be a director, it's a way to be almost transsexual, to be inside both sexes. And for me, it's interesting to work out this ambiguity in my films. I don't believe we have only one way to be sexual. I don't believe in that. It's society that makes you believe that, of course. But this division can escape you sometimes when you meet somebody different, and it's interesting to explore this thing that you can't describe, to explore it in a story. It's an unconscious desire, I believe, because the desire is something very strange—why you desire this certain person at this moment of your life. It's strange, and I do like the atmosphere you can create in a film where the characters are going in a certain direction, but they don't know where they're going. This is something I find myself attracted to in stories.

**Is it a challenge to be a female filmmaker in France? Do you think your gender has any relevance in your filmmaking?**

I never think about being a woman director. In France, of course there are not so many female directors as there are male, but I don't think about it. When some women's festival wants to present a movie of mine, I say no. I don't want to go to a female festival. It doesn't mean anything to me. For me, it's the personality of the director, not the gender. Sometimes a man can speak about women better than a woman.

Everybody asks me the question, because it's something rare and not so easy. It's a space where the machismo of the crews and the producers makes an impact—it's not equal. But in France, nobody can tell you today, oh, I'm suffering because I am a woman director. I think it's a plus, because the producers like that we have another angle to speak about sexuality, to speak about men, of course. So it's really not a problem in France, not at all. I'm lucky to be in France for that.

**Your producers and the people you work with, is it a mixed crew, a mix of men and women, or more women, more men?**

Yes, the last film I just finished in Poland, for example, I took a DP [director of photography] who is a woman. I had thirty-five crew members who were women. But I couldn't do a movie with only women. I think it would be difficult. I like to have both, like a balance. Not to be half and half, because I'm not half and half. I'm more close intellectually sometimes with men, I think. But we have very good female technicians in France now—in sound, in image, great technicians. That was for men before, the technicians, but now there are younger DPs who are women, really amazing.

**How much downtime do you give yourself? I'm curious about your work–life balance.**

For me, it's freedom to work. I work the maximum I can. I am finishing a movie now, and I'm doing a new script for the next one, and another script for the next-next one. I like to have two or three things in my mind, and I need to keep developing stories after I'm done shooting. Because the most difficult part is the shooting. That's really hell and war. And if you can have the new stories to turn to, the imagination and the energy to go there . . . at this moment I try to save my energy to invent new things.

But every day I begin with dance, one hour each morning. I do a classic ballet and barre. So I begin like that, and then I can concentrate on a story.

**And concentrating on story, is that you sitting at a computer all day? What does your writing routine look like?**

No, not at a computer. I do it with my scriptwriter. I speak, and he works with the computer. And after that, I read and rewrite. I don't want to do it myself at the computer. I want to be free and want to work with words that don't always come from me, because if it comes from me, I have more difficulty putting distance between it. I need a scriptwriter to write it. But I do all the scenes, speaking the sentences.

> "For me, it's freedom to work. I work the maximum I can. I am finishing a movie now, and I'm doing a new script for the next one, and another script for the next-next one. I like to have two or three things in my mind, and I need to keep developing stories after I'm done shooting. Because the most difficult part is the shooting. That's really hell and war."

**The scriptwriter, how often do you work with the same person?**
It depends on the story. I worked for two or three movies with the same script-writer, and now I'm trying somebody new. I like not to be too comfortable. It's good to have new blood also—and it depends on the tune of the script that you're working on.

**What happens if you're too comfortable? How does that affect your art?**
For me, it's not possible to be comfortable. I don't know what it is, but I feel that to improve, to be really fresh, you have to be fragile. For example, when I was in Poland with a Polish crew, on location outside in the woods, in this moment I was fragile, and I had to find another way to do things.

It's so difficult to do a movie, because you don't have protection when you're shooting—it can be very violent and very difficult. You can be depressed. And when you have fourteen hours a day, six days a week, trying to find the things you need for the film to work, and sometimes you're not finding these things. You're fighting yourself really. It's complicated, something very lonely in a way, but with many people around looking at you, watching what you're doing. And they're helping you, of course.

**So the shoot, is that your least favorite part of making a film, or is it just the most difficult part?**
The most difficult. The shooting is more violent. It's really something difficult physically, and psychologically. Yes, I find sometimes that it's worse than other experiences. It depends, but I always feel completely down at the end, like I'm a ghost.

**Are you relieved at all, or is it a letdown when it's done?**
When it's done I think it's a miracle. I'm not dead, nobody died. Really, I always pray like it's a miracle.

**Do you have a favorite film that you directed?**
I don't know. I never look at them anymore. When they're done, they're done. It's good to have the adventure. It's like love. You're not always going to love the same kind of people. You're going to love somebody that makes your life different. And with films, it's also like that—it's a love affair. But I try not to look back.

# A VETERAN PRODUCER'S TAKE ON SCREENWRITING

## An Interview With Bruce Gilbert

▶ By Chuck Erven

I was sitting in a café in Indonesia, reading an old Australian newspaper when I happened upon an extraordinary article about a Papuan farmer who took his critically injured niece on an epic journey across New Guinea for medical help. While the article was short and placed well below the fold, I was immediately struck and soon obsessed by it. I quickly discovered the entirety of what the world knew of Iambi Pisau, the Papuan farmer, was contained in that half-page article. Nothing more. Yet, in that article, I saw the outlines of his journey. What I didn't know was that writing would be a journey for me, as well.

Bruce Gilbert

I've spent most of my working life as a college theater professor and playwright and had written only two other screenplays prior to reading the article about Pisau. I suppose I've mostly written for the stage because of economics. If you write a play, you and your actor friends can always produce it. Write a screenplay, and it's far more difficult to find production. Economics. In spite of this rather jaundiced take of playwriting versus screenwriting, I spent a good part of a year writing the first draft. I was simply compelled to write it, whether or not it found production.

I'd given a draft of the script to Blake Ellis, an actor and friend of mine who had recently begun a career in producing. As is often the circuitous ways of these things, Blake then passed the script along to his friend, Bruce Gilbert. Bruce is one of the world's most successful and respected film producers and generously gave his time and keen insight on the script. I understood immediately that this was not typical. I knew that most screenwriters would not be fortunate enough to work with a veteran producer like Bruce Gilbert, and I was grateful, regardless of where it might ultimately lead. I shot Bruce and Blake an extensive revision of the script, and it was then that they placed an option on it.

So much of what has happened has struck me as a personal journey. Writing is, of course, a solitary endeavor, but we also need the input of others. I've always thought it important to seek that discerning eye, to gather those critical voices that give the work real shape and contour. Bruce Gilbert and Blake Ellis have reshaped the script into something I could never have completely envisioned. And I'm sure it will continue to be shaped as new voices join the journey to bring the story of Imabi Pisau to the world.

Bruce sat down with me in a nearly empty Chinese restaurant in Beverly Hills to discuss his iconic journey as a film producer. His vibrant engagement for the process of filmmaking and screenwriting certainly showed no signs of waning.

**Can you describe the relationship between a producer and a writer?**
Well, as a producer, you have to have a sense of story and what will play in the marketplace. But you also have to have a sense of who the right writer is for a project and how to get the best work out of that writer.

**Is this the same relationship between a producer and director, or how does that compare?**
The director has a lot of creative input but also has limitations. So it's not just about who you choose as a director or production designer or cinematographer, or who you choose as the costume designer. They all can have a tremendous impact on the look and the feel of the movie, and the director depends on that— and so does the producer.

But the fact is, the director isn't the author of the movie. They often come on after the script is developed, or mostly developed. That was definitely the rule for the classic producer as I saw it. And so the source of everything is the *story*. It's like with real estate, it's location, location, location. With film, it's story, story, story.

You can't make a good film out of a mediocre script. You can make an *okay* film out of a mediocre script, but you can't make a *good* film.

Bruce Gilbert has produced eleven films, including *Coming Home* (1977), *The China Syndrome* (1979), *Nine to Five* (1980), *On Golden Pond* (1981), *The Morning After* (1986), and *Jack the Bear* (1993).

**I'd like to talk about how you got started in the business. It was an incredible time, the 1970s.**

Luck. I mean, the way I started, luck played a part in it. And I think luck plays a part in everyone's career. When I went to UC Berkeley, they had no film program. I think they had two film courses in the entire university. But I was studying to be a developmental psychologist, interested in the psychology of creativity and the psychology of genius and how children learn. It really focused on the creative process, though, and it turned out to be helpful preparation.

It was a time during the Vietnam War, and I was raising money for "activities" of one sort or another. Berkeley, at the time, was a place where you could really feel the energy—a magical time that kind of gets relegated to images of protest signs and people with long hair and bellbottoms. Nobody has captured the essence of what was really a very exciting time. A lot of energy—creative, political, sexual, cultural.

**And you were able to tap into that energy?**

Yeah. I ran a film society that showed films on Friday and Saturday night and charged a modest amount that would go toward the antiwar movement. The available titles were mostly European films, so I just figured out how to rent these films, 16-millimeter films, mostly from Janus Films.

**And there was an audience for them?**

It was a time when there was an interest in films that weren't Hollywood films, because the Hollywood films were like Rock Hudson and Doris Day and *Pillow Talk*. Mainstream Hollywood films, for the most part, didn't appeal to the campus culture. So I saw a lot of films and collected the tickets, ran the projector—all of that stuff. And I even made the posters. I never thought it would be something I'd end up doing as a career.

**Can you talk about the cultural shift that was happening at the time?**

Yeah, a watershed moment for me was when *Easy Rider* came out. I think it was *Easy Rider* that was distributed by Columbia Pictures, a major Hollywood distribution company—and it was in major theaters. And again, it's hard to re-create the context of the time, but the studios controlled content, and there were only three television networks. It was basically a handful of studios run by these older guys who even when they were making "youth pictures" were really making the older guy's version of that. So you know, it was like *Gidget* and *Beach Blanket Bingo*. They'd stick some contemporary Top-40 song guy in there to relate to the "kids," but the content wasn't representative of what was going on in the culture. *Easy Rider* changed all that.

**So it was a completely galvanizing moment?**
Absolutely. This was a real kind of a watershed moment, not only for me but at the studios, too—because now there was recognition that the people running the studios didn't know who this new generation was. They didn't know how to reach them, and their ideas of what this new group wanted to see was unfathomable.

People talk about the "Golden Age" of filmmaking in the 1970s. That happened because a lot of very talented young people were energized by the times. They had something to say and a point-of-view about how to say it, and they were left mostly alone.

**Coming Home was the first film you produced. How did that come about?**
Well, Jerry Hellman was the producer—I was the associate producer. But luck played into it. I was campaigning against the war as part of the Indochina Peace Campaign. We had a campaign that went through the ten largest states with the most electoral votes to try to affect the election. It was 1972. Obviously, we didn't have that big of an effect on the election.

Anyway, I organized several of those events. And it turns out there's a lot about putting on those events that has some relationship to producing. You have to have a vision of what it is, a great sense of organization and putting together the right team and attending to an infinite number of details.

**And this is how your association with Jane Fonda began?**
Jane was in a lot of these events as one of the speakers. And at the end of these evenings, I sort of fell into a game with Jane and others, which was essentially something like: "If you could make any movie you wanted, what would it be?" Very quickly, it became, "Well, of course, it would be about Vietnam, because that's the central conflict of our generation." Would it be a war movie or a home

front movie? Since we were still at war, it wouldn't be a war movie. What would we do? Shoot it in the Philippines with Filipinos playing Vietnamese? We were very culturally attuned, so that was never going to happen.

**And that's how you got started producing. It grew out of a genuine passion.**

That's how I got started. Then I apprenticed myself to a producer, for free. They already had the story editor, a guy named Syd Field, who would go on to write all these books on screenwriting. I was the low man on the totem pole. Not only did I do most of the reading, but I also had to pick up the producer's dry cleaning and do whatever was asked of me. I can't remember exactly, but I worked either four or six weeks for free before they finally agreed to take me on at some ridiculously low salary. But I was in the door.

**Looking back, what were some of the skills you developed at this early job that have served you well?**

I read scripts voraciously. I kept three-by-five cards of writers and their credits. I would have to update them all the time. I learned who the good writers were, what their credits were, and who represented them. I would try to memorize credits, because often my bosses would say they need a writer for a project: "Bruce, give me a list of ten writers."

I was also writing critiques of submitted scripts, which is sort of ridiculous given that I was probably the least experienced person. At many studios and production companies, this practice continues today.

**Right. So how does a writer overcome that sort of thing?**

It's almost impossible to avoid. It's in the chain of command. No one in authority has the time to read all the scripts. It's one of the great unfair things to writers that I think exists.

**I sometimes feel I learn more from reading bad scripts than I do from reading good scripts. Do you think that's true?**

I used to be able to call up Paramount and get the first draft of *Chinatown* or *The Godfather* or any film you wanted to study. But here's the thing: You don't just read the final draft or see the movie. You read the first draft, the second draft, the third, the fifth, twenty-fifth, whatever it is. Every film goes through a course from first to final draft and shooting.

In my opinion, the best way to learn how to write screenplays is to read and analyze all of the drafts. If there's more than one writer, it's also a good way to tell who can really write and who can't. There are infinite variations on how a story can evolve from the initial idea to the shooting script, and as far as I know, they don't teach that in film school. If they have you read the script, the script is usually the shooting script, right? And by then, it's so refined. It's like taking you to the Cordon Bleu and giving you the finished plate and saying this is how you cook.

As I drove back to my hotel, I replayed the interview in my mind, and what struck me was how much Bruce still enjoyed the art, craft, politics, economics, and comradery of filmmaking. What was especially clear was that he found inspiration from what was happening in the country, the culture, and the wider world. For Bruce, there was no apparent sense of nostalgia or longing for better days. It appeared that the better days were *now*. He was of the moment and ready to explore what the next moment might bring.

I'm not a young man. I've been working at my writing for a long time now, so long that I might be referred to as being in mid-career. But *mid-career* could imply a downward slide, a winding down of creativity and productivity. That is a concept that I can't abide by. I'm impressed by Bruce's long and illustrious career (who wouldn't be?), but what impresses me most is his desire to keep moving forward. And for that, I am both grateful and hopeful.

---

**CHUCK ERVEN** is a member of the Dramatist Guild of America, whose plays include *After Vertigo*, *The Ballad of Chet (On the Eve of His Bliss)*, *Canyon Suite*, *Glynn's Crossing*, and *Painting Landscapes*. *Canyon Suite* won the 2006 David Mark Cohen National Playwriting award from the Kennedy Center. His most recent play, *The Ballad of Chet (On the Eve of His Bliss)*, placed in the top three for the Cohen Award, the best new plays produced at universities and colleges in 2011. In 2006, he was the John Wall Playwriting Fellow at the Sewanee Writers Conference at the University of the South, and in 2009 he was nominated by the Kennedy Center as a "Teaching Artist". Chuck holds a Master's in Theatre from University of Maryland and an MFA in Screenwriting from University of California, Riverside. His screenplay, *Uncle Pisau's Arduous Journey*, is currently under option by Bruce Gilbert's American Film Works and Blake Ellis.

Chuck Erven

Photo by Dan Wong, courtesy of Fresno City College

# NEGATIVE FEEDBACK
## How to Find the Positive
▶ By Hugo Van Laere

In 1999, I started my career as a scriptwriter, and ever since then I've tried to stay true to the credo, "Whatever the question, the answer is yes." I first worked as a staff writer for a comedy series that was broadcast on the VRT, the public broadcasting network in Flanders, Belgium. Soon after, the same network asked me to participate in developing a new comedy show. Although the wages were poor, I said, "yes." We worked for more than a year, but the series was never produced. Still, during that year, I mastered the skills I needed to develop stories for television. So when VTM—the major commercial network in Belgium—asked me to develop a police series, I was able to pitch a mature concept, and I landed my first series, *Rupel*. In the years since, I've developed several series, written documentaries, and until recently I was the showrunner of *Familie*, the longest running soap opera in Europe (VTM).

Saying "yes" has been significant in my screenwriting success, but it took more than that. Hard work, luck, a willingness to exchange ideas and insights—all of these are necessary in a screenwriting career. But one of the greatest challenges a writer must face is negative feedback.

No writer is spared negative feedback. And screenwriters who hope to find success typically go through many years of contending with and responding to negative feedback. Exactly how you respond to the feedback can make or break a career.

But before you can respond, you have to wait for the feedback . . .

## Waiting for Feedback

Congratulations! You've finished the draft of your script. You've worked for hours on end. You've made changes to improve it, and you've even added that genius twist that makes it next to brilliant.

Now it's time to send it to your mentor, your manager, your friend with a foot in the door—whomever you're writing it for. All of a sudden, you're overcome by fear. What if they think you're a lousy writer? What if they find you a pompous ass with your genius twist? What if they don't like you at all?

You're feeling vulnerable. After all, you put your heart and soul into that script. You swing back and forth between pride and fear. It's a feeling even the most experienced writers are familiar with.

You forge ahead, and hit "send." And then you wait . . .

Waiting for feedback is part of what it means to pursue a career as a screenwriter. You put your work out there, and you wait for the response. And you bear in mind that there's a person who *will* have a positive response—you just have to wade through the negative responses first. And you also have to learn how to recognize a positive response when you see it.

# Getting Feedback

In all likelihood—and you probably already have some experience with this— you'll receive a mixture of positive and negative feedback. Some will respond positively and not mean a word they say. They may not have even read your script. They simply want to be nice, "encourage you to death," as the saying goes. Others will respond overwhelmingly negatively and will simply say that the rest is "okay." Still others won't respond at all. Ever. And then, of course, there are those who will respond six months or a year later.

Feedback, whether negative or positive, can be vague or specific:

> Vague: *"I have the feeling that somewhere in the second act your story slows down."*
> Specific: *"The scene on pages 33–37 is far too long."*

The more specific the feedback is, the easier it is to process—and vice versa. But feedback on the early stages of your work will likely be vague. It's important to note, though, that ambiguous comments often concern essential deficiencies. And the sooner you figure out the underlying problem, the less time you lose in your rewrite.

So let's assume you have some feedback on your work. The question now is: How do you respond? We'll begin with how *not* to respond.

# How *NOT* to Respond to Feedback

In the beginning of my career, I worked as a staff writer for a comedy show. The third season had already been ordered when the showrunner received an email from the network. The network considered an episode weak and felt it lacked humor. The showrunner—a very talented writer—replied, "Strange. I think it's a strong episode with plenty of humor." Later, on the telephone, I could hear the showrunner stubbornly defending every single joke. A week later, the show was cancelled—and for years, the writer was out of a job.

What's the lesson here? Be proud, but don't be arrogant or stubborn.

A few months later, I witnessed another scene that taught me it was an equally bad choice to give in too easily. The producer gave a suggestion to have the protagonist of the series react more fiercely when his girlfriend dumps him. He suggested that the protagonist throw his bike at the girl. A fellow writer took the suggestion literally, but the producer had suggested it only by way of illustration. When he read the second draft of the script and the protagonist actually did throw his bike at his girlfriend, the producer was livid. "The man doesn't even have a bike!" he shouted. "This bike-throwing thing was just a matter of speech."

The lesson? Don't be so eager to please that you agree to any suggestion.

# How *TO* Respond to Negative Feedback

Over the years, I've learned that the only constructive way to respond to feedback is saying the magic words, "Thank you," followed by, "I hear you," and possibly followed by, "I'm thinking!" By saying this spell out loud, you show respect and buy some time to figure out the appropriate response. *Respect* is what you have to show your readers, whether they're friends doing you a favor, your superiors, or people in a position to hire you. *Time* is what you need to find a solution to the problem they have with your writing.

And first, you need to make sure you understand the problem. There are two things you need to clarify: labels and levels.

When you receive feedback, you have to clarify that you're interpreting labels the way your reader meant them. People attribute different meanings to the same labels. For example, how would you label the man in this drawing?

What's the Label?

Illustration by Hugo Van Laere

Some will say he's thinking, others will argue he's worrying, and still others will suggest he has a headache. The only way to be certain is to ask him.

With the guy in the drawing, it's impossible to know for sure. But with actual living people giving you feedback, it *is* possible to find out what they mean by the labels they use. Suppose you get notes that your scene could use more violence to make it salable. Instead of promptly throwing in buckets of blood, it might be wise to ask the reader what she means by "violence."

Now you can start to clarify on what level you need to apply changes—story, characters, plot (structure), or production. The tricky part here is that the person giving the feedback often isn't aware on which level the problem lies. But being a writer, *you* should know it before changing anything.

## Story

I once wrote a story about a man, Peter, who fell in love with a mysterious woman. Even though the woman seemed attracted to him, she kept her distance. Peter persisted until he found out that the woman was transgender. His infatuation disappeared, but he understood her problems and was prepared to help her.

When I pitched this story to the network, they refused to produce it unless I turned it into a comedy. This was fundamental feedback on the level of *story*, and I knew it related to a different worldview. I consider transgender issues a question of personality, whereas the network considered it a problem of sexuality. They couldn't convince me to change my story, and I wasn't able to change their minds, so I never wrote it.

Lesson? You can't reconcile fundamentally different worldviews. If the differences are only skin-deep, you can try to compromise.

## Character

Feedback on the level of character can be interesting to unravel. Every writer has heard the remark "this character would never do that." If a character is acting "out of character," there are two possible causes: the writer has misread the character, or the circumstances in which the character acts are wrong. In *Familie*, we introduced a new character, Hanne. In the writers' room, we described her as kind and innocent. When I read the first dialogue in which Hanne appeared, I felt she acted childishly instead of innocently, and I knew I had to talk to my team about the labels "childish" versus "innocent."

If everybody has the same view of the character, and your character is still acting out of the ordinary, you should look into the circumstances. I strongly believe that characters can behave any way we want them to, provided we've created the right circumstances. So when the compassionate, stable mother character suddenly throws the dishes at her adolescent son because he returns home tipsy, and you receive a comment that her behavior is "out of character," you can either scrap the throwing dishes part, or you can set up the mother's outburst. Give her a few sleepless nights, so she makes a big mistake at work, so her boss scolds her, which upsets her so much that she—when she drives home—doesn't see the cat in the driveway and kills it. Now, no one will ask questions about flying dishes anymore!

## Plot

You can also receive comments on the level of the plot—perhaps something like, "the outcome is too predictable." This feedback is about the outcome, but in most cases, you'll have to fix the setup. If it's too predictable that your protagonist will use the knife he received as a gift from his father, throw in more gifts and let your protagonist be excited about the computer game he received. In other words, *snow your setup under*. This comes back to the idea that you don't necessarily have to fix what's specified by the feedback, but you do have to solve the problem that lies beneath. And to do that, you have to develop the skills to figure out the problem.

## Not so fast . . .!

You've clarified the feedback, but you're not ready to rewrite yet. It's always a good idea to check whether the person who gave the feedback agrees with the adjustments you're about to make.

I'll often return notes annotated with three types of color-coded comments. The green comments mean, "I'll change it as asked." The blue comments mean, "To solve your problem, I'll adjust something else." And the red comments mean, "I hear you, but this is why I want to keep things as they are" (for instance, it's a setup for the next episode). The green comments show respect, the blue ones indicate that I give the notes some thought, and the red ones show that although we disagree, I'm still willing to listen.

This is a good practice to consider, regardless of the power level of the person giving the feedback.

## Why Attitude Matters

Learning how to respond to feedback is a matter of adjusting your attitude. I mentioned earlier that you might need to hone that skill of recognizing what positive feedback looks like. That's because we writers, being sensitive creatives, can take a period instead of an exclamation mark to mean that the reader didn't appreciate the work. Sometimes, positive feedback can come in the shape of merely a pat on the back and a willingness to pass the script to someone with pull or stature. The point is, a proclamation of your genius isn't the only type of positive feedback, nor is it realistic.

The fact that someone has read your script to the very end is in itself positive feedback. So is the fact that someone has made the effort to add notes and comments. It means your script is worth it. There are only two kinds of scripts that require little feedback: the best and the worst.

At the beginning of your career, you're better off with a returned script having so many notes that it looks like a battlefield. Every single note is an opportunity to reflect and learn—not only to improve your writing skills but also to hone your positive attitude toward feedback. Is your first impulse on a note, "they misread it"? Or "I miswrote it"? Is your overall feeling, "they don't understand me"? Or "I didn't make myself clear"? Showing your willingness to cooperate will determine the course of your career.

Let me put it to you this way: It's always a pleasure to work with a writer who is eager to learn, willing to rewrite, and capable of expressing his or her gratitude with the simple word, *thanks*.

Being a head writer and showrunner, I also occasionally have to give feedback on someone's attitude. Negative feedback on a script is harmless compared to negative feedback on attitude. It took me months to teach one of my staff writers not to say, "Yes, but . . ." after a remark. I used to say to him, "Let's deal with the *yes* first, and afterward we can talk about your *but*." I really grew tired of hearing *but, however, still* all the time. Finally, I did get angry and told him I wanted him to say out loud, "I hear you." I'm pleased to report that his ability to appropriately deal with feedback has greatly improved since that incident.

However, personality issues or issues with professionalism don't always end well. I once had a gifted writer on my team, but he never met a deadline and always came up with the most dramatic excuses. I accepted those excuses three times, and then I told him to get a grip. He didn't. Although he was one of my best staff members, I had to end our collaboration.

I really began thinking about the importance of finding the positive in negative feedback after meeting renowned script consultant Linda Seger at a lecture in Spain. I had read her book, *Making a Good Script Great*, and wanted her advice about how to give negative feedback in a way that would inspire positive results in the writing. I asked about her experience with writers who received her feedback, and she gave me the following answer: "If someone isn't used to notes, they might get overwhelmed, but my critique is always constructive, so I sometimes have to tell a writer to take a deep breath and read the report several times in order to digest it and get ready for the next stage of the work."

I think this is a great way to look at feedback—as a call for the next stage of a work in progress. A sign that someone has confidence in you. Proof that you're not alone. I strongly believe that if you can turn feedback into a challenge, and if you're prepared to see that challenge as an opportunity, you'll be able to respond in a creative and constructive way. And this is the only way to succeed as a professional writer.

**HUGO VAN LAERE** holds a Master's in Audio and Visual Arts from RITS, Brussels, Belgium. He has written the screenplays for short films, features, documentaries, and television. His feature *Love Belongs to Everyone* won best screenplay at the Shanghai International Film Festival in 2006. He wrote a season of *16+*, a scripted reality series, broadcasted on VRT, the public broadcasting network in Flanders, Belgium, and he created the crime series *Rupel*, also broadcast on VTM. He was head writer of the telenovela *Sara*, an adaption of *Ugly Betty*, and he created his own telenovela *David* for VTM in 2009. For three years, he was showrunner of the soap series *Familie* (VTM). Van Laere is currently developing an international series as well as a Web series.

Hugo Van Laere

Photo by Thomas Geuens

# Notes

1 University of California at Riverside-Palm Desert, Writing for the Performing Arts MFA program, Q&A, December 2011.

2 Leily Kleinbard, "Adapting 'Life of Pi' for the Big Screen Took 170 Script Revisions," *The Atlantic*, November 21, 2012, accessed May 1, 2016, www.theatlantic.com/entertainment/archive/2012/11/adapting-life-of-pi-for-the-big-screen-took-170-script-revisions/265367/

3 Kyle Buchanan, "Meet Allan Loeb, the Most Prolific Screenwriter in Hollywood," *Vulture*, February 11, 2011, accessed May 1, 2016, www.vulture.com/2011/02/meet_allan_loeb_the_most_proli.html#

4 Jim Vines, *Q & A: The Working Screenwriter: An In-the-Trenches Perspective of Writing* (Bloomington, Indiana: AuthorHouse, 2006), 178.

5 "Screenwriter/Producer Terry Rossio (Extreme Interview)," accessed July 4, 2015, http://makeyourbookamovie.com/screenwriter-producer-terry-rossio-extreme-interview/847/

6 Charles Isherwood, "Go East, Young Writers, for Theater!" *The New York Times*, November 13, 2007.

7 Anna Weinstein, "Diva Directors Around the Globe: Spotlight on Anne Fontaine," *Film International*, October 25, 2015, accessed March 1, 2016, http://filmint.nu/?p=16649

# CHAPTER 3

# FINDING SUCCESS

"Here's a secret I have learned in 20 years as a screenwriter: Failure is constant, for everyone. And I mean it. Everybody fails at this all the time. Not just screenwriters, but I think anyone who tries to illuminate the human experience in an authentic way."

Susannah Grant

We know by now that the overnight success story doesn't really exist—that there are always a handful of unproduced screenplays that came before the one that sold. There are files of ideas, folders with half-finished scripts, endless drafts, and pages of notes. There are botched pitches, stolen ideas, and projects bought but never produced. There are broken spirits, journeys to recovery, stories of love and loss and hope and pride.

Success comes after real work, real life, real grief, real mistakes, and real love. You simply can't find true success without first surviving the devastation of real failure.

## Who Knew?

Richard LaGravenese, writer of *The Fisher King*, *The Bridges of Madison County*, *P.S. I Love You*, *The Last Five Years*, and *Unbroken*, has said that he thought his career was over before it began. He wrote hundreds of drafts of his first produced credit, *Rude Awakening*, for no pay, only to have the film tank at the box office.[1] Several drafts into his spec script, *The Fisher King*, which was nominated for an Oscar, he had to rethink the entire story because it was too similar to the premise of *Rain Man*, which had just been announced. LaGravenese's Oscar nomination came after years of struggle and after what felt at the time like actual failure.

There's another thing about success that you probably intuitively know: It often comes with a price. There are lost friendships, lost working relationships, and lost marriages. There is competition, backstabbing, undermining, and bullying. There are the inherent threats that money and respect bring—addiction, greed, fame, and a loss of privacy.

But there's also real opportunity. If you can sew up your wounds and keep pushing forward, you might have the opportunity to create work that will live beyond your lifetime. The opportunity to work with legends, to create art with people you admire, to be a part of something bigger than yourself.

You may very well be someone who will go on to live out your dream career as a screenwriter. Do you know what that dream career looks like? What does success mean to you? Do you want money? Fame? Respect? To stay busy? To simply be paid to write? Do you want to write *and* direct?

In this chapter, we'll look at strategies for achieving the success you're hoping for, and we'll examine several successful careers and try to unravel how these people were able to achieve success. You'll learn about:

- Working with a screenwriting coach and lessons for a successful career
- Building a team of mentors and experts who can help you in a crunch
- How to decide what to write and how much thought to give this decision
- Working with an independent film producer and what the producer–writer relationship can look like
- How to have longevity in a screenwriting career and how much attitude plays into it

- Achieving the top screenwriting honors and some surprises and obstacles that go hand in hand with success
- Why the ability to schmooze is an asset and why it's not as bad as it sounds

We'll begin with employing a screenwriting consultant. A screenwriting coach is one of a handful of people who might become a part of your team.

# BUILDING YOUR TEAM
## Insights From the Screenwriting Consultant
▶ An Interview With Linda Seger

Linda Seger is a renowned screenplay and story coach who has been consulting with working screenwriters since the early 1980s. Her clients include writers, directors, producers, and executives in film, television, and theater. She has worked with Academy Award-winning writers and has lectured on screenwriting in thirty-three countries. She has written nine books on screenwriting, including *Making a Good Script Great* and *From Script to Screen*. She has also trained more than seventy-five script consultants in her method.

Linda Seger
Photo by Katie Gardner

**You've been a screenwriting consultant for a lot of years. Any common threads in terms of the advice you give your clients?**
I'd say the most common advice I give has to do with mentorship. One of the first things a screenwriter should learn is that you don't make it alone. There are a lot of people who say they're self-made, but when you start questioning them, of course, that's not true. They had mentors, maybe a father who runs a studio, or a friend of a parent who works in the business.

But many people don't have mentors. So if you're entering this business and you don't have an uncle in the studio, what do you do? One of the things I did was hire my mentors. I knew I needed a career consultant, a publicist, a media consultant, even a sales consultant.

**When was this?**
This was in the 1980s.

**Interesting. You're a script consultant, and you had enough faith in consultants even back then to invest in them.**
It's these consultants—the team I built—that made my career. You know what you want to achieve, so you put a team around you who can help you get there. They're your mentors.

**How would you explain what mentorship can do for a screenwriter?**
A great deal of what we do that makes us successful is that we *learn*. It's a learning curve. There are people who've said, so-and-so is so lucky. But there's very little about any successful, lasting career that's about luck. There's working hard and working smart—that's important. Finding the right people you can learn from—you take seminars, read books, find mentors or consultants—and don't bother with other people who aren't helpful. I went to a seminar consultant once who didn't seem to understand what I was about—and after two times, I said, "That's not the right person for me," so I found another seminar consultant.

**A seminar consultant?**
To teach me to lead seminars. Even though I'd been a teacher for some time and had experience as a speaker, I was starting to do these three-day seminars, and I wanted to get some good feedback. So I hired a consultant to come to my class. She gave me some really good pointers.

**What an interesting idea.**
It's the same as hiring a screenwriting consultant. People have bad habits that they're not even aware of. For instance, my consultant said that when I told a joke, I wasn't giving the students enough time to laugh, so she taught me to take a breath.

**I imagine you've taught a similar lesson to your screenwriting clients.**
Yes, because these things are universal, aren't they? She told me not to be afraid of silence. This is also true in screenwriting. Letting the script breathe, trusting that a joke will land—not forcing the writing or overwriting.

> "There's working hard and working smart—that's important. Finding the right people you can learn from—you take seminars, read books, find mentors or consultants—and don't bother with other people who aren't helpful."

**How would you describe what success looks like in your clients?**
One of the things successful screenwriters do is invest in themselves. They recognize what it is that they need, and they figure out who can help them get there. Again, in the beginning, it's counterintuitive. You don't have money, so it doesn't seem wise to spend what little money you have. But as you find success, spending money on yourself becomes easier.

There's this general understanding in the business that maintaining a career year after year isn't easy. Your work is up and down, and there are very specific things to do when your work is down and very specific things to do when your work is up—and you have to be wise about making good decisions. I've seen people who have a rapid rise and good things happen, and then they misuse it or abuse it in some way. They spend all the money they made, not realizing they can have lean years. You can make a lot of mistakes. You can get egocentric, say the wrong thing to the wrong people. This is the downside of success, and it's when your team can help.

**Can you give me an example of this?**
I did something once where I didn't say the right thing to a producer, and it literally took me three years to get that relationship back on track. I was determined to get her back on my side.

**What did you say to her?**
I confronted her on something she'd done that was rather rude. But of course, you don't confront your superiors. It's not a good idea. And that was the end of our communication. She had the authority and a lot more power than I did. And she was also a member of Women in Film, so what I did was, every time we were in the same room, for the first year I waved at her. I didn't go over to her, just waved. The second year, I would go over and say hello but keep it short,

no communication, no threat. The third year, whenever she had a movie that was showing, I went to the screening, and I would make sure that I not only said "good work," but I was very specific—whether it was something about the profound theme or the brilliant acting or the arc in the script, I said something specific. And I was always honest. Her work was very good.

**That sounds complicated and a little nerve-wracking. Is this typical in the film industry? This type of interpersonal communication?**
Yes, this is a relationship business. You have to be very careful how you deal with people in the business and be diplomatic. And you need to recognize that this isn't your relationship training ground. This is a well-known person, and you better handle this really well. It takes a lot of work.

It takes a lot of figuring out how to deal with people and having people who can help you with that is important—your team who supports you. Because there are some very tricky situations that come up, and more so in some ways when you're successful than when you're not.

**Is there anything about becoming successful that you think aspiring screenwriters should know?**
Ray Bradbury said, "Pray that your success does not come too soon," because you can have your opportunity, and if you're not ready for it, you might blow it. I've had plenty of clients who just were not ready when opportunities opened up. And the thing with opportunities is they don't come again. You can wait ten years for an opportunity, it comes, you blow it—it will never come again. Maybe it'll come twenty years later, but maybe not. You have to recognize the layers. There's not just the layer of knowing your job. There's the layer of working with people, and handling things, and not being stupid.

> "One of the big things that happens with success in the entertainment industry is that you move from being a private person to a public person. And you have to decide if you want to be a public person, because if you're a public person, people will have attitudes about you even if they're not true."

**Can you talk about failure, or how we perceive and respond to failure?**
What we perceive as being true failure is almost always in response to what we consider a big opportunity. But you have to recognize that just because the outcome of the opportunity isn't exactly what you envisioned in your head, that doesn't mean it's a failure.

I have a story about this actually. When I was starting out, I was asked to speak to the executives at ABC. It was a huge opportunity, and not only did I prepare, I went out and bought a very expensive suit that cost about as much as the money I was going to make from ABC. It was a three-hour seminar, but I felt it didn't go well. So to me, that was failing big.

But here's the upside of that story. About six or eight years after this incident, I was in Berlin, and somebody said I should meet this American who worked at a film company in Berlin. So I spent the day with her, and she said, "You did that seminar at ABC." And I said, "Oh, my gosh, that was one of my biggest failures." And she said, "No. I was in the room. It was terrific. I still remember it all these years later." So we don't always understand our failures and successes. We need to be prepared to redefine what success is. Maybe success is getting an award for a short film, or winning a screenwriting contest. It isn't just getting an Academy Award or getting a lot of money for a script.

We have a saying in our office, "Treat everyone like they're a decent human being even if they're not acting like one." And not everyone is nice, obviously. One of the big things that happens with success in the entertainment industry is that you move from being a private person to a public person. And you have to decide if you want to be a public person, because if you're a public person, people will have attitudes about you even if they're not true.

So people may not like you simply because they're unhappy with themselves and you're successful, and so you become the target. But the thing for me—and this is what I tell my clients—you have to separate this out and not be someone who hurts other people in response. Don't be unkind. Don't be the reason somebody else has a problem, or make somebody else's life difficult. Don't downgrade them or discourage them just because you're now successful and feeling good. And this doesn't mean being dishonest. I just think it's an important thing to keep the focus on, as much as possible, doing good things.

**I'd love to talk a little more about that—success and ego and navigating that road of feeling good finally but also insecure. Do you deal with this with your clients?**

Sure. Ego is significant as you find success. Because there's a point where people start telling you how wonderful you are. To be successful, there's got to be a certain number of people telling you you're wonderful, otherwise you can't be successful. And it's easy to believe you're the best thing ever, so you protect yourself by surrounding yourself with people who are going to keep saying that. So you filter out the people who aren't saying that, and you create a bubble around you to protect your ego.

But you have to find a way to burst your bubble. If you get to the point where you don't allow the negative to get through, then you become unbalanced. You want the negative to get through, because one of the ways you keep your success is by continuing to do well. You want to get that feedback, and you need to have people in your life who you allow in to give you that feedback.

**Is there skill in knowing how to appropriately filter negative feedback?**

Listen. Don't get defensive. Sort out what's helpful, and don't worry about the rest. As you find success, you need to develop a sense of smell. In the beginning, you just presume everybody is nice, and then you get blindsided, or people take advantage of that. But you need to be perceptive about people and protect yourself. Just because somebody says they're nice doesn't mean they are. I get worried actually when people say, "Oh, you can trust me, I'm honest." A lot of the time, those are the people you can't trust.

**How do you develop that sense of smell? Just experience? Practice?**

Yes, but part of it is also fine-tuning your ability to not be a victim. That's an important thing in being successful—to say I don't want to go around being irritated because people have taken advantage of me. So you recognize that you have to have the protective gear in place, knowing who you are and what you need to have a happy work life. It's not just about success in terms of what you achieve—it's also "Am I enjoying what I do?" Success includes happiness and fulfillment on your terms. Being balanced. Letting your success unfold and take you in new directions, guiding your success.

**You might love the writing but not so much the politics or the interpersonal challenges. Do you work on that with your clientele? Navigating the business aspects of their career?**

Screenwriters often say, "I'm not good at marketing." And I say, "Yeah, most of us aren't. So what do you do about it?" It's not enough to say you're not good at it, especially when it's a significant part of what it takes to be successful. So whatever that thing is that somebody says they're not good at, I say, if that's an important part of your job, then you have to find a way to learn it. Because there are always different aspects of your job, and you can always find someone to teach it to you.

**There's the art that you do, and then there's the business. Would you say that learning the business requires a different set of skills, different from the craft?**

For sure. It's art, craft, creativity, and business—and you've got to learn all of them. And of course, especially in entertainment, a lot of things have to do with learning to collaborate, as opposed to seeing colleagues as competition. That can be difficult for screenwriters to learn, but it's an important survival mechanism in the job.

You have fellow screenwriters read your scripts and give you feedback, and you read their scripts and give feedback. Even very successful screenwriters do this. I think there's some statistics that say people in a writing group do better than writers who aren't. So a lot of the time, successful screenwriters will have their writing group, and then they'll have a consultant they turn to for the next step. You need to create a team that has the ability to help you get a better script.

So again, we're back to your team: Who's on your side, and are they really helpful? With screenwriters, you can end up doing a lot of stuff that's not moving you forward, so you're just spinning your wheels and repeating the same mistakes over and over. But your team is your encouragement, your wisdom—and they keep you from going nuts over something or making a big mistake, or maybe they help you clean up a mistake. They're there to help you sort everything out, because there's a lot to sort out in this business.

# INDEPENDENT FILMMAKING
## Working With an Independent Film Producer
### ▶ An Interview With Mary Jane Skalski

Mary Jane Skalski began her career at Good Machine in the early 1990s, where she worked on the breakthrough films of Ang Lee (*The Wedding Banquet*), Edward Burns (*The Brothers McMullen*), and Nicole Holofcener (*Walking and Talking*). In 1997, she produced Bart Freundlich's *The Myth of Fingerprints*, starring Julianne Moore, as well as John O'Hagan's documentary *Wonderland*. In 2003, Skalski was cited as one of Variety's "10 Producers to Watch," and in 2004, she received the Independent Spirit Award for Producing.

Mary Jane Skalski

Skalski has produced four of Tom McCarthy's films: *The Station Agent* (2003), which received a BAFTA for Best Original Screenplay; *The Visitor* (2007), which was nominated for an Academy Award for Best Actor (Richard Jenkins); *Win Win* (2011), starring Paul Giamatti; and *The Cobbler* (2014), starring Adam Sandler.

Her producing credits also include Gregg Araki's *Mysterious Skin* (2004), starring Joseph Gordon-Levitt; Todd Louiso's *Hello I Must Be Going* (2012), starring Melanie Lynskey; and Naomi Foner's *Very Good Girls* (2013), starring Dakota Fanning and Elizabeth Olsen. She also executive produced *Pariah* (2011), directed by Sundance sensation Dee Rees. Skalski regularly participates as an advisor at the Sundance Institute Lab for Creative Producing.

**How did you get your start producing? Was this something you prepared for in college?**

I didn't go to film school, but I always knew I wanted to work in film. I was thinking about that before I went to college, but at the time, film programs weren't as developed as they are now. So I went to the University of Michigan, and I took some documentary classes while I was there, which helped me see how films are actually made. And then I just got it into my head that I would move to New York after I graduated.

**Did you have a job lined up before you moved?**

No, I ended up working in a restaurant, which was great actually, because it gave me time to get the lay of the land. But I saw an ad for this tiny advocacy organization for filmmakers, the Association of Independent Video and Filmmakers, and they were looking for an administrative assistant, so I sent in my résumé. It was a very small organization, and I was there for maybe eight months when a position opened up for Membership and Programs Director. So I applied and got it, and that was really my start, because that's when I met James Schamus.

**How did you meet James Schamus?**

We were putting on seminars, so it was my job to come up with and organize the seminars. And one day, the executive director said, "I met somebody who just came to town. He's doing something similar to what we're doing, and I think the two of you would get along. We should do some programs together." And that was James. So for a couple of years, we put on these seminars together, and then when he and Ted Hope started Good Machine, I went to work for them. That's really what put me on my path to features, where I learned everything about script development and the industry.

**What was the selection process for the films? How did you find your projects?**

In those days, there was Shooting Gallery and Good Machine and a lot of other companies—everybody was making exciting movies. There was just such a vibrant atmosphere at the time. When James and Ted started Good Machine, they came to it to be director driven—that was the mandate of the company. So when they came together to form a company, they each brought a list of directors they wanted to work with, and that was really how we approached things. The script was always something that could be made better, but if it was an exciting director, we were interested.

So we'd see as many films as we could. The Tribeca Film Center would have a screening series of works in progress, and there were all kinds of industry things to go to see the work. We'd also get so many short films in the mail, so at lunchtime we'd all watch them. So we really watched everything, and if we saw something we thought was interesting, we'd call them up. It was just that kind of a world back then.

> "When James and Ted started Good Machine, they came to it to be director driven—that was the mandate of the company. So when they came together to form a company, they each brought a list of directors they wanted to work with, and that was really how we approached things. The script was always something that could be made better, but if it was an exciting director, we were interested."

**Is that how you found Bart Freundlich?**
That's a slightly different story, because I was friends with Bart. I'd read a draft of *The Myth of Fingerprints* earlier, before Good Machine existed, and there wasn't really anything I could do then. But the script came back around a few years later, and at that point I felt like I could do more than just be a fan or friend. I'd seen his short film, I knew he was a student at NYU, and by the time he'd graduated and felt the script was done, I'd been at Good Machine for a couple of years. I'd worked with Ang Lee for a couple of years through *The Wedding Banquet*, so I had a better overall sense of things.

**Did you give him feedback and say, "Before we take this next step, I think the script needs this type of rewrite"?**
No, at that point the script was pretty well there. It was such a fun script. The movie has serious undertones, but the script was a really joyous read and it had its own momentum by then. It really did feel like it was on the way to getting made. I think Noah Wyle might have already been attached, or he was close to being attached, and *ER* was very new, so that was exciting. *The Myth of Fingerprints* came together pretty quickly, ultimately.

**How about *The Station Agent*? How did that come about?**

I didn't know Tom. It was exactly the opposite of Bart—I didn't know him at all, and I got the script and I really liked it, and when I met Tom, he just felt like somebody I'd known my whole life. And because I come from that tradition of Good Machine, where it's so director driven, I don't discount that connection. When you feel there's a connection, that's something to really pay attention to. So that was that—we started working together, and that was certainly a turning point for me, because the film surprised everyone. People really felt like it came out of nowhere.

**I'd love to talk about how much a producer might be involved in the rewriting stage of independent films. What did the rewriting process look like for *The Station Agent*? Was there a lot of back-and-forth between you and Tom before the script was ready?**

It's hard to remember on that film, because now I've worked with Tom for so long. There were definitely things in early drafts that aren't in the movie. The central spine of the story was always there, but there were different ways some of it was teased out. There were some characters that went away, and the ending definitely changed several times. But all the while, we were trying to make the movie. It wasn't a situation where we were like, "Let's do another couple passes of this script before we send it out." The script was in really good shape.

Also, we knew that we weren't going to go out for industry money for that movie, so it's not like we were sending it to Paramount. We were looking for money, and we were looking at budgets. Tom was inspired by a lot of locations that actually existed, so in trying to figure out how to make the movie, it was a question of, "Can we actually shoot in that depot?" We knew that world was very specific and existed, so it was trying to plug into it and put together enough money to be able to make it. And we had the cast. Peter and Bobby and Patty were all involved. It was probably only about fifteen months from the time I first got the script to when we were on set.

**Did you experience any big upsets on that film, where you thought you were ready to go and then it all fell apart?**

We had a couple times where we'd have a meeting and the prospective financier would say, "Let's make this movie. I'll call you tomorrow," and then tomorrow would bleed out, and then it'd be weeks later when we'd finally hear the no. There was some of that where we got very close and then had the brakes put on. But we didn't fall apart. I was involved with Nicole Holofcener's film *Walking and Talking*, and that was a film that was almost up and running and then it fell apart. We were painting the production office, and then the next day the plug was pulled. There are those cases where it's very dramatic, where we're moving forward and then you've got to let everybody know it's not happening. It wasn't like that on *The Station Agent*.

**So your collaboration with Tom since then, do you give a lot of feedback on drafts?**

Tom tends to write until he has questions or wants to talk something through. With all the movies that we've done together, the development process and how I've been involved is always a little different. Sometimes writers just want to get through a draft so they can show you their work. Tom isn't at all like that. There have definitely been projects where the first time I read it it's a complete draft, and sometimes it's half a draft. Often the impetus to send something to me to read is because he has a specific question in mind. And that's great, really, for a producer, because he'll send pages and we'll talk about it, and he'll say, "Did this bother you? What did you think of this?" That's a great way to work.

**For *The Visitor*, did he come to you with the idea, and then you bounced around the idea before he sat down to start writing, or did you see pages first?**

No. There have definitely been times where we've sat and talked about different ideas he has, but that's not really his process. Some people have the process where they talk through their idea with anyone who will listen, and they pay attention to the cues they get from the listener, noticing when they've lost them. They'll talk it through until they have the whole movie in their head and it's killing them not to write it. But that's not really how it's been with Tom. He's someone who will write it out, so I'm usually reading something and then we're talking about it. I'll have a sense of what might be bubbling about in his head, but I don't think too hard about that, because over the years, I've watched how ideas manifest in the script differently than he initially talked about them.

**Can you tell me about your involvement on *Pariah*? Was that a script that you read and knew you wanted to make?**

I was an executive producer on that film, so I was really working more with Nekisa Cooper, the producer. I met Nekisa through the Sundance Producing Lab, so that was a situation where I was giving creative notes to Nekisa and she could decide what to share with Dee.

> "Some people have the process where they talk through their idea with anyone who will listen, and they pay attention to the cues they get from the listener, noticing when they've lost them. They'll talk it through until they have the whole movie in their head and it's killing them not to write it."

**Could you explain how that works? A screenwriter is working with a producer who is working with an executive producer who is giving notes . . .?**

Well, that may or may not happen. I've had projects like *The Hawk is Dying* where Ted Hope was an executive producer, but he would definitely also give script notes. So it depends. It just happened to be that my path into *Pariah* was with its producer, so I was there to help the project. My primary relationship was with Nekisa, not with Dee. But as an executive producer, when I take on that role, I think my job is really to support the producer and the director's effort more than try to bend it or change it. I have my notes and my creative opinion and I give them, but it's different than if I'm producing.

**As a producer, what are you looking for in a project? What are you impressed by in a script?**

I'm looking to have a real gut reaction to something. It has to really strike me in a way. In a sense, it's a little bit like falling in love. I can read something and really enjoy it, but it doesn't mean that I want to produce it. It's something I'm going to be involved with for two to three years, so I need to have that connection. It has to be something that I feel like I am bringing something to creatively, otherwise I'm just sort of facilitating. And that's okay, but it's not so interesting. If I'm going to put together the financing and bring the cast on board, I have to feel that there's something I can bring to it that betters it.

And I have to be able to see its path to production. That's key. I have to see how it starts with me and ends with the movie in front of an audience. Otherwise, I'm not the person to do it either. If I have no idea of how I would do it, then I shouldn't do it. I can't just be like, "I love it. I have no idea how I'll get it done, but I'm going to do it and I'll figure it out later." No, I have to have some idea of how to get it done.

**Does it help if the writer comes to you with her own ideas about that? Or would that be annoying because it's overstepping?**
It does help to have that conversation, because if our expectations are different, then we're going to be fundamentally making a different movie. So if I read something and think it's beautiful and think its budget should be $500,000, but the writer thinks this is a movie that Fox Searchlight will do, then that's good to know. I would love for that to happen, but if I don't believe it, then I'm not the person to pitch it to them, because the writer is going to be disappointed. We may make the movie for $500,000, and I'm thinking it's perfect and exactly what it should be, but the whole time the writer is thinking it's wrong, that I failed her. That's a problem.

So no, it's very helpful. And actually, often when I read something I like, it's the first question I ask the writer, or the writer-director, "How do you see this film getting made?" Because that often indicates their priorities in the making of it. And there's no right or wrong answer, but that's really helpful to me.

**How do you typically get your material?**
A little bit of everything. I'm still primarily filmmaker driven, so a lot of times it's coming from writer-directors or agents or managers. For the most part, pretty fairly industry-standard ways, although I am doing a project now that someone sent out with a query letter. It sounded interesting, so I said sure, I'll read it. I've been reading that through drafts and giving notes.

What I should say, though—it worked because the person had real authority on the subject, so that's what piqued my interest. And the letter was very much about that, like this is who I am, this is what I've done with my life, this is what I've seen, and I've written this script about it. That's what was interesting. I get a thousand queries a day that are like, "Dear producer . . ." I don't even read those, so I don't want anyone to think that they're effective.

**You really get a lot of the "Dear producer" queries?**
Oh yeah, and I literally just delete them. They all come at once, too, because people must use some services that batches them or something. Sometimes I'll be sitting there, and all of a sudden five will pop up.

**So you delete them because experience has shown that this doesn't often result in a positive outcome?**

Mostly because I'm not looking for scripts that don't have directors attached, especially right now. I'm not really looking for anything specific—but right now, to attach a director is really difficult.

> "Build the connections with directors—that should be a first for writers. Because even if you have your script out and you don't have an attachment, you could still say, 'Look, there are a few directors I'm friends with, and I think they'd be great for this project.'"

**Do you have any advice for screenwriters about how to go about getting a director attached to their scripts?**

I would say go to film festivals, watch short films, and meet those directors. Really pay attention to first features and short films that have a different director than its writer, because those are directors who are open to collaborating with a writer. And choose wisely, because I'm not interested to look at an unattached script, but I'm also not interested to look at a script that has a director attached that I couldn't get the movie made with. I have to be realistic.

If you think your movie is commercial and you think it wants to live in that $8 to $12 million range, don't attach a director who isn't going to help that happen. I'm definitely not in the business of coming aboard material and then getting rid of participants who are already attached. So instead, that would just be a non-starter for me.

**Final advice for the writer who wants to go the indie route?**

Build the connections with directors—that should be a first for writers. Because even if you have your script out and you don't have an attachment, you could still say, "Look, there are a few directors I'm friends with, and I think they'd be great for this project." That's showing a producer that you could potentially bring someone to the project, that your project might make sense.

# DECIDING WHAT TO WRITE
▶ By Kira-Anne Pelican

Researchers at Bournemouth University, in conjunction with BT TV, recently claimed to have cracked the code for the perfect television show. Analyzing fifty of the most popular series from the last decade, they found that episodes containing 65 percent drama, 12 percent shock and surprise, 9 percent comedy, 8 percent action, and 6 percent romance made for the most compelling viewing.[2] Closest to matching this formula was the *Downton Abbey* episode featuring Sybil's death (Season 3, Episode 5). Whether we'd soon tire of every episode of our favorite television shows conforming to this dramatic mix isn't known, but what is clear is that audiences across the world have clear preferences for certain kinds of stories featuring certain kinds of protagonists, and television networks and film studios are increasingly keen to make use of predictive research when commissioning new projects.

So how does this impact you as a writer, you might be asking? The answer is: in many ways. Feature film studios and indie producers now use "big data" when making decisions about which scripts to pick up, as well as how they should develop them. Studios already analyze huge amounts of information to predict how well new films are likely to fare at the box office, including a film's genre and subgenre; whether the film is a franchise, sequel, or adaptation; and the film's cast, director, classification, length, critical reviews, awards, and release dates. And with Sundance's launch of their Transparency Project in 2015, indie producers are now able to access similar forecasting data for independent films.

Since many factors impacting a film's financial success start with the script, writers can also benefit from an increased awareness of how certain story decisions impact a film's critical reception and return on investment. If you're wondering whether that means this essay is going to be an unequivocal call for writers to follow formulaic approaches, the answer is not at all. The evolutionary nature of our psychology means that creative innovation will always stimulate our minds and pique our curiosity over and above the familiar. What's more, because every film can be put together in almost an infinite number of ways, film financial forecasting can only make generalized predictions about how well any particular film is likely to fare in the marketplace given the performance of similar films in the past. As two-time Oscar-winning William Goldman famously wrote in his book *Adventures in the Screen Trade*, "Not one person in the entire motion picture field knows for a certainty what's going to work. Every time out it's a guess, and, if you're lucky, an educated one."[3]

That being said, today's guesses are certainly better informed than they were in 1989, and while a string of "flopbusters" produced over the last decade stand testament to the fact that studios still aren't always getting things right, Hollywood studios are probably getting things right on around 70 percent of their films.[4]

But returning to the point—if you're an early career path writer about to start crafting your next spec script, wouldn't you rather know, before you start writing, how producers are likely to evaluate your script, rather than six months of work down the line? So let's look at how you can evaluate your ideas in terms of the marketplace, starting with multiple idea generation.

# Generating Ideas

At the earliest stages of idea development, most writers have a whole series of concepts floating around their heads. Some may be fully sketched out original ideas, and others may just be newspaper clippings or a few notes on a new character.

The first stage of the sifting process is to throw out ideas that don't stick. If you're not interested in an idea after a couple of weeks, it's highly unlikely anyone else will be. Then test your ideas with their first audiences by pitching the concepts to friends and colleagues. Next, consider your ideas in relation to your personal goals. What is it that you're hoping to achieve with this spec script? That might be a sale, and if that's the case, ask yourself whether there's a particular genre that you're best at writing and if it's likely that as an up-and-coming writer you have a good chance of selling a script in that genre. Maybe your next goal is to raise your profile and take a shot at placing in one of the major screenwriting competitions, but you're wondering whether you'd have a better chance of winning with your hi-concept thriller idea or your art-house drama. Or you may be set on finding critical acclaim, or on navigating a route through the indie market.

Whatever stage you're at as a writer, and whichever creative path appeals to you most, the genre you choose to write next is likely to have a significant impact on the outcome of your script.

# Impact of Genre

For writers set on commercial success, it's unlikely that you'll have missed the fact that over the last decade action-adventure films have dominated the US domestic box office, making up over a third of films ranking in the top ten, with animation and fantasy films the next most popular. Action genre spec scripts have also been outselling every other genre spec script since 2012. However, and here comes the big *but* . . . in the last decade, only two spec scripts in this genre were sold by "first-time" writers who haven't previously sold a script but may have been writing for up to fifteen years before their first option.[5] Action and animation scripts are the two genres that new writers are least likely to sell. Proven track-record writers, hired by the studios, write the vast majority of action films, while the animation studios develop nearly all animated films in-house.

So what's the bestselling genre for spec scripts written by writers who aren't yet established? Thrillers. High concept loglines dominate the lists of recent spec sales, with action thrillers selling best in recent years, followed by sci-fi thrillers. Over the last decade, comedy scripts were the next bestsellers for newcomers. And in recent years, high concept action comedies and road trip scripts have been going down particularly well.[6] Bear in mind, though, that comedies are particular to the culture they're written in, and they rarely translate well to global audiences.

For writers drawn to darker material, horror films continue to perform well at the domestic and global box office, and horror is the only genre that predicts a movie's return on investment. Which subgenre you choose to write makes a big difference in terms of any resulting film's likely box office success. Slasher movies perform best at the US domestic box office, while zombie films perform least well.[7]

Dramas are notoriously hard to get off the ground, primarily because they're highly unpredictable when it comes to forecasting a film's return on investment. They are, however, the best genre of choice for up-and-coming writers set on critical success. Narratives that are accessible to a large audience yet deal with serious issues tend to be longer than average (though it's not known if this translates back to the original spec scripts), and adaptations of a bestselling novel or piece of nonfiction are more likely to find critical acclaim. Interestingly, adaptations of classics tend to be less well received by the critics. And since award-winning films are more likely to be released during the Oscar run-up period (over the winter holidays), you might want to think twice about setting your potential Academy-winner on the beach.[8]

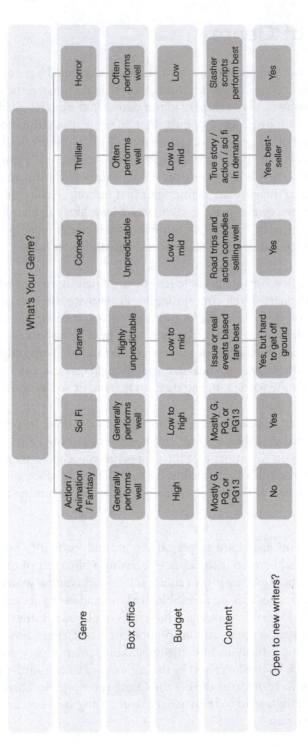

| | Action / Animation / Fantasy | Sci Fi | Drama | Comedy | Thriller | Horror |
|---|---|---|---|---|---|---|
| **What's Your Genre?** | | | | | | |
| Genre | Action / Animation / Fantasy | Sci Fi | Drama | Comedy | Thriller | Horror |
| Box office | Generally performs well | Generally performs well | Highly unpredictable | Unpredictable | Often performs well | Often performs well |
| Budget | High | Low to high | Low to mid | Low to mid | Low to mid | Low |
| Content | Mostly G, PG, or PG13 | Mostly G, PG, or PG13 | Issue or real events based fare best | Road trips and action comedies selling well | True story / action / sci fi in demand | Slasher scripts perform best |
| Open to new writers? | No | Yes | Yes, but hard to get off ground | Yes | Yes, best-seller | Yes |

What's Your Genre?

Dramas have also been the most popular choice amongst winners of the Academy Nicholl Fellowships between 2010 and 2014. Many of the fourteen winning drama scripts, out of a total of twenty-four, were concerned with powerful issues, and some of these were based on true events. Interestingly, the 2014 entries reflected an apparent shift toward comedies and comedy-dramas, but no long-term conclusions can be drawn from a single year's data—and it's useful to remember that all the figures I'm citing here may just be results of recent trends. In addition to the recent slew of comedies and tough-hitting dramas, three thrillers, one romance, and one historical action-adventure have also made the Nicholl selection in recent years, while sci-fi and fantasy scripts have consistently made the finals. Given that a number of Nicholl Fellowship scripts have gone on to sell, this would seem to be a particularly good route for getting the very best dramas noticed.

## Who Assesses What?

When assessing how well a script is likely to perform at the box office, Hollywood producers usually draw up a list of five to ten comparable films, similar in genre, budget, and possibly also theme. This comps-based approach helps inform financial projections of how well a new script is likely to perform, as well as helping determine the best routes for casting, release season, and windows.

As an alternative to writing an original spec script, some writers are drawn to the possibility of adapting a novel, short story, or other source material.

# Writing the Adaptation

If you're considering adapting a book or magazine, bear in mind that it can sometimes be an expensive process. The more popular the book, the better the adaptation is likely to fare at the box office, since bestselling books come with their own fan bases.[9] While optioning a lesser-known book from an independent publisher for twelve to eighteen months might cost as little as $500, the development process often necessitates buying two eighteen-month options, typically costing upwards of $7,500,[10] with the options for blockbusters selling in the high five- or six-figure range. The rights for highly coveted, long-form magazine articles may go for similar figures—that is, if you even have a chance to buy them. The "based on a true story" thriller genre is in such demand that 20th Century

Fox have a two-year first look deal with Epic, a new online platform for edgy nonfiction, launched by the journalists behind *Argo* (2012). If you can't afford to option one of the articles that Fox has passed over, there are a number of other investigative journalism magazines now online, or with some serious digging you might just scoop your own story.

# Market Research

## Research Whether Your Idea Has Already Been Made

Having gathered together your first set of ideas, you'll next need to check that no similar films have been produced, are in production, or are even in development. This is where market research becomes vital. Extensive Google and IMDb searching by title, subject, and themes will confirm the subject matter of existing films, while films currently in production and development are listed in the Hollywood trade papers, as well as websites including Movie Insider. Since faithful remakes tend to lose money at the box office because of market saturation, you'll likely want to avoid remaking an idea unless you're radically transforming the original, coming to the creative process completely afresh.

Once you've checked that no one else is developing a similar film, you'll probably soon start thinking about your protagonist.

## Find the Right Protagonist

Certain genres lend themselves to certain kinds of protagonists, but it's also useful to consider your target audience when creating the main character. While 18 to 39 year olds remain the largest audience, in 2014, the number of theater tickets sold to 40 to 59 year olds was at an all-time high. And the 60-plus demographic has also been steadily on the rise since 2011.[11] For writers, this means that following the success of *The Best Exotic Marigold Hotel* (2011) and its (2015) sequel, producers will be on the lookout for scripts catering to this emerging market. When it comes to gender onscreen, US domestic audiences are equally split.[12] That means that as the industry plays catch-up in addressing the gender imbalance onscreen, following the recent successes of *The Hunger Games* (2012) film series, *Frozen* (2013), and *Gravity* (2013), this is a good time to be writing strong female roles.

As part of my own research, I've been interested in whether audiences have preferences for any particular qualities in film protagonists, and whether any preferences are universal or vary with culture from nation to nation. With international sales now accounting for between 50 and 70 percent of a film's total box office, appealing to the global market has become vital for a film's financial success. The suggested answer, in screenwriting manuals, is often to write stories featuring characters with universal emotions, problems, and motivations to create stories with global box office appeal. But what does this actually mean?

In an attempt to find out, I compared the protagonists of 100 top-ten, domestic hits released in the United States and China between 2009 and 2014 with the protagonists of fifty films ranking at the bottom of the US domestic box office for the same years. The results demonstrated that whether a film was a top-ten box office hit, regardless of genre, could be predicted by three protagonist qualities: impulsivity, altruism, and physical ability. Main characters in the most financially successful films tended to be highly impulsive and driven by the desire to help unrelated characters while displaying their physical skills. Given that these three traits are equally important in predicting the success of films at the US and Chinese box offices, they may well be universally popular qualities in screen protagonists.

This, of course, isn't to say that films without protagonists exhibiting these typically male, heroic qualities don't perform well in the box office. Bilbo Baggins in *The Hobbit* trilogy (2012, 2013, 2014) and Dr. Ryan Stone in *Gravity* (2013) have recently demonstrated this. But part of the appeal of these less-active protagonists may be in their pairing with more heroic supporting characters. We don't yet know. Or it may be that more private female heroism is celebrated in different but equally popular character traits on screen.[13] Another conclusion that I drew from my research is that protagonists in the most financially successful, recent films tended to display a greater emotional range, and often more intensely. Taking *Avatar* (2009), for example, the world's all-time greatest box office protagonist (as of 2015) Jake Sully rates highly on nearly every universal, primary emotion—from happiness and sadness, through showing fear, surprise, disgust, shame, excitement, pride, guilt, love, and compassion.[14]

Creating a compelling protagonist is also vital for a future producer to package the film. The more interesting the role, the better the chance of attracting talent to the project. And it doesn't just stop there. For the highest-budget films, attracting "A-list" actors to roles has become a vital way of attracting finance to the project.

Once you've honed down your concept, you'll soon be starting to think about where your script should be set.

## Locate Your Story

Some stories come with a natural setting, but for those that don't, locations may have a significant impact on the chances of a film being made. Your script's genre, together with the film's likely budget and audience, will have the biggest impacts on where you should set your film. If you're writing an action-adventure blockbuster, you'll be writing for a budget that probably now requires settings across the world to maximize the film's global appeal. There's a good reason why *Mission: Impossible – Ghost Protocol* (2011) features segments in Moscow, Budapest, Prague, Mumbai, and Vancouver (standing in for Seattle). The production of low-budget indie films, on the other hand, may require finding locations that maximize local tax incentives, while still having good film infrastructure and local talent. In their analysis of 106 Hollywood films released by the majors and mini-majors in 2014, Film LA found that 64 percent of these films were filmed in the United States, 11 percent in the United Kingdom, 11 percent in Canada, and 6 percent in the rest of Europe. Nearly thirty different US states and foreign countries were used as primary filming locations, but those topping the list were California, the United Kingdom, New York, Canada, Georgia, and Louisiana.[15]

Government subsidies in the form of regional development financing may be another reason to reconsider the setting of your screenplay. In the United Kingdom, for example, "Microwave" is Film London's micro-budget feature filmmaking scheme that provides development financing and support to selected writers who set their films in London. And iFeatures is an equivalent, micro-budget development scheme for writers locating their screenplays in the English regions. In Canada, a number of similar development schemes exist, some of which specify that films must be primarily located instate. You can find details on the Writers Guild of Canada site.

# Writing for a Budget

Whatever genre you're writing, it's imperative that your script stays within the likely production budget for that genre. Action-adventure, fantasy, and some sci-fi films will generally cost upward of $80 million—and twice as much if they're top-ten blockbusters. For that budget, audiences have come to expect A-list actors, multiple "destination" locations, often including China and India for secondary market appeal, as well as complex visual and special effects. Following the critical success of *Moon* (2009), produced for just $5 million, there has also been recent interest in lower-budget sci-fi films. These will inevitably require confined sets or locations, a minimal cast, very few action sequences, and limited visual effects. Thrillers vary widely in their production budgets but are often in the $50–60 million range, with action thrillers coming in much higher and psychological or erotic thrillers being produced for under $10 million. Mainstream comedies tend to be produced for between $10 and $50 million, generally with a few extravagant set pieces and limited cast.

Drama budgets also vary widely but are frequently under $20 million. The black comedy drama *Birdman* (2014), for example, was made for $18 million, and *Boyhood* (2014) for just $4 million. With these kinds of budgets, scripts require creative thinking about a limited number of cast and locations and very few complex action sequences, if any. Finally, horror films generally leverage financing for between $5 and $20 million, and therefore inevitably draw a lesser-known cast, limited sets and locations, and creative use of visual effects and props to create the right atmosphere while keeping budgets down.

## What About Rating?

Unless you have a great concept that can only be well told as an R-rated movie, it's generally advisable to maximize your future audience by ensuring that your narrative is suitable for children aged 13 and over, gaining the studio's preferred G, PG, or PG-13 ratings.[16]

Now that you're up to date with current research on how a film's genre, subgenre, protagonist qualities, locations, budget requirements, and content impact the likelihood of your script finding critical or commercial success, you're in the best position to make judgments about which of your ideas to take forward and how.

Ultimately, however, a script will only be produced if it's good enough, and no amount of research is going to improve your writing. As Ray Bradbury once said, "The important thing is to *explode* with the story, to emotionalize it, not to think it. If you start to think it, the story's going to die on its feet. It's like anything else . . . People who take books on sex to bed become frigid."[17]

So now, before you become self-conscious, please forget everything I've said.

**KIRA-ANNE PELICAN** is an independent script consultant, a Visiting Tutor in Screenwriting for graduate students at the Met Film School, London, and a screenwriter, commissioned by the BBC and ITV. She is set to complete her PhD in Screenwriting in 2017. Prior to her work as a researcher and script consultant, Kira-Anne spent twenty years working in the film industry, first assisting Stanley Kubrick on *Eyes Wide Shut* (1999), and then working in visual effects production on films ranging from *The Ladykillers* (2004) to *The Matrix Revolutions* (2003).

Kira-Anne Pelican

# A WORKING SCREENWRITER'S JOURNEY IN AUSTRALIA

▶ By Susan Macgillicuddy

It goes without saying that things are different here in Australia, but for screen-writers, the keys to success—to having a career that can span decades once you've had that first, strived-for lucky break—are the same as anywhere else.

I remember standing in a producer's office eons ago, and as he gave me what I would later learn was called a "soft pass" at my first screenplay, I looked over his shoulder and saw a poster with the following slogan:

"Success is a journey, not a destination."

Well, I *was* successful, or so I thought. I'd sold my first serious radio play and had it produced and broadcast nationally by Australia's media Colossus, the Australian Broadcasting Corporation. Actors from the Royal Melbourne Theatre Company had performed in it, and my phone was ringing off the hook. I thought I knew what success was already. What did that annoying poster have to teach me?

Everything.

Now, almost thirty years later, I'm still awed, amazed, and delighted by one of the great truths about writing as an occupation—and a vocation—that there's no Chairman of the Board position to aspire to when you're a writer. You write. That's your natural state, beyond the hype and lessons and myths about writers as a breed. You have a monkey on your back, and that monkey is called *story*, and only you know the stories you're going to tell, and the monkey will make you do it. Success *is* a journey, and the wonderful thing is, no two writers have the same one.

> Remember that there never has been, nor will there ever be, nor is there today, another you. Great philosophers like Plato have reminded us of this, but you must keep the belief that your experience of life and the way you use your imagination are unique. Your gifts and achievements that led you to this threshold point—as well as your magnificent failures—are unique. So no one else can approach story the exact same way you do.

Here are a few of the things I've learned on my own, unique journey as a working screenwriter in it for the long haul.

## "Come On In, the Water's Fine!"

Don't let the gloom-mongers and naysayers discourage you. A lot of screenwriting gurus and teachers focus on how hard it is to make a living if you're contemplating a career as a writer. And, yes, while that's true—that it's hard and will cost you everything—it's also important to remember that in the arts, as well as in life, miracles happen every day. People get breaks, and careers start and grow from strength to strength, but successful writers—and artists across the board—all have one vital thing in common.

Persistence.

Now they also have talent, sure. But talent without persistence is nothing. There are countless people out there who aspire to write, and many *will* write, but they only have one story in them, because they aren't able to face rejection or criticism about their work. No one can help you with this. You have to get used to it, because here's a little secret:

The rejection never stops.

You will have your work bought and your services as a writer/developer commissioned, and you will also face countless rejections. There's no guaranteed, magic formula for success or sustaining it once you have it.

Get used to the idea that for any number of reasons—likely too many to waste good writing time and energy pondering—someone said "no" to your latest masterpiece. It's not the end of the world. You will live. Even when some gruff actor throwing a tantrum hurls a script at your head, comparing it to excrement in the loudest of voices, you'll get over it. You have to, because if you don't, those rejections, disappointments, insults, and criticisms will *become* your stories. Then bitterness sets in. And before you know it, you haven't written anything new in a year.

The road to a screenwriting career is littered with people who have given up when they were just getting started, and also those who have faced the dragon of rejection and are now too terrified to return. You must avoid these people like the plague.

A lot of people say you need tough skin to survive working in the arts, but to me this presupposes negativity and the wont to fail. I saw the opposite of this mentality when I was fortunate enough in the late 1980s to meet Frank Herbert, the author of the seminal science-fiction fantasy saga *Dune*. It was at a science-fiction fan convention, an environment immersed in story for days at a time, and I approached him to say hello, and he asked me where I got my sandwich. I said, "Here, have mine," and we had a nice chat about his impressions of Australia. I asked him the quintessential budding writer's question: "What advice can you give me about becoming a writer?" I was afraid he'd say the same as everyone else—that I'd need rhino skin and that the odds of my not succeeding were great. But he didn't. Instead, he smiled—a warm, genuine smile of welcome—and said, "Come on in, the water's fine." I went home feeling high from the rush of that powerful, positive, and generous validation of my aspirations and wrote the first twenty pages of a novel. It never came to anything, but it helped me get started. And Frank was right—the water *did* feel fine.

# Do It Your Way

As a lecturer at university, I see students making the same big mistake over and over: copying others. Australia has long held a fascination and admiration for American film and television shows, and I've read countless *Walking Dead*-type zombie apocalypse scripts, ditto *Breaking Bad* and *Game of Thrones*. And yes, while those shows are awesome and popular, they're someone else's stories and they've been done. If you're copying someone else to get that next writing job or keep your current writing job, it's because you're afraid—and what you fear is doing it your way, because that has brought you rejection in the past and you don't want to revisit that particular corner of hell again.

Stop! If you don't give your stories a chance to emerge, they'll be like teeth. And what happens when you ignore your teeth for long enough? They go away.

It's perfectly okay to come up with lame, derivative ideas, so long as you only allow yourself to do this for test-drive purposes. Sometimes it can take try after infuriating try to get a story right. Other times it will appear in your head as if by magic. But either way, it's up to you to put your own unique spin on it, without judgment or anticipating what others will say. You have to thrill yourself first, and if you achieve that with your own material, there's a good chance you'll be able to do it again, and again, and again, and again as long as you allow yourself to do so.

Dr. Seuss's Note to Susan

When I was a kid, growing up in Hong Kong during the 1960s, at the age of 10 I won a big-deal drawing competition, and the Judge was Dr. Seuss. He'd just written "The Sneeches and Other Stories," and after giving me my prize on live TV, we were filmed for several other news and current affairs, as well as children's shows over the next couple of days. He showed me things about drawing that I've never forgotten, and I'm now applying these to my first online animated graphic novel. The main thing he said was, "Do it your way." He told me that it's all well and good—advisable even—to have teachers, but you must never allow them to make you think about your art in a generic way. I didn't understand what "generic" meant until much later, and whenever I doubt what I'm doing—that it's weird or too "out there"—I recall Dr. Seuss saying those fateful words, and I obey. As a result, especially when this applies to developing and creating TV series, it can mean you unexpectedly get a "yes," because networks, just like producers, often only have a vague idea of what they're looking for until it appears in front of them.

# Be Fearless

I'm not suggesting that you go about bragging or challenging people *not* to read your work, I'm talking about the other, equally important side of having a career as a screenwriter. You must be fearless when it comes to promoting yourself. It may take you a while to find an agent, and after that, the *right* agent for you. But even then, just like the act of writing itself, this aspect of the job never stops.

There's absolutely no escaping the fact that you will have to learn to become adept at networking. You will also have to become used to approaching total strangers, either by phone or in person (under the right circumstances), and let them know you exist. People talk about writers, and you need people talking about you. You never know how that next new contact will pan out. It could lead to the right person hearing about you, or to your next job. Writers can be solitary creatures by nature (it goes with the territory), but you'll also have to learn how to be social and win people who connect with your ideas and stories.

I always have a cool, edgy business card that stands out. I had one that was so popular that I'd see it in the offices of people I hadn't even met when I went in for a meet-and-greet. Your card says who you are, as much as how you look. Create an image that suits you, with the help of a professional stylist if you're clueless. Don't think for a second it doesn't count. This *is* show business after all, right?

But above all, be authentic and genuine. A fake stinks from a great distance, so be yourself. This will also attract people who admire that quality. I became close friends with the late Heath Ledger, because we both had admiration for how the other started out. He drove across Australia in his mid-teens to seek fame and fortune, and I sat on a couch in a producer's front office for ten hours straight until, bemused, he agreed to give me five minutes at the end of the day, which led to my first paid job as a writer.

You need to be fearless to face the unknown and thrive. The path of the writer is like no other, and it will lead you to places you can't imagine if you're brave enough.

## Lie If You Have To

I'm talking about lying to retain your anonymity. When people know you're a writer (especially when you've written or created something they know), they start acting funny, by either censoring their behavior, or worse, boring you all evening with their bestselling story about the joys and sorrows of breeding Shetland ponies, which they're *certain* would be a mega hit if only they (or you!) had the time to write it. When people ask me what I do, I say, "I enter data in a mainframe computer at such and such hospital." It sounds so boring that I've never been asked to elaborate and can simply observe away unhindered. It's also a great way to observe the reactions of your audience and learn from them.

In all other work situations though, it's *never* okay to lie. A lot of producers have been burnt by writers who lied or couldn't deliver. So always, in professional circumstances, speak the truth.

## Can I Buy You a Drink?

This isn't a suggestion that you should encourage others to drink. Coffee or lunch will work just as well, but in my experience, offering to buy someone a drink is casual, friendly, and not as much of an intimidating (and breakable) commitment as lunch.

Writers need to understand people and life, and screenwriters need to know how to condense life. A medical emergency or situation that takes a day in real time to unfold has to be squeezed into a forty-five-minute commercial hour for television. The only thing that will help you achieve this with any credibility is *authenticity*.

You will need to get whatever area of human experience you're writing about from the horse's mouth. If, say, you're writing about something that happened a long time ago, like the sinking of the Titanic, and no survivors exist, then you should talk to present-day survivors of shipwrecks, descendants, people who still do the same jobs today—historians, doctors, crew, etc. Allow each thread to unravel where it will, because it may lead to gold and something we've never seen before on the screen. Part of the success of James Cameron's *Titanic* was its ring of authenticity, right down to him studying the late ceramicist, Beatrice Woods, as his model for his free-spirited heroine, Rose.

Offering to buy someone a drink and listening is another one of those key skills that you need as a contemporary screenwriter. Audiences expect authenticity now, and you can't just flub medical dialogue by having your characters run around yelling "stat!" Buying someone a drink is seen as a generous act and will allow your subject to relax and spill the beans. Never write in front of them—and please, put the damn phone away. Give them your full attention and authentic reactions to what they impart. Always get their contact info so you can reach them for permission later, but you'd be amazed how many people say, "Go ahead, use it," when they've told you something truly amazing in a relaxed, informal setting.

# Say *Yes* to Everything

Unless you have another, reliable form of income, you'll need to plan your career carefully. One of the best ways to ensure longevity as a screenwriter is to constantly challenge yourself by working outside your comfort zone. Many writers cling to the one genre or one bouquet of themes—and without realizing it, they cut themselves off from great opportunities.

It's great to specialize when you've proven yourself to be good at something, of course. It can help build your brand as a writer. Stephen King is a good example, but he also wrote *Stand By Me*. Woody Allen is a master of writing comedy, but he also wrote dark, conflicted dramas like *September* and *Interiors*. If you're going to work for decades, you need to expand your range. Learn outside your comfort zone, and view and write outside it as well. It never hurts to try something different. I've won awards writing martial arts and action, and I had just as much fun and success writing TV for kids.

You'll never know what you're capable of if you don't give yourself permission to experiment. These days, you can jump mediums as well if you have a mind. The Internet has opened up an interdimensional vortex of possibilities for writers. I've often seen people limit their careers for fear of rejection or criticism. Talent often manifests itself in more than one way, so you owe it to yourself to see what else you can do.

Writers can earn big bucks, and royalties are a joy and a pleasure to receive, but if you limit yourself to one genre, and it goes out of fashion (as genres are wont to do), you could find yourself in the awful position of not having worked for a considerable period of time. People who *could* hire you have decided that you only write material that's old hat.

You never want to put yourself in this position, so say yes to other jobs: that quirky kids' show, or doctoring scripts, or helping develop a new TV drama, or writing a movie for an actor who likes your work, or scripting that controversial documentary, play, graphic novel, whatever. It will force you to learn new skills, approaches to writing, formatting and dialogue, and it will keep you on your toes mentally. You want that. There's nothing sadder and more painfully obvious than a bored, play-it-safe writer who's walled themselves into a particular genre or medium and can't get out.

# It's Only a Phone Call Away

It never gets tired, that call, out of the blue offering you work on some great new show, or to write a feature script, or work with someone you've only ever read about or seen in movies. Screenwriting is one of the few professions where your life can literally spin on a dime. One minute you're in your pajamas, eating toast, and bemoaning the fact that you didn't get that soap, and the next, you're frantically throwing things into a suitcase, yelling "Where's my passport?!" Life will never be dull, even the dull parts. I've seen some amazing things and met some truly unique people, none of which would have happened had I not been a screenwriter.

I'm always shocked when I see young writers watch an unknown number come up on their phone and refuse to answer it. That *could* have been a job, or led to one, and whomever it was might now be calling the next name on their list. My experience on *Heartland* (the Australian mini-series starring Cate Blanchett and Ernie Dingo) was the result of answering an unknown phone call one Sunday morning. A producer I'd never heard of had seen an experimental piece I'd done as a favor for a friend, who ran a theater with a leaky roof and held a benefit night with works donated by writers. He told me he'd been in the audience, watching an actor he wanted to hire, and thought my piece was "courageous." He asked me to dinner, and I met the other producer and was hired on the spot to write two episodes of what became a groundbreaking Australian Indigenous drama.

As part of the job, I had to go to a remote coastal region in South West Australia, where you needed permission from Indigenous Elders to enter Tribal land, and where I lived with them in very primitive conditions. I learned lessons I will never forget. The experience changed my life and made me a better writer. Early one morning, I woke to a scratching on my tin door. One of the Elders, the main one who had refused to speak with any of the writers, came to fetch me. In silence, I followed him down to the ocean as dawn broke, and we got into his boat and he took me across the water, over to an island. "Take off your shoes," he ordered. It was the middle of winter and extremely cold, but I did as I was told. "The Government came here one time," he said, "to put down a bore and take samples, because this is where my people have cooked their shellfish and food since the beginning." He beckoned me to follow him across a blinding expanse of midden, covered with bleached white shells and bones. "The sample they took was carbon, dated over 30,000 years old," he said, "way longer than your mob have been around. These are my people, and these are their stories, beneath your feet. That's why I wanted you to take your shoes off, so you could let them in."

I followed him around the midden, my feet crunching the bones and shells of his ancestors, listening to him sing his strange, moaning song. These songs, or song *lines*, were the way Indigenous Australians created maps. A song that leads you here, or there, over the hill and beyond to places you've never been.

A writer's life is like that, if you let it. If you're brave enough, you'll lead a singular life and learn more about the nature of story and your part in telling it than you ever could have imagined. Happy trails!

**SUSAN MACGILLICUDDY** has written for Australian television for the past thirty years. Her credits include *H₂0: Just Add Water*, *Heartland*, *Wicked Science G.P.*, and *Medivac*. She co-created *Raw FM* and has helped develop many successful Australian series. Susan has also written for radio and fringe theater, and wrote several episodes of the US series *The New Adventures of Flipper*. She teaches screenwriting part-time at The Queensland University of Technology and is currently working on an online animated graphic novel.

Susan Macgillicuddy

# THE PATH TO WRITING AN ICONIC FILM

## Navigating the Business of Hollywood

▸ An Interview With Barry Morrow

Emmy- and Oscar-winning screen-writer Barry Morrow began his career in the 1980s when he wrote about his experience befriending and eventually becoming the legal guardian of Bill Sackter, a man with developmental challenges who spent forty-four years in an institution. Morrow was living in Iowa at the time, and portions of his original story, called "The Triumph of Bill," were published in the *Des Moines Register*. Bill's story found national attention and was eventually turned into the television movie *Bill* (1981), starring Mickey Rooney, Dennis Quaid, and Helen Hunt, which earned Morrow an Emmy Award and propelled him on his journey as a screenwriter. Morrow moved with his family to California and wrote the sequel to the movie, *Bill: On His Own* (1983).

Barry Morrow

Gregg DeGuire/ WireImage/Getty Images

After Bill passed away in the early 1980s, Morrow became involved with The ARC, a national association for people with intellectual and developmental disabilities. There he met Kim Peek, the inspiration for his screenplay *Rain Main* (1988), starring Dustin Hoffman and Tom Cruise.

*Rain Man* is widely considered one of the great films of the past four decades. The film was nominated for three BAFTA Awards, four Golden Globe Awards, and eight Academy Awards. Of the eight nominations, the film took home four, including Best Picture, Best Actor in a Leading Role (Dustin Hoffman), Best Director (Barry Levinson), and Best Screenplay (Barry Morrow and Ronald Bass). Morrow famously gifted his Oscar to Kim Peek.

Morrow has close to twenty credits as a screenwriter and producer, and he's currently in postproduction on his new film *Smitten!*, which he wrote and directed. Morrow continues to work on behalf of people who struggle with intellectual and developmental challenges.

**I know Bill is intimately tied to your early days getting started as a screenwriter, but I'm curious about what came before. What were you doing before you met Bill?**
I was really a Jack-of-all-trades master of none back then. I did a little of everything. I had a rock band, and we'd make some money playing weekend gigs, and I sold encyclopedias for about two days. I was doing a lot of oddball things in those days, but I wasn't a screenwriter.

**How did you meet Bill?**
Bill was a dishwasher at a country club where my wife Bev worked in Minneapolis. And she would get off her shift about 1:00 or 2:00 in the morning, and I'd be waiting in the car in the parking lot, and I'd see him working in the window, scrubbing pots and pans. And he'd always wave to me, so I started waving back. Then finally at a Christmas party at the country club, I sat down with him. And the next day I was picking up toothpaste for him, and the next day he needed hair spray—or "wig spray," as he called it—and then I couldn't shake him. But I didn't want to. It was the hippie days, early 1970s, so having a guy like him with you was cool.

> "If you're going to be a storyteller, you've got to have ammunition. That's why I always say, if you don't engage in the world, especially the fringes of the world, where are your stories?"

**Had you befriended someone with special needs before? Did you immediately feel comfortable with Bill?**
Yeah, it wasn't hard once you get over your initial shyness. People just open up,

and it's kind of been my MO wherever I go. You make friends with different people at different socioeconomic and education levels, and then one day you wake up and realize you have some really interesting stories to tell. It's not Mother Teresa stuff at all, what I do. It's pretty selfish.

**In what sense?**

I just really enjoy the hell out of it, and the fact that Bill came with a whole trunk full of problems didn't phase me because I figured, well, we'll fix the ones we can and we'll ignore the ones we can't. What else could I do? I'm not a social worker. We eventually moved to Iowa, and I ended up working as a media specialist for the School of Social Work, but even though I was working there, I never used social services for Bill. I just wasn't oriented to that, and it was always simpler to just fix it myself or with the help of friends.

**There's that beautiful scene in *Bill* when Dennis Quaid's character tells him that they're going to move to California, and he asks if he'd like to move with them, and Bill gives him his lucky two-dollar bill. Can you tell me the story behind that?**

That really happened. I said, "Bill, Bev and I are moving to California. We're going to see if we can get this movie thing going, and we want you to come with us if you'd like to." And Bill thinks about it and says, "Well, Buddy, I don't want to hurt your feelings, but I got a good home now and I got a job. I have to stay." And then he reaches into his pocket and pulls out his lucky piece, which is a two-dollar bill that he'd carried with him all those years, and he gives it to me.

I don't know how he got it in the institution. He thought his mother sent it to him. A two-dollar bill has a picture of Thomas Jefferson on it, and Thomas Jefferson was born on April 13th, which is Bill's birthday, and that's why it was his lucky piece. But he figured having that lucky piece was what got him out of the institution and brought him to me. So he handed me this two-dollar bill and said, "Buddy, if you're going to California, you're going to need this more than me."

It's still in my wallet now.

**Do you think about Bill regularly? Does he still feel a part of your life?**

His picture and Mickey Rooney's pictures are on my wall right now. There's a great one of us on our way to the Golden Globes. Oh my God, I'm so young and he looks so handsome and happy. We're all dressed up in tuxedos. He's all around me.

**Living your life befriending people who need help or maybe just need a friend, how much would you say that continues to inform your creative work?**

I don't feel that I can write something without having some authority over the material. I once turned down an offer to adapt the book *The Perfect Storm*, which was a huge movie, but I just knew that my writing it was ill fated. I would be doing it for the money and hoping I could fake my way through it.

I like to start with something organic in my life, like this movie I just finished in Italy, *Smitten!*. Twenty years ago, an Italian friend of mine showed me this obituary column of a woman who died and left a sizeable fortune to preserve an abandoned 400-year-old wooden cottage in northern Italy, and I was like, why would she do that? I had to go to Italy to try to find this place. So I went, and the story that I found was a grand story of love and loss.

**You're talking twenty years ago?**

Right. And after I visited, I came up with this idea that if you sleep in this cottage, when you wake up the next day, you'll instantly fall in love with the first soul to meet your eyes, sort of a *Midsummer Night's Dream* thing. So that was my idea. I kicked it around for a long time. I wrote a treatment, and I took it to a couple of places, pitched it, but nobody was particularly interested. A woman who worked for me at my production company at the time, she's a producer now, and two years ago, she called me and said, "That was always my favorite story. Why don't you write it and we'll get it going?" So I did. And we got the financing, and I shot it in Italy—I'm working on post now. But writing for me, it has to be organic. It has to be a story that's meaningful. I'd been kicking this story around for years.

**Had you had opportunities to direct before this film?**

I had opportunities to direct after *Rain Man*, but I had two kids, and I know what it means to direct a picture. It means nobody counts other than this movie for a year. Nothing can get in the way. If people die, unless it's your spouse or child, you can't leave. And even then, after two days you come back and finish the picture. I just never wanted to risk what that meant, so I didn't pursue it.

I never really cared to direct, but then I never really cared to write either. I just started doing it and found out I could. I don't go to many movies. I don't read the Hollywood trade papers unless my wife says my name is in it. Then I'll look. But I've never lived in Hollywood. I'm always at least an hour away.

**Even when you initially moved to California in the 1980s, you didn't live in LA?**
No, we moved to Claremont. It's an hour or more out of LA. I got a job right in the heart of Hollywood, but I commuted every day because I didn't want to raise my kids in LA. But eventually, it got too small, because after *Rain Man*, a tour bus drove up in front of our house one day, and I could hear the guy inside saying, "This is the house where the man who wrote *Rain Man* lives." So my wife and I, as soon as the kids left for college, we sold that house and came to Santa Barbara. We've been here now for seventeen years.

**So you've never been somebody who's been a part of the Hollywood machine.**
No, and it's cost me opportunities, but it's left me free to be not ground up by that machine.

> "I don't know anybody who didn't get divorced that I knew when I started in this business in 1981, or isn't dead or hasn't struggled with addictions. I don't know anybody who has been married forty-seven years. I'm very happy with my life, with my wife."

**When you say ground up, what do you mean exactly? What would your worry have been?**
Mostly it would be to the family and the kids. I don't know anybody who didn't get divorced that I knew when I started in this business in 1981, or isn't dead or hasn't struggled with addictions. I don't know anybody who has been married forty-seven years. I'm very happy with my life, with my wife. Our kids are within an hour drive of us. My son Clay is a producer at Disney, and my daughter is a schoolteacher, and they each have two kids. So I'm way too lucky, but I don't think it would have worked out this way had I gotten in the fast lane in the 1980s. The Hollywood lifestyle just didn't appeal to me. It still doesn't. Look, I can count on one hand the really genuine, straight shooter people in this business who wouldn't stab me in the back.

**Do you still have friendships from the 1980s?**
Some, yeah, but you've got to have something that binds you together, and my writer friends and I never talk about writing. We're afraid to.

**Why?**

Because it'll get into some sort of competition, and you'll end up saying, "Well, that's good, but what do you think of this?" And by the time the night's over you've had a bunch of drinks, you let all your ideas out of the bag, and then you start getting paranoid about it. So you've got to find something else to do together, like playing softball or going to the racetrack, golf, or traveling.

**It's interesting that you say that, because what you hear so often is that you want to befriend other screenwriters so that you can speak the same language, and maybe you join a writer's group and exchange work.**

If you go and join a writer's club in LA, nothing good comes out of that. The only people who are there are ones who aren't busy writing, and they're usually bitter because they've gotten screwed. But hey, everybody does. That's just the entry into the club. You've got to be stabbed in the back and screwed over a hundred times—then you get to be taken seriously.

**What is it about the film and television business that you keep hearing about people doing this to each other?**

Well, there's Washington, DC, and there's Hollywood, and they're similar in many ways. They represent power and money, so when you've got those attractions, greed isn't far behind. And people are fallible. They'll break a promise because it's in their best interest to go with somebody else to get a deal done. There are the actors who say they want to do your picture, and then they do something not only different from that but something that destroys your project. That stuff happens a lot. And for you, that actor might be the only hope you have of getting this picture made, so you pin all your expectations on that. And when it falls apart, you say, "In the room, he told me he was going to do it!" But you can't believe it. At that moment, it was genuine, but there wasn't money or there wasn't a director. It just didn't have the kismet going.

**Do you need to just forgive and move on because that's to be expected in the business, so you can't take it personally? Like that's the norm—they just stop returning emails or calls?**

It's the norm, and you *can* take it personally, but the sooner you learn to stop looking in the rearview mirror, your future becomes clearer, and that's where you need to keep heading. I have a writer friend who is more talented than me, smarter than me, better read than me, his vocabulary is five times mine, but he never worked out in Hollywood. First of all, he couldn't schmooze, refused to do it. And after getting screwed over five or six times, he just said that's it, packed it in, and became a teacher. The teaching world is really attractive for smart people, because you're communicating your knowledge and wisdom, and it's generally appreciated, and it's paid for and secure. Screenwriters have got none of that going.

**I'd love to talk about this ability and need to schmooze. What's the difference between schmoozing in a good way and schmoozing in a schmucky way?**

Schmoozing is really storytelling. You know, I woke up last week, and I couldn't hear out of my left ear. This actually happened to me, and for five days I couldn't hear out of that ear. I was talking to a guy today who said, "I know this woman who can help you with these mushrooms." Well, where is she? She lives in Marin County. Now, if you don't know Marin County, there are a lot of people there with a magical sense of the world. Anyway, he said, "But I'm going to warn you, when you call her, she's going to talk your ear off." And I said, "Oh, maybe that's how she'll solve my problem!"

So I just schmoozed you with a joke that occurred to me when he said that today, but this was about something that happened that was kind of scary for the last five days. I couldn't hear. So schmoozing is just talking about something that really happened mixed in with a little self-deprecation and possibly a joke at the end of it. What you're doing is showing a producer or director or actor that you can tell a story.

When you're pitching, you don't want to just sit down and wait for them to say, "So, why are you here?" You want to walk in the door telling a story. You start with something besides the task at hand, which is selling them on a film that's going to cost millions of dollars. Get them to recognize you for your real talent, which is storytelling, and then convince them that you also have the craft to execute it in 115 to 120 pages of a screenplay.

**Do you have any examples of schmoozing that you've done before a pitch? Any come to mind?**

I remember pitching the head of DreamWorks, and I wore brand new red Converse tennis shoes. This was a meeting of all suits. This was the studio—they were suits and ties, but writers are expected to come sloppily dressed. So I'd just bought these tennis shoes, which I hadn't broken in at all, and I knew if I wore them, they would ask about them. And I had the perfect story.

I'd heard on the radio that Converse had filed bankruptcy and was going out of business, and I couldn't believe it because all I wore at the time were Converse tennis shoes. So I hear this on the radio, wherever it is I'm driving, and within twenty seconds, I see a shoe store—Converse closeout special. I swing into the parking lot and go in and buy a 10½ of every color they have. A week later, I read in the newspaper that Converse had been bought by a Japanese company. Nothing will change, and they'll continue to make the shoes. So I had all these tennis shoes in green, yellow, white, blue, red, black, pink, flesh, and orange. So I wore them to the meeting, and first thing, the guy comments on the shoes. And I said, "Yeah, there's a funny story of how I got these."

**Were you ever nervous about pitching? Or was that something you were always comfortable doing?**

I was way too comfortable with it when I was young and brimming with confidence, because the stories I had nobody else had. But when I was still trying to stay in the studio game, which would be around 2000, by that time, they weren't doing my kind of story. They weren't doing *Rain Man* or *Forrest Gump*, or *My Left Foot*. It all switched into the indie world, and I was still trying to get big paychecks, and I wasn't really successful.

First of all, many of the executives who knew me and liked me had died, retired, or moved into different businesses. So I was starting over with way younger people, UCLA graduates in their early 20s. And that's when I got nervous. I was thinking I was losing my touch, but I wasn't. The market just wasn't there. I had to make a complete change of gears and figure out how to get into the world of independent filmmaking. I learned that you're not just selling your script on a pitch and getting paid. You write it, and then you go find somebody who will put in enough money where you can hire attorneys to do the paperwork and then incorporate, and then more money, and on and on it goes. And you do everything. You're the studio here in your little office. It took me a long time to get to be good at that, enough to where I could actually pull off this movie that I just made in Italy.

**So you're wrapping up postproduction now. What will you work on next?**

I've got four projects out there that take up some time every week, nurturing them along. Some still have a few missing pieces, and some are ready to go. I put everything on the backburner to make this picture, but soon I'll be dusting this stuff off again. I'll say, which is the most viable? Which is the one I should put my time into?

> "You can't expect to make it big by moving to Hollywood and peddling your one script. You've got to write five or six crappy scripts before you even have a craft that you can depend on."

**Looking at your IMDb page, I'm curious about *The Bridge to Jabez*. Is that one financed? The logline is intriguing.**

*The Bridge to Jabez* was fully financed prior to my leaving for Italy, and I'm planning to do it with a very respected producer, Mike Medavoy, who did *Black Swan*. But I recently found out there was a divorce between the principal people who owned the financing, and everything came to a screeching halt. So now I have to look around, and say, "Well, what's the next step with this?" But I also have a Bob Marley project, and there's a small indie picture that a named producer is serious about doing, and I'm likely to write a movie as a co-production with a Chinese company, so there are a lot of projects.

**This recent development on *The Bridge to Jabez*, the more you do this, does it become less painful when you get news like that?**

It's not painful at all. Believe me, I refuse to get depressed over this stuff. I have in the past, and it's just wasted emotion. It doesn't go anywhere. You infect your spouse and your friends with that. I mean, it's disappointing, but it's never surprising.

**So when you get good news about something that looks like it might happen, have you found a way to be excited about it but not too excited?**

I refer to this as, When to Open the Champagne. When things were starting to gain momentum on *Rain Man*, I met with Dustin Hoffman, and on my way home, I stopped at a liquor store and got a much more expensive bottle of champagne than I deserved. And I brought it home and told my wife what was going on, and I said, "We're putting this in the refrigerator. As soon as it's signed"—or I don't know what the demarcation point was—"we'll drink this."

Six years later, we still hadn't opened it, because I was never certain of anything. With every bit of good news, there was always some setback. *Rain Man* went from a picture that had this huge burst of momentum, lost almost all of it, and then was resurrected and went on to be the little engine that could. So through all of that, that champagne remained unopened. Then, the night of the Oscars, we came back, and the house was full of flowers and cases of champagne from anybody I'd ever met in Hollywood. And all that champagne was way better than what I'd put in the refrigerator. So I told my wife, "From now on, when I bring home a bottle of champagne, we're drinking it."

So that's a longwinded way of saying that I'm very happy to celebrate. But I know that it can sour, and it likely will. That's why you have to be operating on many fronts, with lots of stories that you have rattling around. And this is true for everyone. You can't expect to make it big by moving to Hollywood and peddling your one script. You've got to write five or six crappy scripts before you even have a craft that you can depend on. And you've got to have something that nobody else has.

**Meaning a story that nobody else has?**
You've got to have a great story. If you want to break in, and you don't have experience, you don't have credits, you don't have a reputation, then you've got to have something better than most veteran screenwriters—that great story. And if you're going to be a storyteller, you've got to have ammunition. That's why I always say, if you don't engage in the world, especially the fringes of the world, where are your stories?

After spending a lifetime in that institution, Bill was wide open to the world. So the lessons that you learn from a man with an IQ of 47 or whatever it was—which I don't buy at all, by the way—they weren't lost on me.

If you look at the *Bill* movie, it's this young man who befriends an older man, and they form a buddy relationship, and they triumph. Then with *Rain Man*, I just took that same model and stood it on its head. Tom Cruise would be me inside out. His Charlie Babbitt was not a good person. When he discovered he had a brother, his instincts were not to embrace him as a human being but to use him to get the inheritance that he felt was rightly his.

I took almost every step that Bill and I faced and turned it into a selfish motivation. But look where they end up. The end of *Bill*, you have Dennis Quaid and Mickey Rooney looking at each other over a little coffee table in Bill's coffee shop, and their foreheads almost touch as Bill gives Barry his lucky two-dollar bill. And the end of *Rain Main*, Tom Cruise and Dustin Hoffman, the Babbitt brothers' heads do touch—same ending, but the journey is completely different because the people are different.

You have to meet people, make friends. You have to be really living. That's when you'll find your stories.

# Notes

1 Geoff Berkshire, "Richard LaGravenese on His 'Rude Awakening' to Hollywood," *Variety*, February 27, 2015, accessed May 1, 2016, http://variety.com/2015/film/news/richard-lagravenese-on-his-rude-awakening-to-hollywood-1201441753/

2 BT, "Decoded: The Secret to the Perfect TV Episode," *BTplc.com*, 2014, accessed August 25, 2015, www.btplc.com/news/articles/showarticle.cfm?articleid=%7B585 a9931-8865-4bce-aed8-d435d3fe4d56%7D

3 W. Goldman, *Adventures in the Screen Trade: A Personal View of Hollywood and Screenwriting* (New York: Warner Books, 1983).

4 Sergio Sparviero, "Hollywood Creative Accounting: The Success Rate of Major Motion Pictures," *Media Industries*, May 21, 2015.

5 Jason Scoggins, Cindy Kaplan, and Landon Rohwedder, *The Scoggins Report: Year-End Spec Market Scorecard* (Los Angeles, n.d.). Scott Myers, "The Definitive Spec Script Sales List (1991–2012)," *Go Into the Story*, accessed July 21, 2015, http://gointothe story.blcklst.com/2012/06/the-definitive-spec-script-sales-list-1991-2012-2005.html

6 Scoggins, Kaplan, and Rohwedder, *The Scoggins Report*.

7 B. Deniz and R.B. Hasbrouck, "When to Greenlight: Examining the Pre-Release Factors That Determine Future Box Office Success of a Movie in the United States," *International Journal of Economics and Management Sciences* 2(3) (2012): 35–42.

8 D.K. Simonton, "Cinematic Success Criteria and Their Predictors: The Art and Business of the Film Industry," *Psychology & Marketing* 26(5) (2009): 400–20.

9 X.L. Liu, "Do Popular Books Always Make for Popular Movies?" Duke University, 2015.

10 Carl Wilkinson, "Adapt or Die?" *Financial Times*, February 10, 2012.

11 MPAA, "MPAA 2014 Theatrical Market Statistics Summary," 2014, accessed August 25, 2015, www.mpaa.org/wp-content/uploads/2015/03/MPAA-Theatrical-Market-Statistics-2014.pdf

12 MPAA, "MPAA 2014 Theatrical Market Statistics Summary."

13 S.W. Becker and A.H. Eagly, "The Heroism of Women and Men," *American Psychologist* 59(3) (April 2004): 163–78.

14 A.H. Eagly, "The His and Hers of Prosocial Behavior: An Examination of the Social Psychology of Gender," *American Psychologist* 64(8) (November 2009): 644–58.

15 Film LA, *2014 Feature Film Study*. Los Angeles, 2014.

16 Mohanbir S. Sawhney and Jehoshua Eliashberg, "A Parsimonious Model for Forecasting Gross Box-Office Revenues of Motion Pictures," *Marketing Science* 15(2) (1996): 113–31.

17 Lisa Potts and Chad Coates, "Ray Bradbury Quotes on Madmen, Friends, Love and Writing," *Blank on Blank*, 1972, accessed August 25, 2015, http://blankonblank.org/interviews/ray-bradbury-interview-on-madmen-writing-farenheit-451-friends-driving/

# CHAPTER 4

# GETTING AHEAD

"Develop your own compass, and trust it.
Take risks, dare to fail. Remember, the first person
through the wall always gets hurt."

Aaron Sorkin

**This chapter is about what it takes** to jump off your plateau and move to the next level of your career. This doesn't only apply to screenwriters who have found Oscar-level success. Keep in mind that *success* is a term you'll define for yourself. And that definition will change as your career evolves.

## Who Knew?

Acclaimed writer-director Boaz Yakin (*Fresh*, *Remember the Titans*, *Now You See Me*) struggled for decades to settle into his career as a studio screenwriter and director. In the *Directing for the Screen* book in the PERFORM series, you'll find an interview that has a lot of insight for screenwriters as well as directors. The biggest takeaway, though, is just how important your definition of *success* is to your outlook.

In Yakin's words, since *A Price Above Rubies*, he's had a "zero batting average" when it comes to getting his independent films produced. If that were the yardstick he used to measure his success, then yes, he'd come up short. But if his yardstick had notches for profitable studio films that he wrote and/or directed, or for 12-year-old boys who were forever touched by *Remember the Titans*, there would be no denying his success. And as he says, sometimes it just takes time—reaching a stage of your career where you can look back and reflect, and then you're able to appreciate your success for what it is.

As you read in the last chapter, one of the most exciting things about making a life as a screenwriter is that you never know when your phone will ring. You just have to be ready to answer it. Be ready to jump.

And being prepared to take that leap involves a commitment to taking risks. Getting ahead in any career requires calculated risk-taking. When you stay in your comfort zone, it's unlikely that you'll achieve success in a way that surprises. And that element of surprise—both in your creative work and in the business of your career—is what you're striving for.

So let's talk about setting yourself up for successful surprises in your career. In this chapter, you'll read about:

- How to trust your storytelling instincts and run with a compelling narrative that's taking your career in a new direction
- The process of writing and directing independent films
- The casting process in independent films
- Practical strategies for surviving and thriving in your career
- Why your personal truth and being able to tap into it is a key to success
- The relationship between creativity and craft and the many hours it takes to build a craft you can count on
- Overcoming significant challenges on the road to screen storytelling
- Pursuing screenwriting later in life and keeping risk in perspective
- Addressing mental and emotional health issues such as high sensitivity, anxiety, and depression

We'll begin with the idea of making a career-altering move. What might happen if you choose to run with an unexpected story and see it through to the end? This is how Mary Harron broke into filmmaking in her late 30s. On her second feature, *American Psycho* (2000), she made the difficult choice to hold out for the actor she wanted, which got her fired from the project. Bold move, but a move that ultimately propelled her career forward.

# A BOLD MOVE
## Running With an Unexpected Story
▶ An Interview With Mary Harron

Mary Harron wrote and directed the feature films *I Shot Andy Warhol* (1996), co-written with Daniel Minahan, *American Psycho* (2000), co-written with Guinevere Turner, *The Notorious Bettie Page* (2005), also co-written with Guinevere Turner, and *The Moth Diaries* (2011). She's directed television shows such as *Homicide, The L Word, Six Feet Under, Big Love, The Nine, The Following,* and *Graceland*. In 2014, she directed a short film as part of *We the Economy: 20 Short Films You Can't Afford to Miss*, an anthology of shorts that sheds light on how the economy impacts our lives.

*I Shot Andy Warhol* was nominated for an Independent Spirit Award as well as the Grand Jury Prize at Sundance, and in 2005, Harron received the Filmmaker on the Edge Award at the Provincetown International Film Festival.

Mary Harron

Photo by John C. Walsh

Mary Harron is often referred to as a feminist writer-director, though she's reluctant to label herself as such.

**Would you describe yourself as a feminist?**
I would, in the sense that without feminism I wouldn't be making films at all. However, when people say "feminist film director," they often imply that your films are ideologically driven, which mine are not. They're not message films. Most films are written and directed by men, so if you're a female writer or director, you are going to present a different view of women. I don't feel I have a

responsibility to present noble female characters, or role models—I'm more interested in characters that are flawed. I do think I have a responsibility to present all of my characters as truthfully as I can. I'm just presenting my perspective, which happens to be a female perspective.

**What was your big breaking-in moment? Or did you have one?**

Really, the big thing that happened to me—I think it was in 1992 or 1993—was that I was introduced to my producers on *I Shot Andy Warhol*. I was at a dinner party in New York. I'd moved to New York to do a series for the BBC, but really I moved there to get my movie made, because I knew I had to be in New York to research so I could write the script. And I gave up everything to do that. I gave up my career at that point in England. It was just, I'm going to go to New York to try and make this film before I die, kind of thing.

**How old were you at the time?**

I was 39. I was old, because I had been a journalist for a few years before I started in documentaries and television, so I'd worked for twenty years in England at that point. It seemed quite old to be starting your life anew, but I was just so compelled to do it.

**When did you first have the idea for *I Shot Andy Warhol*?**

I think it was in 1986. I was researching a documentary by Andy Warhol, and on the way to work I always passed a leftwing political bookstore. And one day, I looked in and there was a copy of Valerie Solanas's *SCUM Manifesto* in the window. But it was about seven years before I really got the traction to start making the film.

> "When people say 'feminist film director,' they often imply that your films are ideologically driven, which mine are not. They're not message films. Most films are written and directed by men, so if you're a female writer or director, you are going to present a different view of women."

**Seven years is a long time to stick with something before you find success.**
It's funny, I wasn't thinking about success really. I just thought I wanted to make this movie, however it was going to get done. And finally after all these years, I found a producer at the BBC who supported my idea and said, we'll give you $150,000 and you can go find more money.

**This was before you moved to New York?**
Yes, before. So I went to New York, and I was trying to get the script done, and I was at this dinner party, talking to someone, and I said, I'm trying to do this movie about Valerie Solanas, this crazy radical feminist who shot Andy Warhol. And he said, oh, then you should meet my friend Christine Vachon—she's looking for projects. So I met Christine and Tom Kalin, who was producing with her, and it was just one of those incredibly lucky moments, because it was the very early stages of the independent film scene, and Christine and Tom were people who would take a chance on someone who hadn't made a film before.

**Was that common at the time?**
It was the culture, I think. You don't always get in during those moments where people are willing to take a chance. And this was a project that when I showed it to most people, they thought I was completely out of my mind. They just thought, why would you make a film about this awful person? I'd say, but she's interesting and brilliant, and yes she's crazy, but she's also very interesting. But people didn't see it, and it scared them in some ways, I think.

**But it didn't scare your producers?**
Christine and Tom, they weren't scared by it. The things that other people were scared by, they liked—the outrageousness and the idea of it. And it was a New York film. So I was very fortunate that they took it on.

**So you began to write at that point? Or did you already have a script?**
I had written a forty-page treatment that was very detailed, and that got everything rolling. And it was with that treatment that we got Lili Taylor to sign on, who was then up-and-coming as an indie film star. She really liked it, and she'd read the *SCUM Manifesto* and thought it was interesting.

**Did you get financing from the treatment as well?**
Nothing happened until I actually wrote a script, which I think is generally true. If you don't have a script, it doesn't matter how good your idea is, nothing will move forward for people to read and see what the film is going to be. So I started writing with my friend Dan Minahan in Manhattan, but we're talking two years before we actually went into production—first to get the script done, and then the inevitable delays. I've never been involved in a movie that didn't get delayed by at least a year. And I had to make a living during that time, so I worked in TV and also did some journalism.

**You're not someone who makes a film every year. Is the gap between films due to these inevitable delays? Or is that partially by choice?**
Of the four features I've done, I've written or co-written all of them, so I'm always involved in the script, and that's a lot of time. I think people who write as well as direct tend to make fewer movies. But after *American Psycho* came out, and I was nine months pregnant at the premiere with my second child, then I took a year or two off. Not entirely off, because I'm always working on something, but I had two children, so I didn't have time for much else the first few months.

**What's it been like balancing motherhood and your career?**
Well, I've turned down work. When *American Psycho* came out, I remember having to turn down working on the first season of *Prison Break*. I had to say no because my younger daughter was starting kindergarten and I couldn't go to Chicago—I just couldn't be away for that. In some ways, I haven't been able to focus as single-mindedly, but it's also meant that during those long periods when you're not working anyway—and that happens to everyone—it's been good to have that time filled with something I can devote myself to. Not everybody wants kids, but it's helped keep me sane.

Everybody has their ups and downs as a director, and certainly all of my projects have gotten delayed anyway, but when I found out I was pregnant with my first child, I was already attached to *American Psycho*—and I thought, how am I going to tell everybody I'm pregnant and have to delay? In fact, this happened twice. I had to call Christine and tell her that I was pregnant with both children when I thought I was going into production—first one, and then three years later, the same thing again. But in the end, for completely other reasons, both *Bettie Page* and *American Psycho* got delayed anyway. Everything gets delayed. In movies, everything's pushing a boulder up a hill.

**Do you think gender plays into that difficulty at all?**

I'm sure it's harder, but it's hard to say precisely why. I think, for whatever reason, you get fewer chances to fail as a woman. You don't get cut as much slack. That's just an assumption really. But the other thing that makes it difficult is if you do a film with a woman as the main character, it's harder to get made, especially if it's not a romantic comedy. But also, I've been very specific about casting and haven't wanted to cast big stars, and that will delay a project.

**In all of your films?**

With *Bettie Page* and *The Moth Diaries* I didn't have big Hollywood names. I'm very specific about casting, and I thought these people were the right ones. And same with *American Psycho*. Christian Bale wasn't a star when I cast him, and that film would have gotten made a lot faster if I'd cast somebody with a bigger name.

**Were there bigger names interested in playing the part?**

Yes, lots of big names.

**Do most directors have that much input in terms of casting?**

In an independent film, you have tremendous say about cast. The bigger the budget, the less say you have, but it depends on what the film is and who you are. Over the last few years, even in independent film, there's certainly been tremendous pressure to cast big names so they can do presales for financing. People just feel more comfortable with a big name, even if this person isn't great for the role.

> "There's a lot of rejection and a lot of people telling you no or telling you your project isn't any good ... Whatever your story is, it has to be something you really care about so you're devoted to the project."

**That sounds like a tough business decision to make, not to cast the major star.**

Yes, I was actually fired from the *American Psycho* for a few months, because a bigger name wanted to do it, and Christian wasn't well known. He'd done European films, smaller films, but I just felt that he understood the role, and I'd already cast him when this other actor decided he wanted to do it. So I was fired, and then it fell apart with the other actor, and I was brought back. You have to have tremendous resilience. It's a very difficult job.

**You started as a writer. Any thoughts about how you got people to notice and appreciate your work initially?**

Really it's about having a lot of focus and determination, and a lot of people fall by the wayside because it just takes so long to get a film made. I think I did always go for unusual ideas, and I just saw them through. I didn't water them down. So it's good if you have a very strong take on something. My first film was a very strong take on the story of this female, would-be assassin. But somebody could do very well with romantic comedy. I think you have to be true to what you have to say. And there's a lot of rejection and a lot of people telling you no or telling you your project isn't any good.

**What kind of self-talk do you go through when you're up against that kind of rejection?**

My first film, I just believed so much in that story, and I was so involved in bringing this forgotten piece of history to light. It was the story that carried me. I never got bored with it. I never tired of it in those many long years, and that's important. Whatever your story is, it has to be something you really care about so you're devoted to the project.

**For someone who's a writer and thinking about becoming a director, what would you suggest this person do to get started?**

The material is always first, having the material. With *I Shot Andy Warhol*, I had this idea for such a long time. But when I was a researcher in television, I don't think anybody would have looked at me and said, oh, you're going to be a film director. I'd only been a writer, and at that time, there were very few women directors. There were a lot of hotshot male directors who were sure they were going to make films, and I didn't have that kind of confidence. They were sure— "I'm definitely going to go to Hollywood. I'm definitely going to make films."

But I just had this desire and belief in my *idea* for my first film. That's why I say you should have the material you're devoted to. You always have a lack of confidence before you start directing, but if you can feel like, whatever happens, this is my story, and I have something to say about this, that will keep you going. I didn't have experience as a director, but I felt I had something to say that hadn't been said. So instead of just a *take* on the 1960s, I had a piece of history.

**So would you say that you learned how to direct on *I Shot Andy Warhol*?**
I guess so. I'd been on a lot of documentary shoots, but I had a great DP, Ellen Kuras, who was very supportive, one of the most successful female DPs. I brought in certain things that I was interested in visually, and we did the shot list together. I always come in with photographs when I'm working with a cinematographer, so I had certain visual ideas that I knew I wanted, but then together we worked up a look. And she was a huge help to me on set, helping me understand things.

And then the rest of it is working with actors, and I think that was quite easy for me actually. When you're in the casting process, actors are reading the scenes and you're trying to direct them in their audition, and I remember thinking, oh yeah, I have a good feel for working with actors. And then because I'd co-written the script and it was based on real-life sources, the actors trusted that I knew a lot about their character. So if you've written the script, it gives you a certain authority I think.

**Are there things over the years that you feel you did right, that contributed to your success?**
I think sticking to my guns over casting has always served me well, even though it's caused me so many problems. I think in the end, no great movie was ever mis-cast. I feel strongly about that, and when you feel very strongly about something and you can't see the film any other way, it's good to stick to that.

**What about the opposite, any mistakes? Things you know now that you wish you knew then?**
I'm sure there are mistakes, but they're probably more about projects that I wish I'd taken or projects that I didn't have time for.

**The fact that you're not quickly jumping to a list of mistakes, that probably says something about your personality.**
I'm always filled with self-doubt with everything, so it's funny that I can't think of anything.

**Can you talk a little bit about that, about self-doubt and how you tackle that?**
I've learned to be more accepting of it. There is doubt, though, because I'm very often puzzling things out on set, and I take my time. In a way, doubt isn't a bad thing, but you need to have the strength to show that and also to be sure that you still know what you're doing. That's part of your process.

**What about in terms of writing? Or when you're waiting two years between projects—how does the self-doubt play into that?**

That's very hard, very difficult. You have to really work on resilience about all the rejections. Nobody's on the rise all the time, though. Every career has highs and lows, and you have to go through the bad times. Not everyone's going to love everything you do, and that's when you really need to be strong. It's easy to be strong when everybody's telling you how fabulous you are. So I think it's hard, and doubt is part of being an intelligent human being. You need to be open to what might be wrong.

**Do you have a support group of other writers and filmmakers who you can lean on during the difficult times?**

Well, I'm married to a director-writer, and we write together. We've written a number of scripts, several pilots—in fact, that's how we make a living in between movies. We haven't gone to series, so you won't see them listed, but it's quite a good thing to do. And we talk a lot about all this, so that's helpful. And then I have a lot of friends who are producers and directors, too—so yes, there's a good community. But probably my husband is the one I talk to most.

Mary Harron is currently shooting a segment for *XX* (2016), an anthology of female-driven horror-movie segments.

# SURVIVING AND THRIVING IN HOLLYWOOD

## Eight Principles to Empower Your Writing and Your Life

▶ By Jim Jennewein

Becoming a successful screenwriter—or any kind of professional storyteller—is as much about attitude and commitment to a certain kind of behavior as it is about learning the many elements of story craft. It's a disciplined way of thinking and behaving—on paper and off—that determines your ability to develop the stories you want to tell.

Here are a few things I've learned during my journey as a professional screenwriter and teacher of writing. You want to make a living as a screenwriter? Join the club!

## It Isn't a Story Until You Write It

Yes, of course you live and write in your head. That's what we writers do. It's an occupational hazard. We have to spend time there to dream and think.

But we externalize these dream-thoughts only by taking action on the page. In other words, it's only through the difficult word-selection and decision-making process—also called "writing"—that we discover the true nature of our story. It's the disciplined act of sitting down day after day and putting pen to paper (or fingers to keypad), whether we feel inspired or not. *That* is the action that makes a story real.

An old mentor of mine put it this way (you might want to write this down and put it above your desk like I did):

> The worst thing you actually do put on paper is always better than the "great masterpiece" you keep in your head and never write at all.

The point is, no matter how vividly you can see your story in your head, it's not fully realized until it's words on a page. *So get it out of your head and onto paper.* Get past your fear of it being imperfect. There's no such thing as a perfect first draft. A first draft is meant to be crude and clunky, the messy product of your urgent need to expel it from your brain. It's as much raw impulse as hard logic—and when you read it for the first time, you'll understand why we've coined that term "vomit draft."

But once it's out of you and living on the page, this is when you can see it more clearly, with all its failings and flaws and strengths—all of which enable you to more easily begin the work of rewriting. And *that* is when the real creativity begins.

# Give Your Readers a Polished Draft, Not a First Draft

Don't be too eager to share your first draft. Yes, you've been laboring to birth this creature, and now it's out. It's alive and well, and you're finally holding printed-out pages in your hand. You want to share these pages, I know. You want a reaction, approval—perhaps a celebration of your genius.

Please hear me on this, though. Resist that urge. Don't show it to anyone. Not even to your closest friends or family members. If it isn't the best you can do, don't show it. And generally speaking, a first draft is never the best you can do.

Early on in my writing years, I had an idea for a short story and spent several days and nights feverishly typing away. When I finally reached the end, or what I thought was the end, I proudly took my stack of pages to a friend and urged him to read it.

He did. I actually made the mistake of *watching* him read it, which I also recommend that you never do.

And when my friend finished, instead of doing what I thought he would do—tell me how great it was—he began to go through my story page by page, enumerating all the points that didn't make sense, the many inconsistencies of syntax and errors of grammar and punctuation. And every time he pointed out something to me, I found myself saying, "Oh, I have a fix for that," or, "Yes, I'm going to cut that," or "Right, that part's not done yet."

My friend finally gave me a harsh look and said, "Well, if you're not done with it yet, why did you ask me to read it?"

Point taken. Also, the saddest part was, he was so blinded by the manuscript's obvious and superficial flaws that we never got to discuss the deeper issues of the story itself.

This is what happens when you ask someone to read material before it's ready. So don't disrespect your readers by asking them to read a sloppy first draft. When you think about it, it's pretty inconsiderate.

Here's another reason I don't share first drafts, and this might even be more important: I don't want to put that kind of pressure on myself. If I know that no one but me will read my script, it frees me to just write—to free myself of the thing that haunts and possesses me. Once I get it down on paper, no matter how rough, I have confidence that I can muster the energy and inspiration to finish it.

And that's what we writers do: We finish things. No matter what. We push on— past the doubt and uncertainty and terror—until we reach the end. No matter how uninspired we feel.

## In my opinion . . .

Speaking of inspiration, allow me to correct another myth about screenwriting: You need inspiration. I think this actually might be the cruelest myth newbie screenwriters absorb, because it keeps you away from your chair and that much further from completing your script.

Inspiration is overrated. For me, writing is 90 percent perspiration, 9 percent inspiration, and 1 percent caffeination. (Well, maybe 5 percent caffeination, depending on deadline.) You just have to sit down and do it, no matter how you feel. Or as I tell my students:

*Motivation is a product of activity, not a prerequisite.*

The crystal-clear clarity of vision that guides us as we write is a result of hard work, not some inspiration that lives outside of us. It's the reward we get for sitting in the chair and concentrating until the juices start flowing. It's the prize, not a pre-existing condition.

# Write to Please Yourself, Not Someone Else

Shakespeare said it best: "To thine own self be true." And generally speaking, that's the best advice a writer could ever get.

But Shakespeare didn't live in Hollywood, where writers are expected to "collaborate" and receive "notes" from all manner of studio execs, producers, directors, and movie stars. He didn't live in a world where scripts go through multiple drafts in the "development process" and writers are expected to make changes to their work that aren't always in sync with their original vision for the story.

Oftentimes, to survive—to keep a project alive and increase its chances of getting produced and earning a critically important writing credit (not to mention money)—you've got to write multiple drafts, incorporating the ideas of others.

But what do you do when an idea that begins as a workable compromise—an interesting new way to tell the story—ends up muddying everything and threatening to destroy the very thing you worked so hard to create? Which set of notes do you listen to?

At the end of the day, there's only one person you should be listening to: you. When serving so many masters, it's easy to lose connection with the passion that got you there. Doubt sets in. But as *Chinatown* producer Robert Evans famously said, "Success is betting on your instincts." Your *own* gut instincts. Not someone else's. It's the only way you truly test the value and power of your original ideas—and usually, it's the very thing that leads to the highest levels of success.

Yes, you must be open to the opinions and ideas of others. Good writers always are. But don't let fear and confusion hold you hostage to other people's wishes and whims, tuning out the most important voice of all. If you've done the work of becoming a disciplined storyteller, and if you've acquired the requisite tools of craft, then chances are your instincts about the story are sound.

*Listen to the voice inside you. That is your talent speaking.*

Trust the voice of your creative subconscious, the creative intelligence from which all your unique powers flow. If you write (and rewrite) to please *this* voice, you'll always end up with work you can be proud of.

# Write What You Feel Passionate About, Not What You Know

The old truism "write what you know" is often overused and far too limiting. Yes, this advice can help newbie writers find familiar subject matter to jumpstart their writing journey. But to really grow and develop as a writer—to put down roots into the soil of your *you-ness*—you must move beyond the limited pool of your direct experience and into the realm of imagination.

Let yourself go. Write about what you can't stop thinking about. Write from your heart, from the gut—from the strangest part of you. Here's something scary but true:

> *Whatever you think makes you weird, chances are that's where you'll strike writer gold.*

Don't try to chase market trends. Instead, get in touch with your inner truths—your dreams and obsessions, your worries and wisdoms. This way, your work will be authentic to you and also very likely universal. When you do the work and write the stories that only you can write, you'll be on the road to finding your unique style—the thing that makes you *you*.

# Serve Your Story, Not Your Ego

Big ego does not equal big success. If you want to succeed as a writer, you need to be willing to do the work. You need to be so emotionally engaged with your material, so lit from within by the burning desire to create it, that you successfully muster the passion to write as many drafts as necessary to bring the story to its fullest expression.

Simply put, *focus on serving the material*, not on making it serve you.

We've all seen what happens when writers lose their sense of humility and fall in love with the gigantitude of their talent. It isn't pretty. A reputation for being "difficult to work with" has quickly ended many promising careers. But even worse, basking too long in the limelight can blind you to the simple human themes that once gave your work value. And it can disconnect you from the more vulnerable parts of your psyche, the places from which all creative passion flows.

So build an attitude of service toward the story. Make the story bigger and the writer smaller. Devote yourself to the act of creation, not self-glorification. This will put you in a far better frame of mind to birth your story. And when success does come, you'll be more grounded and better able to keep things in perspective.

As three-time Oscar-winning screenwriter Paddy Chayefsky (*Marty*, 1955; *The Hospital*, 1972; *Network*, 1976) once said:

"Focus on mastering the craft. Let others decide if it's art."

Amen, brother.

# Measure Success Creatively, Not Financially

I don't need to tell you that the road to success in Hollywood is loaded with obstacles—crushing rejection, crippling self-doubt, whims of the marketplace, movie star egos. You already know this. And unfortunately, there's no correlation between the time you spend on a script and your chances of selling it. You can't control what people think of your screenplay and whether a studio gives you a six-figure deal. Those outcomes are beyond your command.

What you *can* control is the work itself—the quality of your story, the richness and vitality of your characters, and the time and energy you spend bringing it to life on the page. You can control your level of commitment and devotion.

But what happens to your work when it goes out into the world is anyone's guess. Even having representation is no guarantee of a sale. If you're lucky enough to someday sell a script—or two or three—go ahead and celebrate. You deserve it. But after you've cashed your checks, get right back to work, creating a new and better story.

Keep focused on the *process* of writing, on outdoing your last effort. Measure success by how well you nailed your narrative—by how artfully you pulled readers into the world of your story, made them feel the hopes and dreams of your characters, and compelled them to keep reading until the very end. Measure success by the emotional response from your readers, not the financial returns of your stockbrokers. By the quality of your ideas, not the quantity of zeroes on your paycheck.

# Failure Is Something You Do to Yourself

There are far more scripts that exist on the page than on the screen. It's just a fact of life. Many scripts are written, and few are bought. The same is true for the many thousands of story pitches writers perform in any given year in Hollywood.

Rejection, whether in the form of "no," "pass," or a phone call that never comes— it's inevitable in the life of a screenwriter.

But we mustn't let these temporary setbacks cause us to lose confidence or doubt our own talent. As Henry Ford sagely said, "Failure is only the opportunity to begin again, only this time more wisely." To survive the long haul, you must learn to accept failure as a necessary part of the learning process, not an end to your dreams.

Be open to criticism—in fact, seek it out. Surround yourself with people smarter than you, and eagerly accept their input. Do everything possible to learn from your missteps and strengthen your story skills. Expectation of perfection not only kills confidence, it kills careers. I've seen many writers along the way who were far more talented than me, but they failed to find success because they gave up too easily. They failed to persist.

In effect, if you succumb to self-pity or egotism, you beat yourself. I've known writers who felt they were so talented that nothing they created could ever be faulted or criticized. But in truth, they were simply undisciplined and unable to live with the idea that they had to work harder than they wanted to.

In writing, as in life, there are no shortcuts. There's simply no substitute for hard work. And no matter how low you may sometimes feel, always remember this:

*You have power.*

You can do what few actors, producers, or studio executives can do. You can create something from nothing. You possess the awesome creative power to lay down a vision on paper and make it real for others. You have the power to be the seminal creator of a movie or television series that has the potential to pull in an audience of millions. This unique talent—the strength of your ideas joined with the skill of your craft—is the only real power you have. So don't forget about that power. You'll harness it when you're up, and you'll depend on it when you're down.

Up or down, the power is yours.

# Above All Else, Tell the Truth

I'll end with a story that, to me, sums up the most important principle of screen-writing: truth.

In my days as a working screenwriter, I've had the good fortune to receive credit on several produced movies. One of these films, released way back in the Stone Age of 1994, was the Universal Studios comedy *The Flintstones*. Exec produced by Steven Spielberg (dubbed in the credits as "Steven Spielrock"), it starred John Goodman, Rick Moranis, Elizabeth Perkins, Rosie O'Donnell, and the beautiful Halle Berry.

When I learned I was going to spend a day on the set watching them film, excited as I was, it wasn't Halle Berry I most wanted to meet. It was someone far sexier. Cast in a small cameo playing Wilma Flintstone's mother was none other than the legendary Elizabeth Taylor.

When she stepped on the set dressed in Stone Age furs, she drew a standing ovation from the cast and crew—and I was probably clapping louder than anyone else. After she did a short scene with Fred, her son-in-law in the film, I saw Liz conferring with the director. And then, a few moments later, the 1st assistant director approached me and said that Ms. Taylor had a problem with the dialog. She wanted to talk to the writer, he said. In her trailer.

I was supposed to meet Liz Taylor . . . *in her trailer?*

Most writers hate to change their dialog, but in this case, I could have rewritten all day long!

So I was waiting in her trailer, when finally the door opened and in she came, still wearing the fake fur. She plopped on the sofa beside me, and an assistant gave her an iced tea and then quickly left.

There I was, alone with Liz Taylor.

As I stared into her famously blue-violet eyes, mesmerized, I said, "Ms. Taylor, what would you like me to do?" And batting her eyelashes, she said, "Please call me Liz."

As it turned out, fixing her lines was all too easy. In all of a minute, I was done, and I realized my time with her was over. It was time to go. But I didn't want to. I was sitting with one of the greatest movie actresses of all time. I wanted the moment to last. I wanted to keep talking, to make some kind of personal connection. I wanted to learn her secrets.

So I said, "Ms. Taylor—I mean, Liz—you've lived such an amazing life and have had one of the longest acting careers ever. I just have to ask you. What's your secret? What do you attribute your success to?"

She put down her iced tea and closed her eyes, pausing to think. Then her eyes flew open, and she reached out and put her hand on mine. She leaned closer, and squeezing my hand, she said, "Truth."

"Truth?" I said.

"Yes," she said. "I tell the truth, in my life and in my work. The truth is my secret. And it's also *my secret weapon*!"

I'd always known that at the heart of great stories were great truths. But to call truth her "secret weapon"? This was a compelling reminder of the rare power that comes from having the courage to speak the more painful truths—the ones most of us fear and don't want to face, yet we so deeply need to tell and hear these truths over and over again, from generation to generation.

So I'll let Liz's lesson be a reminder to us all. In art and in life, there is real power in the truth. Tap into it. Pay attention to the truths of life, both big and small—the deep, abiding, everlasting truths of human nature *as you see them*. The more truth you put in your work, the greater your stories will resonate with others. And getting your readers to feel something? Well, that's what it's all about.

---

A veteran screenwriter, author, and teacher, **JIM JENNEWEIN** has received writing credits on such films as *The Flintstones*, *Richie Rich*, *Getting Even With Dad*, *Stay Tuned*, and *Major League II*. He is also co-author of the RuneWarriors trilogy, a comedy-fantasy series of young adult novels published by HarperCollins. A member of the Writers Guild of America since 1990, Jennewein holds a BFA degree from the University of Notre Dame, and an MFA degree from the Graduate Program in Creative Writing & Writing for the Performing Arts at the University of California, Riverside. He is currently an Artist in Residence at Fordham University in New York City.

Jim Jennewein

Photo by Tom Stoelker, Fordham University

# FROM CREATIVITY TO CRAFT IN SCREENWRITING

▶ By Mark Readman

We talk about creativity as if it were some kind of essence. In fact, the British Broadcasting Corporation (BBC) includes in its statement of Mission and Values: "Creativity is the lifeblood of our organization,"[1] the implication being that creativity somehow flows around the BBC body, enriching it and supplying it with oxygen.

But this rhetoric around creativity masks the fact that it is merely an idea or a concept, not a thing with universal meaning. Once we recognize that creativity is more or less subjective—and only ever meaningful in relation to other things (such as certain kinds of products or personal attributes)—we can then start to work with it in more useful ways.

As a screenwriter, you may feel that you are, by definition, a creative person, but you may also struggle to articulate exactly what that means. When you try to pin down creativity as a *thing*, the problems with it quickly become apparent. Is creativity a quality of a person? A quality of a piece of work? How does it relate to other activities and qualities, such as *craft* and *art*?

The solution is not to try to answer these questions head-on and come up with a definitive answer, but instead to look at the specific details of the contexts in which these terms are mobilized. It's not uncommon to hear of *creativity* and *craft* treated as separate entities and often pitted against each other. We've heard screenwriters, screenwriting teachers, and scholars discuss the relationship between creativity and the craft of screenwriting; and all aspiring and working screenwriters will eventually ponder—at one time or another—whether as craftspeople they can also be creative. But this pondering—this questioning—is meaningless out of context. By attending to the context, however, we can take control of the meaning.

> "As a screenwriter, you may feel that you are, by definition, a creative person, but you may also struggle to articulate exactly what that means."

So let's begin with context. We can start to disentangle the meanings of *creativity* by identifying particular binary oppositions. In positioning creativity in opposition to craft, we put it in the realm of what we tend to think of as "art." Related to this, but on a more fundamental level, creativity can also be opposed to commerce—in other words, there is a common idea that creativity can only exist if it is free from any relationship with money. This is not a new idea. English poet and printmaker William Blake's etching *Laocoön* includes the words: "Where any view of money exists art cannot be carried on."[2] Similarly, the maverick English artist and filmmaker Billy Childish asserts, "the true artist, by nature, is always an amateur and never a professional."[3] At the heart of this opposition, of course, is the idea of creative *freedom*—that any kind of limitation or constraint must inevitably compromise creativity.

Although this is a seductive idea, most of us would probably agree that it's difficult to separate these two areas of life, especially if one is attempting to make a living out of creative work.

And there are other oppositions worth considering, as well. For example, there is the opposition between what we might call a *selective* conception of creativity and a *democratic* conception of creativity. On one hand, creativity is the preserve of exceptional people—of "geniuses"; and on the other hand, creativity is conceived as an essential human quality we all share and one that simply needs to be released and nurtured. When Hungarian psychologist Mihaly Csikszentmihalyi selected his case studies for his analysis of creativity, one of his criteria was that "the person had to have made a difference to a major domain of culture."[4] Their specialness, in other words, was indicated by their impact on culture. As an alternative to this selective version of creativity, we find, for example, educationalist Ken Robinson arguing that "we all have creative abilities and we all have them differently."[5] This is one of those tensions in the creativity literature that will never resolve, because there is a fundamental contradiction between the idea that creativity is a characteristic of exceptional people or a quality that everybody possesses.

One way of dealing with this problem is to differentiate between different types of creativity, which is what some psychologists have attempted to do. Anna Craft, for example, differentiates between "big C" and "little c" creativity—the former being "the extraordinary creativity of the genius."[6] Similarly, Margaret Boden distinguishes between "P-creativity" (psychological creativity, concerning ideas that are novel to the individual) and "H-creativity" (historical creativity, concerning ideas that are novel in human history).[7] Psychologists and cognitive scientists Lawrence Barsalou and Jesse J. Prinz make a similar distinction with "exceptional" and "mundane" creativity, suggesting that everyone possesses mundane creativity, but exceptional creativity is the preserve of a gifted minority.[8]

But this creates another problem—judgment. Who or what decides what is "extraordinary," "historical," or "exceptional"? We know that history isn't necessarily characterized by good, right, or inevitable decisions and that a whole range of factors including politics, influence, money, class, opportunity, and sheer accident can be instrumental in making one thing succeed over another. Creativity then, as an inference drawn from historical significance, is—at the very least—questionable.

It might be more useful to look at sociological approaches to creativity, to examine the ways in which creativity is *attributed* to individuals and come up with theories about how these judgments are reached. Instead of looking for a creative disposition in individuals, we could look for the ways certain products and people are judged to be creative. Psychologist Joseph Kasof, for instance, looks beyond the individual mind and instead talks about "the human tendency to attribute creative behavior to dispositional causes rather than situational causes."[9] He draws our attention to the "creative person stereotype," which as he says, may be based in truth but is "exaggerated beyond reality."[10]

Let's circle back to screenwriting now and see how this might fit in. Researchers in organizational behavior, Kimberly Elsbach and Roderick Kramer conducted a fascinating study that seems to confirm these theories of attribution. In their research into perceptions of unknown screenwriters in Hollywood pitch meetings, they found that executives (the "catchers" in the pitch/catch relationship) make decisions largely on the basis of how writers conform to particular "prototypes." According to the study, these executives often rely on cues that "indicate characteristics . . . that are the opposite of those known to be correlated with *actual* creativity." As Elsbach and Kramer explain, if a writer is awkward or dull in a meeting, this inability can be perceived as a positive characteristic because the executives can assume that the writer has a fascinating internal world and can't be bothered with the performance of presenting it. "This finding suggests that having a perceived handicap (such as being unpolished) sometimes leads catchers to judge a pitcher as more creative than individuals who appear more conventional." Being a bit quirky, in other words, might lead executives to believe the writer has creative potential. In fact, Elsbach and Kramer coined the phrase the "Woody Allen effect" to describe the positive effect that a writer's nerves and neuroses might have on their perceived performance in pitch meetings.[11] Of course, this attribution probably owes something to the clichéd notion that genius and madness are connected[12] and that manifestations of neuroticism may be signs of hidden talent.

The takeaway from this research and from the varying opinions about creativity is that this is not a simple discussion, nor is there a singular definition of *creativity*. It's not a universal quality, and often when people talk about it, they're talking about very different things, using different kinds of evidence to support their judgments. It's important to have a sense of this complexity, particularly when making judgments about your own work and identity.

You almost certainly want to believe that you are creative—you probably *need* to believe this—and you may well have struggled with some of these contradictions. So let's return to that apparent contradiction between creativity and craft and consider how you can make sense of these terms in relation to your own process and output.

# Are You Creative?

Several years ago, I interviewed a group of undergraduate screenwriters and asked them these two questions: "What is creativity?" and "Are you creative?" Their responses were revealing in the way people tend to talk about creativity. In response to the first question, some of the answers were as follows:

- "Everything you do could be classed as creative."
- "Creativity. Being spontaneous and expressive."
- "Creativity? Originality. Being individual."
- "Creativity is an expression of your imagination."
- "Creativity is expressing new ideas in an innovative way."
- "Creativity? Expressive. Different. Risks?"[13]

We can identify here some themes and categories. First, for example, we can see what I like to call "credo-like utterances," which assert a *belief* in creativity. There's also a tension between the notions that creativity is exclusive or inclusive—in other words, whether it's a universal quality or something that only special people possess. The language the students used is also interesting. We might notice, for example, the tautologies in these statements—"expressing new ideas in an innovative way" is an overdetermined statement of "newness," which attempts to convey the specialness of creativity. Also evident is the way the students mobilize particular alternative words to communicate the idea. *Individual*, *imagination*, *spontaneous*, and *expressive*, for example, are all words rhetorically enlisted in the service of creativity. And finally, there are also instances of syntax breaking down—as in the last answer, where it appears that conventional sentence structure isn't adequate for the task of conveying the idea of creativity.

In response to the question "Are you creative?" some of the answers include:

- "Yes . . . I continually think of new ideas and try to try new things whenever I can."
- "Yes! Isn't everyone?! Nothing is unimportant. I see ideas and novelty in things others would ignore. I think that counts for something."
- "Yes, because I can be inventive."
- "I think I am, because I see the potential for creativity in many things around me."
- "Yes. I believe everyone is in their own way. I think I am because I regularly use my imagination to the best I can to think of new, fresh ideas."
- "Yes, with the ability to imagine and transfer to word or image, I am creative."
- "Yes, but I can't prove it . . . interesting."[14]

We can see some tautological statements here, as well, particularly the claim that the student is creative because he sees "the potential for creativity." And again, we see that tension between inclusivity and exclusivity, actually presented as a contradiction in the second response, in which "Isn't everyone?!" sits uneasily with "I see . . . things others would ignore." But we can also see the appearance of "creative identities," a sense that these screenwriters are forming their identities around the idea of creativity.

Although a writer can derive strength and determination from the production of a creative identity, we might also describe the creative identity as Romantic. I use an uppercase *R* to invoke the nineteenth-century literary mode that came to equate literature with "imaginative creation" that depended upon, as the literary theorist Terry Eagleton puts it, "the intuitive, transcendental scope of the poetic mind."[15] This conception of creative identity is seductive, perhaps, because it isn't dependent upon external validation.

In other words, a writer can feel a sense of certainty that he or she is creative despite the fact that nobody can recognize it. At its worst, this creative identity can serve to endorse the individual's retreat from the world that isn't equipped to appreciate her or his refined artistic sensibilities. For a poet, perhaps this isn't a problem; but for a screenwriter pursuing a career, it isn't a model for success.

# Creative Identity

As we've seen, creativity tends to most often align with being an "artist" or a "genius" or a "game changer"—certainly idiosyncratic, and certainly distant from the compromises that money brings. But most of us, sadly, must accept that we don't meet these criteria. We might console ourselves with the idea that we have Anna Craft's "little c creativity" or Margaret Boden's "P-creativity," but we also need to believe that we are capable of doing something special and extraordinary, otherwise what is it that distinguishes us from everyone else?

So let's discard the word *creativity*—just the noun. We can still use the adjective *creative* as a label to distinguish, say, writing a story from adding up a column of numbers. But the noun *creativity* is too freighted with contradictions, unrealistic expectations, and fantasies. In its place, let's recuperate the word *craft*.

We have long discussed the relationship between creativity and craft in screenwriting, particularly in emphasizing the need for a writer to have a firm grasp of the craft before being permitted to be creative. But this argument depends upon an idea of difference between craft and creativity, suggesting that the final screenplay form represents a synthesis of these two qualities. We've heard creativity aligned with art, originality, individuality, inspiration, talent, and passion; and craft aligned with experience, formulae, collaboration, and reiteration. As screenwriter and scholar Jill Nelmes writes, "Creativity may be essential in writing an original screenplay but, even if the writer has the greatest story idea, without craft he or she cannot express the story in terms of a screenplay."[16]

This is a persuasive argument, and it seems to make good sense. But does it contribute to an idea of creativity as something elusive and magical that exists in a nonmaterial realm—something inferred through the materiality of the screenplay? There is also the implication that the process of crafting the screenplay is not creative but rather a routine process. Screenwriter Amy Holden Jones (*Indecent Proposal*, 1993) subscribes to a similar conception of her practice: "I'm not an artist . . . An artist would put his own vision ahead of the project, and I try to fit my vision into the project; I try to make them work together . . . It's a community effort more than most arts, which are more singular."[17]

It may be true, that the business of screenwriting involves a more collaborative process than other forms of writing. But there are examples of novelists who have worked closely with editors and whose work has been shaped by this collaboration. American short story writer and poet Raymond Carver, for example, collaborated so closely with his editor Gordon Lish that his trademark style is now seen as attributable to the editing process. As journalist Gaby Wood said of their collaboration, "If you are a Carver reader who mainly associates his work with a certain style, then you may be surprised to find that the style itself—the sentences and paragraphs, the blunt, mid-air endings of his stories—was in many cases engineered by Gordon Lish."[18]

The question isn't whether it's most common that screenwriters must work within a collaborative production model and whether the very nature of that collaboration requires a firm grasp of craft. Nor is the question whether the crafting process is routine or creative. What I would like us to acknowledge is that the distinctions between art and craft, creativity and craft, and the individual and community effort are all artificial constructs and rhetorical (rather than actual) oppositions. With this acknowledgment, we are better able to understand the work of the screenwriter in coherent, pragmatic terms.

> "We have long discussed the relationship between creativity and craft in screenwriting, particularly in emphasizing the need for a writer to have a firm grasp of the craft before being permitted to be creative. But this argument depends upon an idea of difference between craft and creativity, suggesting that the final screenplay form represents a synthesis of these two qualities."

# Toward Craft

I have suggested that we treat creativity with skepticism and avoid indulging its Romantic connotations. This is because the word is inherently problematic and because individuals who have absorbed the myths of creativity may make it difficult for themselves to operate in complex contexts involving institutions, finance, collaborators, technologies, audiences, and grueling development processes.

It's no secret that the chances are slim for any individual to become a working screenwriter. It's an unlikely profession to succeed in, and we've heard endless stories of working screenwriters who are treated disrespectfully, whose writing is simply in service to the end product (the film or television show), who are rewritten mercilessly, whose phone calls are never returned again after the producer has lost interest, and on and on.

So you can see how a Romantic creative identity might be too fragile to endure these bleak conditions, particularly given that it's founded on myths and rhetoric.

But what about the craftsperson?

To think of oneself as a craftsperson recognizes that craftsmanship is founded on "skill developed to a high degree," as sociologist Richard Sennett points out. He argues that at its higher reaches, "technique is no longer a mechanical activity; people can feel fully and think deeply what they are doing once they do it well."[19] You might recall hearing that to become a master at something, you need to devote at least 10,000 hours of practice. This is Sennett's research,[20] and for the screenwriter, it can be comforting research to latch onto.

This means embracing practice. It means acknowledging and working with a range of creative limitations. It means being prepared to collaborate. It means accepting notes and feedback and responding to them. It means enduring disappointments and failures. And it means acknowledging that although the idea of the "artist" is a seductive one, there is integrity in being a craftsperson.

Remember, too, that whether others perceive you as being creative isn't necessarily based on anything concrete. Nor is this perception necessarily any indicator of whether you will get the job. Perhaps one person wants to hire the "creative genius" and another wants to hire a "practical professional." Neither scenario has any basis in reality (what/who you are), nor can you hope to predict what the person reading your script or sitting across the table from you might want. You can't predict this, and you can't control it, but by understanding the language and preconceptions, you will be better able to position yourself positively in relation to these industry players, and your craft can extend beyond the script and into the "game."

---

**DR. MARK READMAN** is a Principal Lecturer in Media Education at Bournemouth University, UK. He has published on screenwriting for the British Film Institute (BFI), has a PhD in the rhetoric of creativity, and has worked as a script editor. He has an unproduced sitcom in a bottom drawer but now concentrates on researching other people's creative practice.

Mark Readman

# WRITING FROM PERSONAL EXPERIENCE

## A Strategy of Forward Motion

▶ An Interview With Claudia Llosa

Peruvian director Claudia Llosa, described by *Variety* as one of Latin America's fastest-rising *femme helmer-scribes*, has written and directed three features, including *Madeinusa* (2006) and *Milk of Sorrow* (2010), which was nominated for an Oscar. Her most recent film, *Aloft* (2014), is her English-language debut, starring Jennifer Connelly and Cillian Murphy.

Claudia Llosa
Photo by Vanessa Montero

Llosa's story as a writer-director is one of bravery—daring to write from personal experiences and pain, allowing for healing and also forward motion in her career. By tapping into her personal truths and exploring and sharing her fears, she has positioned herself to put stories into the world that reflect global and interpersonal struggles that are both universal and unique. Her 2014 film *Aloft* tells two interconnected narratives several decades apart, ultimately about the reunion between a mother and son.[21]

**What was the inspiration for *Aloft*?**
It's never easy to know the exact inspiration. My process is very intuitive. It's funny, but if you read the first drafts of my script, you'd probably think the atmosphere feels the same—but really there's a completely different story there. You start with a notion of what you think you want, but somehow the story has its own nature, and it tells you where to go. So you start by writing something,

and little by little, the story arises, and without knowing it, you end up writing what you always wanted. But the inspiration for this story, I'm a mother now, so this has something to do with it, I'm sure.

**How old are your children?**
I have a son. He's 3, and he came with me to this shoot in Winnipeg. It was a great experience for him. He went to a Montessori school for a couple of months—lots of new friends, playing in the snow. He still remembers his trip to Canada. For me, it was challenging, the shoot, but for him this was a good experience.

**What made the shoot challenging?**
I guess everything. Working with higher budgets, higher expectations. Convincing this amazing cast to be a part of this dream. Shooting in a foreign county, and directing in a different language. Working with almost every member of the crew for the first time. As I said, I guess everything was a challenge. Also everything was uncertain. And to turn this uncertainty into our ally was the main goal. But I've had the best teachers in my crew—the producers and the rest of the team—everyone was amazing and accompanied me on the journey, through the whole process really.

**How did you get your start in filmmaking? Was there a game-changing moment?**
When I was maybe 23 or so I went to Madrid to study. I was working in advertising at the time, and I wrote a script in the evenings. I wanted to share my story, but I couldn't find very many readers—well, only my mother read my script. So I decided to send it to the Havana Film Festival. This was the important moment, because I won the first prize and also €150,000 to start production. I quit advertising and started knocking on doors, finding a production company. Actually, I was also looking for a director to shoot the picture. At that time, I was only known as a copywriter, never as a filmmaker. I never studied film. And that's how I found my producer, Jose María Morales. He read the script and said he wanted to produce my film but only if I directed it. And I was like, what? Are you sure? He said, if you wrote this, you'll be able to shoot it. Directing is easy! So that was the moment for me. And that was the script for *Madeinusa*, my first feature. But of course, it wasn't easy.

**You've written all three of your films. Do you consider yourself a writer first or director first?**
I was always a writer, a storyteller, even as a small child. I'm dyslexic, so reading and writing was always difficult for me, but I would tell my stories, and someone

in my family would write them down for me. I never dreamt of being a director, though—only a writer. But at least when you're a writer-director, sometimes it's much easier to find your way, because you're never waiting for someone to give you a story.

> "I was always a writer, a storyteller, even as a small child. I'm dyslexic, so reading and writing was always difficult for me, but I would tell my stories, and someone in my family would write them down for me. I never dreamt of being a director, though— only a writer."

**With dyslexia, do you think your stories grow more visually initially? Do you see the film as you write?**
I suppose yes, my visual world became kind of a way through as a child. I could always see the world of the story more clearly visually, and it wasn't as difficult or painful as reading or writing. I could hear the words, say the words, but to free them out of my body, that was always a challenge. This is sometimes very hard for a child, an adolescent. And even now, it's difficult for me. But I couldn't live without that part of the creative process.

**Was this your inspiration to some degree with *Milk of Sorrow*? She can sing but not speak? The idea of being stuck, in some ways mute?**
*Note: The film is about a woman who puts a potato in her vagina so it would be physically impossible for someone to rape her.*

The movie remembers the traumas generated by violence and terrorism, and the need for those victims to heal. The singing works as a great vehicle to express, to recreate our memory or oblivion. Sometimes, this is the only way to let out the pain. It has to do with the roots of our country and how to create a balance with our memory, the need not to forget but to forgive. Finding a balance between two opposing worlds, modernity and tradition.

**How much do you draw on your personal experience when you're writing?**

It's more about empathizing and understanding. I grew up in very different circumstances than the character in my film, but I did experience fear a lot of times. We were living in a difficult moment in my country during my youth, so I couldn't go to a cinema, for example, because it could explode from a bomb. I never experienced the cruelty that was experienced in the Andes, of course, because I was born and raised in Lima. But I could grasp that feeling. There's something about the muteness of the culture, the Andean culture, that I can relate to. This idea of holding something that you're carrying and how to deal with the weight of that—and the pain.

**This is because of the fear that you experienced growing up?**

The fear is the pain, yes—the feeling of not being able to do anything about it. So it's knowing that shutting it up, this is all you can do. It's so deep, and the reasons are so complex, and it comes from so long ago, and then building and building as a big sort of lock or shield. But something is there, growing. It could be dangerous, and it could be painful, but it's yours, and the only way out is to let it grow into something new and better.

**I'm curious about storytelling as a means of resolving conflict. Do you think the process of storytelling helps you grow, or helps your viewers grow?**

Storytelling, it's a dichotomy. Because it's on the one hand very personal, and on the other something you want to share. And sure it's to heal. My goal is to make the viewer live an experience, the experience of the film. And the only way to do this is if you let yourself live the same experience. Sometimes people won't connect to your stories, but others might, and that's why we never stop trying. The risk is always there, and you have to be willing to accept it. But it's remembering that it's not only the result that matters. This process of creating—*how* you create—this is living. And healing.

**What are your thoughts about female storytelling, the importance of women sharing their stories on screen?**

I have to say that I think gender doesn't dictate anything. Not an overwhelming sensibility or a specific interest, and it doesn't make a difference in the creative process, at least not from my perspective. It influences, no doubt—part of the sum of things that define us as individuals: our nationality, or idiosyncrasy, sense of humor, or genetic memory. That said, I think it's very important to find more stories with the point of view of women. Because the more we understand the psychology of women, the more we'll understand ourselves. But I don't feel I need to create female characters because I'm a woman. It's not an obligation for me. It's something that's part of who I am and what I want to share. It's something that comes naturally in my case. It's not preconceived.

> "I don't feel I need to create female characters because I'm a woman. It's not an obligation for me. It's something that's part of who I am and what I want to share. It's something that comes naturally in my case. It's not preconceived."

**Can you describe how you learn from films? What is the experience of watching film for you?**

It's like I'm hungry to watch films all the time. For me, it's about the inspiration. And there are filmmakers who teach me the craft and others who teach me the profundity and complexity of life, and then others who teach me tenderness. I just take what I can from each one. But I admire filmmakers who have their own voice for sure.

**Were you always drawn to that? Filmmakers with a voice?**

It was difficult to see films as a child because we have so few cinemas, so it was difficult to access the kind of films that I saw later on in university. But I suppose I've always liked the stories with a voice. I had a hard time as a kid, trying to communicate, to open myself. That was part of the challenge. But I needed to write my stories. That's why when people say, "I want to be a filmmaker," I just think that's amazing. Because for me, it never was that clear. I knew I wanted to do something in the arts, but it could have been anything. But I was always finding my voice, I think. And even now, if I couldn't shoot anymore because something happened, well, I would always write. I'll never stop. I'll always find a way to tell my stories.

# RISKS AND REWARDS

## Following a Passion

▶ An Interview With Jay Paul Deratany

Jay Paul Deratany received his law degree from DePaul University and his MFA in Writing for the Performing Arts from the UCR-Palm Desert. He is the founder of The Deratany Firm in Chicago. In 2016, he was selected as one of the Top 100 Illinois Litigation lawyers by the American Society of Legal Advocates (ASLA).

Deratany's courtroom successes include winning the largest jury verdict in Lake County history ($23,000,000). He has served on boards such as Howard Brown, Chicago House, Perspectives Charter Schools, and Community Support Services. He won the Eckroth Award for his federal lawsuit advocating on behalf of disabled women who were being discriminated against in housing, and he was featured in *Foster Families Magazine* for his continuing fight on behalf of foster children.

Jay Paul Deratany

Photo by Natalie Ginele Miller Photography

Screenwriting and film producing is Deratany's second career. His first feature film, *Saugatuck Cures*, was released in 2015, and he's currently putting together financing for his most recent film, *Foster Boy*. His play *Haram Iran* was nominated for a GLAAD theater award and has played in Chicago, Los Angeles, and London.

**When did you first know that you wanted to write?**
I always knew I wanted to write creatively. I took creative writing classes in college and enjoyed them, but I never thought of it as a potential career—more just as

something that I enjoyed doing. I kept journals and wrote poetry, which I wouldn't show to anybody—short stories and plays. I wrote a lot, but I considered it a hobby.

And then I got to the point in my early to mid-40s where I wanted to take it more seriously. In my law career, I was writing legal articles, but obviously that was a very different type of writing. But part of my law career is human rights, and I read a story about two boys who were killed in Iran for being gay, and it hit on several themes that were important to me. It hit on my legal background, because they were tried in basically a kangaroo court. It hit on my gay background, because they convicted them of being homosexual. And it hit on my background in writing. I'd always been a writer but just never *considered* myself a writer. So I wrote that play, *Haram Iran*, and that's where it clicked. I said, "You know what? I want to be a writer."

> "Just because I might be successful in one field doesn't mean I'm not going to make a complete ass of myself in another. You get older, and you start having doubts about yourself."

**At what point in the writing process did you have that thought? Or was it after it was produced?**
Yeah, it was after. When I was nominated for the GLAAD Award and getting this attention, and when they were going to do it in London, that's when it helped my confidence. Sitting watching the play one day in LA, I thought, "I want to go back to school and really learn how to write."

**And how old were you at that time?**
Forty-seven, and I had incredible doubts. I kept thinking, "Are you kidding? You're a fool." So many of those negative thoughts popped up that made me think I couldn't do it or was too old or was having a mid-life crisis. I didn't want to tell people I worked with.

We all have insecurities. Just because I might be successful in one field doesn't mean I'm not going to make a complete ass of myself in another. You get older, and you start having doubts about yourself. Sometimes people think they have to do something because their family told them or because they went to school for it, but if you want to make a mid-career change and you think you're too old, you have to push that negative demon away. It's not healthy. So many people make a difference later in life. Colonel Sanders became a millionaire at 80. There are plenty of stories where people struggle for ten or twenty years, people who find their stride when they're older.

**Does that stuff inspire you?**
It really does. And I'm so glad I've taken this journey the past few years. I've done some plays. I've made a movie. I'm making another one. It isn't about making money. It's about having the freedom to be you.

**Do you feel like you can't be yourself in law?**
I just have much more freedom of expression in writing. I've met so many new people the past few years, and I've experienced such joy seeing my play on stage and watching this little indie that I made make it to iTunes. Obviously, I've been excited in different points of my law career, winning cases, but I think some of us aren't meant to do just one thing all our lives. I wasn't.

**Are you ever concerned about your two lives bleeding together? Your film, *Saugatuck Cures*, has a strong take on religion. Do you worry that people in the legal world might be offended by something you're doing in your creative work?**
At this point, I'm successful enough in the business of law that if someone doesn't want to be my client, then what can you do? Obviously, in my film, I poke fun at religion, and I suppose some clients can see that film and have an opinion. But my film isn't mean. It's poking fun and making a statement about the right-wing Christian take on homosexuality. So sure, some people might take offence at that, but it's my view. The idea of curing homosexuals is ludicrous. I'm at a point where I'm comfortable in my own skin, so if a client doesn't take me seriously or wants to fire me because of something like that, then that's their business.

I had a client once who said, "I found out you're gay, and I don't want to hire you because I don't know if you'll be effeminate in a courtroom." This person hadn't even met me. There's always going to be somebody who doesn't like you for something, and you don't want to associate with those people. Yes, money is money and business is business, but I prefer to represent clients I like anyway.

**Any concerns about what clients or colleagues might think about the fact
that you're a writer-producer as well as an attorney? Do you worry that
they won't take you as seriously? Like it should be one or the other?**

I know some clients think that. Can I be a full-time lawyer for them if I'm also
a writer? The way I put it is this: I have time to be a lawyer for you, and I have
time to do my writing. If I didn't, I wouldn't do it. I have a successful law firm,
and we work hard and do very good work. But yeah, when I ran in politics, I had
some clients leave because they didn't think I could be a politician and represent
them as a lawyer at the same time.

**Tell me when the politics started.**

About 2004. In Chicago, the Democratic Party is somewhat split. Long story
short, the assessor and a congressman asked me to run for county commissioner
to represent the progressive wing of the Democratic Party. I got roped into it,
but I thought it was a good idea. And that consumed about a year of my life,
and then I lost. It was pretty devastating. But had I not run and lost, I wouldn't
have been in a mindset to find the human rights article about the two boys that
inspired my play [*Haram Iran*]. I found it only a week after the election loss.
I was going through a very bad time. I lost the election, spent a lot of my own
money. I lost half of my clients, and I was feeling pretty down.

But I pulled up these human rights articles, and I read about these boys, and I
thought, "Wait a minute. Why do I have any reason to complain?" I got consumed one weekend, writing and writing, and I literally didn't change out of a
pair of pajama bottoms and t-shirt until I finished the first draft of the play. So
things happen for a reason. The political race wasn't successful, but then I wrote
that play, and my business came back.

**Which led to you going back to school, studying screenwriting, and then
writing and producing *Saugatuck Cures*. Tell me where the film is now in
terms of distribution.**

It has a distribution agreement. It's released throughout the United States on
VOD, iTunes, and Amazon. At one point we were seventh out of 7,200 LGBT
films. In the independent film world, you don't usually make a ton of money
unless you happen to make *Little Miss Sunshine*, but you *can* make money. It may
come in residuals or contract deals, but it comes back.

**Can you tell me about your decision to buy a house in Los Angeles? Seems like a bold move when you've been established in Chicago all these years.**

Yeah, I downsized in Chicago and bought a place in LA. I still have to practice law for about two more years, because I don't make money yet as a writer. But I say, jump off a cliff, you know? You still have to have a plan. I'm not that crazy and adventurous. Adventure, but have a plan, that's what I would say. If you have a good financial base and can pay your bills, then you don't have the pressure of trying to make money all the time, so you can have some creative freedom.

**I look at your careers, and you have the ability to delegate work so that you can pursue a lot of different things. Does that come naturally to you, delegating?**

No, it doesn't come naturally. For a long time as a lawyer, it was very hard for me to not be involved in every single case. I want to know about the cases that I'm working on, but I have amazing lawyers. I have my law partners Michael Kosner and Megan O'Connor, and I trust in their abilities. But delegating has come slowly for me over the years.

**Learning to trust the lawyers in your firm and your partners, do you think that helped you in making your first film? The collaborative nature of it?**

Yes, I couldn't do it without trusting people. I was nervous, but then at some point I let go. There were scenes that Matthew [Ladensack, the director] cut that I had a very hard time accepting. I thought, "Why did you cut this scene? I worked so hard on it." You think it's the best scene in the world. Then the director cuts it, and in editing they're chopping and slicing. Even these two great actors, Max Adler and Danny Mooney, they came from an improv background, so they were throwing in some of their own lines. But you have to put your ego aside and say, "Well, actually those lines are better than the ones I wrote."

If you're going to collaborate, you've got to let other people's visions come in. It's difficult, but I don't ascribe to the idea that you can be the writer/producer/director/actor of your own project. It'll make you narrow-minded, and your work can't really bloom that way. Plus, you want everyone to shine, and if you accept their input, then they can have that opportunity. You're not just serving your audience with your film—if you're the one in charge, then you're serving your collaborators too.

> "If you're going to collaborate, you've got to let other people's visions come in. It's difficult, but I don't ascribe to the idea that you can be the writer/ producer/director/actor of your own project. It'll make you narrow-minded, and your work can't really bloom that way."

**Is being of service important to you? I know you do a lot of humanitarian work, but how would you describe service fitting into your life and work?**

Being a lawyer is about more than just a business—it's about your ethical responsibility. If you conduct your life ethically and with an idea that you're supposed to serve people, then your reward comes so much more, and financially too. I'm not a martyr. I make money. I'm a businessman, but I do think—with both the law and writing—that if you don't behave ethically or in the most responsible way you can, then you won't get financially rewarded. You'll also sleep better at night.

**I'd love to talk about financial rewards and the risks involved. How old were you when you started your firm and hired other people?**

I always wanted to work for Legal Assistance Foundation to be a lawyer for the poor. Back then, Reagan did a big hiring freeze, and I couldn't get a job for anything but $8 an hour. So I went into the private sector for five years, and then I wanted to start my own firm. I was 28. The first year I made $11,000, and then I had a big case. I had a line of credit and borrowed over $100,000, and then I lost my line of credit. It was a timed loan, and I had to pay it back. I had a trial the next week, and I had no more money. I wasn't paying myself anything. I paid my secretary with my credit card, worrying about the taxes later, eating macaroni and cheese for a month—which to this day, I can't eat. I went to trial, and I couldn't even afford my rent. Luckily, talk about pressure, I won the case. And after that, I built up my money so that when I went for months without earning a percentage of a case, I could still pay the bills. I really didn't start making money until I was 40.

> "I'm not a martyr. I make money. I'm a businessman,
> but I do think—with both the law and writing—that if
> you don't behave ethically or in the most responsible
> way you can, then you won't get financially rewarded.
> You'll also sleep better at night."

**You clearly perform well under pressure. How do you handle it when
you're under massive stress? Or does it just not get to you?**

It totally gets to me, but this is where I think my father comes in. I agree that's
a stressful situation, being in debt, worrying about the case, but our parents
went through the Depression and world wars. It was tough, but I wasn't in a jet
dropping bombs or getting shot at.

**So you're able to keep perspective.**

I just thought, "If I lose all my money, I'll go work for somebody. It's not going
to be the end of the world." I didn't like it, and I was definitely stressed out and
couldn't sleep at night. But I was focused on my clients' cases. Representing
somebody who's been wronged in the law was a big passion, and it still is. You
can have more than one passion.

I'm fortunate. I haven't gone through anything like what our parents and grand-
parents went through. That's a perspective we can all have. My dad lost everything
at the age of 50. He had five children, and I was there when he lost his house a
few weeks before Christmas.

**When was this?**

In 1967. My father had restaurants in Detroit, but nobody went back to Detroit
after the riots. Downtown shut down. He lost everything, and he had five kids.
I was the youngest. At 10 years old, I remember my father packing our stuff,
having to find a place to live, and then working as an assistant manager at a fast-
food restaurant. He went from owning several restaurants, doing very well, to
working in fast food. This was a self-made man. His father had to leave his home
country of Syria for reasons of persecution, just like now.

**Other people might watch their father go through this and make the decision to play it safe for the rest of their lives . . . "I'm never going into business for myself, because this is what happened to my father."**

Right, but he inspired me—also because he made it back. He had that fighting spirit. I was always proud of him for that. He was just an amazing man, a beautiful man.

**Can you tell me about your next project?**

It's a movie about the foster care system, a legal movie. I have a great actor who's considering directing and starring. I'm working on financing now. We have commitment of passive financing, but we still have to work on the rest of it. I think it will happen. It might take time, though.

**Any closing advice for aspiring screenwriters?**

Just do it. And look for the people who will give you emotional support. That's enough to get you through. Don't worry that you're going to have self-doubt, because you will. Take the chance, and believe in yourself. And it's okay that you won't always believe in yourself at times, and it's also okay that you fail every once in a while. We had a terrible review in one of the papers for *Saugatuck Cures*. It was mean. I don't think this guy was very nice at all. And by the way, I also had an awful review in *Variety* about *Haram Iran*, but a week later it was nominated for best theatrical play in LA. You can't let any one little step backward make a difference in your life. You've got to just keep going and believe in yourself.

# SCREENWRITING AND MENTAL FITNESS
## Thoughts From a Mental Health Professional
▶ An Interview With David Silverman

David Silverman graduated from Stanford University with departmental honors in psychology. He is a practicing therapist in Los Angeles and uses evidence-based methods to treat anxiety, depression, compulsive behavior, and psychotic symptoms. He works with creative professionals of all kinds, but especially Hollywood writers. He coaches writers on overcoming writer's block, strategies to improve writing skills, the psychology of writing, career burnout, reinvention, and breaking in.

David Silverman

Before Silverman became a therapist, he was a screenwriter for twenty-five years. He worked on over thirty TV shows, including *Mork & Mindy*, *One Day at a Time*, *ALF*, *Newhart*, *Dilbert*, *Duckman*, and *South Park*. He pitched, wrote, and sold screenplays to studios, did rewrites on features for Amblin, and created five TV shows, including two half-hour comedies and a long-running animated show called *The Wild Thornberrys*, which spawned two feature films.

**You went to Stanford intending to be a therapist, but you ended up a writer. How did that happen?**

When I got to college, I met all these people who were interested in writing as well as psychology. So I started taking creative writing classes and ended up writing my honors thesis combining creativity and psychology. It was a 300-page book on the origins of comic geniuses—Chaplin, W.C. Fields, the Marx Brothers, Lenny Bruce, Woody Allen, Mae West. And then when I graduated, I was more interested in the writing part for some reason, so I decided to go to USC and started writing scripts, mostly comedies. That's where I met my writing partner. We wrote shows like *The Jeffersons*, *Alice*, and *9 to 5*. We ended up doing more animation as our careers went on, and we gained a reputation for shows like *The Wild Thornberrys* and *Dilbert*. And then later, we got into darker shows like *Duckman* and *South Park*.

Truth is, I'd always wanted to be a therapist, though, and I always knew there would be a time when it'd be best to get out of writing. It took twenty-five years, but it was pretty clear that you don't want to be 60 years old and working in Hollywood as a writer.

**Why do you say that?**
There are a number of reasons. One is that you become overqualified and used to a big check. With TV staffs, the head writer usually has his own favorite writers he wants to work with. They'll look at our samples, but generally they don't want people in the room who have more experience. They get intimidated by that. Plus, they can get three or four baby writers for the cost of having my partner and I on staff.

> "It's tough for writers in Hollywood. Hollywood is full of a lot of narcissistic people, studio executives, and big stars. So people who are highly sensitive tend to absorb more when they're dealing with these people. They need to learn about self-care."

There's an ageism in Hollywood, so I figured it was time to get out—and I had a plan B. I always wanted to do therapy, so I got my license in psychotherapy and clinical psychology, and I decided I would cater to creative people. I can understand what writers go through with the rejection, procrastination, isolation, and trouble with motivation and productivity. Writers need to know how to take care of themselves.

**How do you work with clients to tackle these problems? To learn how to take care of themselves?**

To start with, a lot of writers are highly sensitive in the sense that they feel more empathy. They also tend to live inside their heads. When you're sitting in front of a keyboard all day manipulating ideas, you're not really out there like a more extroverted person. So a lot of people have problems with that. They're overwhelmed with a lot of sensory stimulus or going to six meetings every day. It's best to pace themselves. Studies have been done actually, connecting creativity with high sensitivity.

**Could you describe the highly sensitive person? How does that play out in most people?**

Elaine Aron is a psychologist who found that about 20 percent of the population have this sensitivity, which involves different things depending on the person. Some people are more highly sensitive to loud music, or they might be highly sensitive in a movie theater. They would feel things more deeply or they would be more moved during certain scenes, or they might feel pain if they see somebody being knocked around on screen. It has to do with empathy, that they're willing to connect with people emotionally.

Basically, these are people who spend a lot of time alone. They might have social anxiety or shyness. I think all of that overlaps in a writer. It's tough for writers in Hollywood. Hollywood is full of a lot of narcissistic people, studio executives, and big stars. So people who are highly sensitive tend to absorb more when they're dealing with these people. They need to learn about self-care. So I teach a lot of that to the people I work with, both writers and non-writers actually.

**What would you say is the most common mental health problem in your screenwriter clients?**

They're just like everybody else. A certain percentage have anxiety disorder. That seems to go along with writers. They have anxiety over where their next idea will come from, deadlines, paying rent.

**Anxiety about rejection?**

Rejection, too. One thing that can help with rejection is having a writing partner. I worked with my partner for most of my career. It's a huge advantage to have a partner, especially in the beginning. The rejection doesn't feel as bad when you have somebody to commiserate with. You have someone to prevent procrastination, somebody to hold you accountable. There's less isolation. You can write in the room with your partner. I used to write Act 1 and my partner used to write Act 2, and then we would come back together and go through the whole thing. The process is more social. It also helps with your motivation because if one guy is down, the other guy can be the cheerleader.

But having allies keeps you from getting nailed by this horrible rejection. There are other ways to deal with rejection, too. It gets easier to deal with once you realize that every writer gets rejected. Writers get a thousand no's and one yes.

**How do you work with clients through the no's? Or how do you help them get through the writer's block that can result from the no's?**
The essence of writer's block is the fear of being judged. Once you put it on paper, then it can be judged. So as long as it's still in your head, you don't have to worry about that, that's the general idea. One solution is to write about the block. In other words, just write.

There are other difficulties in Hollywood careers, too, like getting hot for a while and then cold. It's hard to have control over that, but what I try to do is give my clients ideas for how to reinvent themselves. Almost every writer eventually tries something a little different at some point, and maybe it's because the trends are changing. For example, I told you that my partner and I wrote for some dark animated shows like *South Park* and *Dilbert*. We weren't always doing that. We were doing more straight-up, big laugh comedies, but we intentionally made the choice to try writing for those shows. Once that happened, a lot more things opened up for us.

**How far along in your career were you at that point?**
That was probably about halfway through.

**So you reinvented how you were perceived in order to jump off a plateau?**
Yeah, but you also just become a better writer over time. You start to learn some of the subtleties in terms of what a scene should look like, when to enter the scene, when to leave the scene, and whether the scene even needs to be there. You get a better sense of that. But sometimes reinvention is what you need to do. We did it.

**How would you advise your clients in this situation?**
Looking at different genres is a possibility. Paying attention to trends and the marketplace. Some of the best stuff is being written on TV now, and writers

are taking more chances. Take the success of a show like *Breaking Bad*. That's a perfect example of a very dark show. If you have a guy who's written for mostly family shows, I would try to encourage him to write a *Breaking Bad* spec script or a pilot that has that feel to it.

If you're not working and need to reinvent yourself to get the work, it's tough, because there could be a mild depression and certainly a lot of anxiety. I help treat the symptoms so they can write again, whether they're symptoms of depression, anxiety, or panic. Sometimes, I provide stories from my own career to help, since twenty-five years steadily writing for television or film is a pretty tough thing to do. The guilds are filled with thousands of writers, who may or may not be working at any given time. So we talk too about my experiences and how I got through them.

**If somebody is in the midst of a panic, what might that be about?**
It could be about a deadline. More realistically, there could be more complicated issues too, like intimacy problems, alcoholism, addiction. Or you could have a deadline, and you can't write. You could have writer's block, and you start to drink. I've had clients who couldn't hold down a job and lost their house. They get so preoccupied that they don't see it as merely a setback, and sometimes they fall prey to irrational, catastrophic thinking.

## Building Blocks for a Long Screenwriting Career

Silverman says that for a career to last decades, you have to reinvent yourself over and over again. "We were known for being 'big joke' guys, then for being 'women's writers,' then for being animation writers, then for being 'darkly comic' one-camera writers, and for writing dark and edgy humor. You can't rely on your old scripts and your résumé to keep you working. You have to keep reinventing yourself, writing new spec scripts based on the latest shows, or writing sketches, plays, features, and even Web series."

Silverman also says if the goal is to keep working, it helps to have a great reputation for being amiable, flexible, good in a room, and able to adapt to changing trends. "You have to reach outside of your comfort zone in your writing and networking. All during your career, you have to think about reinventing yourself, writing outside of your comfort zone. The alternative is getting stuck in old-style shows and finding it hard to move forward."[22]

**For a client who has had success as a writer, what would you say this person can do to take his or her career to the next level? To keep moving forward?**

The key is to keep writing, to try writing new things—going back to the idea of reinventing yourself. I know a guy who never stopped writing. He made a lot of money from *Home Improvement*. He hadn't worked for years, but he never stopped, just kept pitching pilots and movie ideas for years. At a certain point, he was leaving a pitch meeting, and he turns around and pitches, "What about Godzilla in a retirement home?" They were interested. He based his idea on a movie called *Going in Style*. In that movie, a bunch of retired bank robbers get bored with life in the home and decide to pull one more big heist. So his idea is, Godzilla is in a retirement home with a bunch of other monsters, and he gets them psyched up to go on a last rampage.

They bought that and paid him to write it, and now they're paying him to direct it. At some point, he contacted a friend of ours, another writer who was out of work, and said, "Hey, you want to help me write this script?" So it's a good idea to keep in touch with other writers, especially the ones who refuse to give up. Persistence definitely pays off.

# Notes

1 "Inside the BBC: Mission and Values," BBC, accessed September 28, 2015, www.bbc.co.uk/corporate2/insidethebbc/whoweare/mission_and_values

2 "William Blake *Laocoön* 1826–27," accessed September 28, 2015, www.blakearchive.org/exist/blake/archive/object.xq?objectid=laocoon.b.illbk.01&java=no

3 Billy Childish, "Do it For Love," *The Idler* (August–September 1998): 12.

4 Mihaly Csikszentmihalyi, *Creativity: Flow and the Psychology of Discovery and Invention* (New York: Harper Collins, 1996), 12.

5 Ken Robinson, *Out of Our Minds* (Chichester: Capstone, 2001), 12.

6 Anna Craft, "Little C Creativity," in *Creativity in Education*, edited by Anna Craft, Bob Jeffrey, and Mike Leibling (London: Continuum, 2001), 46.

7 Margaret Boden, *The Creative Mind* (London: Abacus, 1992).

8 Lawrence W. Barsalou and Jesse J. Prinz, "Mundane Creativity in Perceptual Symbol Systems," in *Creative Thought: An Investigation of Conceptual Structures and Processes*, ed. T.B. Ward, S.M. Smith, and J. Vaid (Washington, DC: American Psychological Association, 1997), 267.

9 Joseph Kasof, "Explaining Creativity: The Attributional Perspective," *Creativity Research Journal* 8(4) (1995): 311.

10 Kasof, "Explaining Creativity," 328.

11 Kimberly D. Elsbach and Roderick M. Kramer, "Assessing Creativity in Hollywood Pitch Meetings: Evidence for a Dual-Process Model of Creativity Judgments," *Academy of Management Journal* 46(3) (2003): 292.

12 Anthony Storr, *The Dynamics of Creation* (London: Penguin, 1991).

13 Mark Readman, "What's in a Word?: The Discursive Construction of 'Creativity.'" (PhD diss., Bournemouth University, 2010), 263–4.

14 Readman, "What's in a Word?" 261–2.

15 Terry Eagleton, *Literary Theory* (Oxford: Blackwell, 1983), 19.

16 Jill Nelmes, "Some Thoughts on Analysing the Screenplay, the Process of Screenplay Writing and the Balance between Craft and Creativity," *Journal of Media Practice* 8 (2007): 112.

17 Joel Engel, *Screenwriters on Screenwriting* (New York: Hyperion, 1995), 63–4.

18 Gaby Wood, "Raymond Carver: The Kindest Cut," *Guardian*, September 27, 2009, accessed October 6, 2015, www.theguardian.com/books/2009/sep/27/raymond-carver-editor-influence

19 Richard Sennett, *The Craftsman* (London: Penguin, 2008), 20.

20 Sennett, *The Craftsman*, 20.

21 Anna Weinstein, "Diva Directors Around the Globe: Spotlight on Claudia Llosa," *Film International*, January 14, 2014, accessed March 1, 2016, http://filmint.nu/?p=10564

22 http://blogs.psychcentral.com/hollywood-therapy/2015/03/career-longevity-in-hollywood/

# CHAPTER 5

# STARTING AGAIN

> "And then the dreams break into a million tiny pieces.
> The dream dies. Which leaves you with a choice:
> You can settle for reality, or you can go off, like a fool,
> and dream another dream."
>
> Nora Ephron

**We've been talking about the lack of rules** in building a screenwriting career—what works for your friend may not work for you, and vice versa. And it's true. There's no such thing as a right or wrong. But there's one thing that's a definite: If you give up, you're out. Not for good, necessarily. You could give up today and change your mind tomorrow. But this is one of the few things you can control in this business—whether you choose to persist.

In the last chapter, you read about writers who moved into a screenwriting career after first succeeding in another career. And you read about how some writers decide to move on to a different career after a few decades in the film and television business. As you know, though, retirement isn't a necessity for screenwriters. There are plenty of inspiring stories of writers who achieved their greatest heights in their third act.

## Who Knew?

If you're unfamiliar with Ruth Prawer Jhabvala, just take a quick glance at her IMDb page to see the span of her half-century career and where she landed in her latter years. (Hint: She was the scribe for Merchant Ivory and won two Oscars, one in 1985 for *A Room with a View* and one in 1992 for *Howards End*.) You might also look up David Seidler, who in 2010 won the Oscar for *The King's Speech* at age 74. He began his career writing for television in 1965.

But this chapter isn't necessarily about beginning again later in life, after an accomplished career. This final chapter is really about the stark reality that all screenwriters, no matter their age or level of success, must begin again regularly. After a solid day of writing. After a murky day of writing. After finishing twelve drafts. After a significant fall. After a minor slip.

Recall what writer-director Anne Fontaine said about her work process—that she has several stories going at the same time. She finds shooting the most challenging part of the filmmaking process, so when she returns from a shoot, she makes sure she comes back to a story that's already in progress.

You might find that you're somewhat similar—that in order to avoid the rut of not writing, you have multiple projects in various stages of development. So if one isn't working at this moment in time, you always have another you can turn to. Recall that Barry Morrow said this exact thing—that when he returns from his shoot, he'll evaluate his projects and determine which makes the most sense to work on.

Let's look at some strategies for starting over, and the different shapes that might take in a screenwriting career. Here's what the essays and interviews will cover in this chapter:

- Why reinventing your career is the often the way out of a screenwriterly rut and into working again
- How two celebrated screenwriters reinvented their careers
- What the screenwriter's internal struggle looks like in dealing with writing for art versus commerce
- How the television industry works when writers follow their producer bosses
- How all writing is writing and why that allows for new opportunities if you keep an open mind

- Choosing between writing and directing for a living and how the day-to-day life differs
- Writing habits of successful working writers
- Why picking up and moving mid-career is sometimes the best answer
- How family fits into a screenwriter's life and career
- Business and life lessons from a two-decade career writing for children's television
- How to take control of your career and ask for what you need

We'll start with the notion of reinvention. If you haven't done this yet, you will at some point in your career. You might do it out of necessity after you've already established yourself in the industry, or you might choose to do it now, regardless of where you are on your path to becoming a screenwriter.

# REINVENTION
## Writing the Next Great Script
▶ By William Rabkin

This is how it feels now:

You're standing outside a great door. You've been standing here for what feels like forever. Every once in a while the door swings open to admit someone else, and for a brief flash you get a glimpse of the beauty and riches inside. Then the door slams shut in your face and you're frozen out again.

It's impossible to say how long you've been standing outside this door. You've been given a series of tasks to complete, and there have been vague promises to the effect that if you finish them all successfully, you'll gain admittance—but every time you do what's been asked, you're told to keep waiting.

You hate it here. You want to leave. You hear from your friends back home and they're getting married and having children and rising in careers, and your entire life is on hold until that door opens for you.

And yet you keep waiting, because you know that the door will finally swing open to let you in. And once you've passed through, you've made it. You're part of the life inside the walls—the happy, creative, productive people who are paid vast sums to do what you'd be willing to do for free.

This is how it feels now as you churn out your spec scripts, as you enter contests, as you cold call agents, as you scurry to follow up on a rumor someone else half heard that there might be a new program to help beginning writers break in if only you can figure out where and what it is and whether you fall into the particular group they're helping. It feels like there's a great Outside where you wait, and a beautiful Inside where you'll live happily ever after, and a gatekeeper that stands between them.

If this is indeed how you feel, I have some good news for you: It's not actually true.

If this is indeed how you feel, I have some bad news for you: It's not actually true.

So let's start with the good news: There may be a door, but there is no gatekeeper. Certainly not the way there used to be. Even when I was trying to break in thirty years ago, there was no single gate through which everyone had to pass—but it was a lot more like that then. There were four television networks buying shows from a dozen or two production companies, and if you wanted to get into any of them, you needed to first be vetted by one of the relatively few literary agents who'd actually consider new writers. And those agencies were the chokepoint that everyone had to get through.

> "There may be a door, but there is no gatekeeper."

The agencies are still there, of course, and they're still the primary feeder for new writers to get into the studios and networks. But they're not the only way in anymore. With the vast technological changes of the last decades, you can now write, produce, and distribute your work online, essentially for free. You don't need to ask people to read your script—you can put it out on the Web and build your own audience, and the studios will be coming to you to ask if you'd like to work for them.

So you don't need to wait outside that door anymore—you can build a ladder or dig a tunnel or just smash right through it.

As I said, that's the good news.

And here's the bad:

You know the pretty part of that image? How you get through the door and then you're on the inside forever? I know this is how I felt when I sold my first spec script—when I was allowed to join the Writers Guild, when I landed my first staff job. I'd made it, and I'd made it for life. Because I'd gotten through the door.

It took several years and a number of rude shocks to learn what really lies behind that door . . .

Landing your first job in TV is an amazing, life-changing event. But it's not going to change your life *forever*. Only you can do that.

# Luck + Talent + Hard Work =

I know a showrunner named Howard Gordon. I met him thirty or so years ago. My partner and I had just sold a spec episode to ABC's detective series *Spenser: For Hire*, and the gentlemen who were running the show suggested we might want to meet the young writing team who'd had their first professional sale on *Spenser* the year before.

Howard and his partner Alex Gansa were brilliant—literate, ambitious, and terrific writers. After a short time freelancing, they were hired on a prestigious drama called *Beauty and the Beast*, where they worked for the show's entire run. When that was cancelled, they joined a new show called *The X-Files*.

Howard thrived there, staying for the show's full run even after his partner left. He formed a great relationship with the show's studio, 20th Television, and he stayed with them to create his own show, the short-lived *Strange World*, and then to work on *Angel* and *24*. In that series' fifth year, he became its showrunner and made what are frequently referred to as its best seasons. After *24* ended, Howard reteamed with Alex (and with writer Gideon Raff) to create *Homeland*, one of the most respected and awarded series in recent history. And that led to deal after deal, with Howard placing shows at multiple networks and becoming one of the most important writer-producers in the business.

There are two reasons why Howard's story should be important to you:

One is that this is the television career everyone dreams of. Even while you're sitting in your tiny apartment or escaping to Starbucks to write yet another spec, you're visualizing the life you'll lead once you break through. And while everyone's fantasy is different, they're all based on the idea that you'll be given the opportunity to do good, meaningful work, that this work will be successful, and that every success will lead to a greater opportunity.

The other is that a career like Howard's is about as common as a winning Powerball ticket—that is, if buying that ticket involved tremendous talent and a tireless work ethic. I don't know anyone who begrudges Howard the slightest bit of his success—because through it all he has stayed one of the nicest people in the business. But even he would have to concede that for all his hard work and inspiration to have paid off so completely required a massive streak of luck. If *The X-Files* had tanked in its first season, as so many earlier science-fiction shows had; if the studio changed management and a new executive had taken a dislike to him; if he and Alex had been offered a staff job on *Houston Knights*, the meat-and-potatoes cop show they'd sold a freelance script to before *Beauty and the Beast*—who knows where Howard's career would have gone?

Most successful people, if they're honest, will admit that luck played a big part in getting them where they are. There's nothing in this world more powerful than the combination of talent and luck.

The fact is, though, most of us are not this lucky. (Even fewer of us have the level of talent necessary before luck can figure in. I'm writing this essay on the assumption that you're not only one of those, but one who is willing to put in the hard work that's even more important than talent.) We get our first job in the business working as a staff writer on a new show, and our future looks great for the four months we're working before the series premieres. Then it hits the air, gets decimated by critics, draws fewer viewers than an infomercial, and is cancelled after one episode.

And your experience on that short-lived show—your wonderful, glorious, life-changing experience working (and getting paid!) as a professional TV writer—you do know what that means to the world outside, right?

Nothing.

Maybe less than nothing. Because before you got the gig, you were a complete unknown, offering nothing but potential. Now you're part of a massive, humiliating flop, and even if the failure was in no way your fault, the stink sticks to you.

Unfair? Absolutely. If you're looking for fair, it's probably best to consider a different career . . .

Now it's possible you might get lucky. Someone above you on the flop might land another show and bring you on. Or an executive at the network might be aware of the good work you did and look to give you a second shot.

But you can't count on luck.

You spent years working for your shot, and now it's over.

*What do you do?*

# Follow Matthew Weiner's Lead

You've probably heard of Matthew Weiner, the writer-producer who, in creating and running *Mad Men*, did more to change the art of the television drama than almost anyone in history.

But have you heard of Matthew Weiner, executive story editor of the long-running Ted Danson sitcom *Becker*? Supervising producer of *Andy Richter Controls the Universe*?

Matthew Weiner spent the first years of his career writing situation comedies. And these were pretty good comedies—the ones that weren't commercial hits were critically respected; the ones the critics didn't fall for got big audiences. This was a career and a career path that would have made a lot of writers very happy.

Not Weiner.

It wasn't the career he wanted. It wasn't the life he wanted.

But here's the thing about the TV industry—you're not really a part of it until you've got a box they can fit you in. This guy writes procedurals; she's good at romantic comedy; this team does action. And once you're in that box, they can't see you any other way.

Unless you force them to. Unless you reinvent your career. Unless you reinvent yourself.

You're standing outside that door, and you're convinced that once you get inside everything will be great forever. Because you can't see what lies behind this door: Another door. And another. And another.

What you don't understand is that unless you have a blessed career, every stage of your working life will mean fighting your way through another door. You'll have to fight for every job you ever get.

Many years ago, Fox picked up a pilot called *Bones*, a light crime drama about an FBI agent teamed with a forensic anthropologist. My partner and I had just come off several years of working on similar light crime dramas, including a successful period running *Diagnosis Murder*. Our agent pitched us for the show. The studio executive—with whom we'd had a good working relationship on previous series—said he probably couldn't get us read for the job, let alone schedule a meeting. "You have to understand," he told our agent, "I'm looking at a stack of literally 100 scripts, all by writers with credits as good as or better than your guys'."

This is the reality of the TV business for the vast majority of writers—99 out of 100, as it happened here. You achieve some level of success, you're typed by that success, and you compete for the same kind of job with every other writer who has been assigned the same type. If you're lucky, you get the jobs. If you're not, you keep searching for the next similar one.

And even if you're working now, unless you're lucky enough to land on hit after hit, the work is going to run out. Because the TV business has the same kind of attention span as a 13-year-old fixated on a pop idol: When they love you, they love you unquestioningly, but pretty soon they're going to find someone else to adore. Whatever box you've let them put you in, eventually they're going to get tired of seeing you there and start looking for your replacement.

How did Matthew Weiner escape that trap? How did he go from mid-level sitcom writer to one of the most influential, powerful figures in dramatic television? How did he completely reinvent his career and himself?

He did it in the one way that's open to all writers: *He wrote a script.*

To be more precise, he wrote a script that represented not who he was or how he was perceived. He wrote the script that defined the writer he wanted to be.

This script was the pilot for *Mad Men*.

Now, of course, that's widely considered one of the greatest pilots ever.

His agents didn't want to send it out.

And if you want to understand everything there is to know about your future career in the TV business, reread those two sentences: *The script is widely considered one of the greatest pilots ever. His agents didn't want to send it out.*

Because they had Weiner in his box, and him being in that box was making money for everyone. He was at the supervising producer level in sitcoms. He'd be starting out at the bottom in dramas, if he could even get a job.

> "How did Matthew Weiner go from mid-level sitcom writer to one of the most influential, powerful figures in dramatic television? *He wrote the script that defined the writer he wanted to be.*"

But Weiner wouldn't let them keep him in his box. He demanded—and demanded and demanded—that they get the script to David Chase, creator and executive producer of *The Sopranos*. And Chase read the script and hired Weiner . . . and Matthew Weiner had successfully reinvented himself as a writer (and later executive producer) on what was at the time the most prestigious drama on television.

## Write Yourself Into the New You

It's not just writers who need to reinvent their careers. It happens to actors, directors . . . anyone in the entertainment industry.

The difference is that we can do something about it. It's true that we get defined by the shows we've worked on. But we can change that definition just by doing what we do, by writing. We can turn out sixty pages that will show the world who we are—that will allow us to define ourselves.

We all do this at the beginning of our careers—we have to. But the further we get into the business, the harder that becomes. We get accustomed to writing for money, and the thought of turning down a paying job (or taking time off the job search) to write something on spec feels like taking huge steps backward. We get accustomed to having our work welcomed by studios and networks that know exactly what they want from us—an unsolicited spec risks a level of rejection we haven't faced since we were starting out.

But here's the fact that every writer has to understand: No matter what we do, sooner or later that rejection is coming. And when it's the old you—the successful you—that's being rejected, the only way to triumph is to have the new you ready to go.

Which leads inevitably to a hard and scary question: Who do you want that new you to be?

Most writers are, at some very basic level, insecure. We don't trust our talent. We don't really understand where our stories come from. At some level, almost all artists' deepest fear is that they'll be revealed as the fraud they know they are.

I think this is what makes the thought of reinvention so terrifying to so many writers. As long as we're being hired—and even put into boxes—by people in power, we can rely on their judgment to tell us we've got talent. "Hey, CBS thinks I'm good at writing procedurals—I'll do it!"

To attempt reinvention demands that we stand up and proclaim who we believe we really are. The business has said we're only good enough to work on mid-level sitcoms, and we have to be willing to reject that and insist that we're worthy of writing high-end dramas. It feels like arrogance. Hubris. And unlike most of the people who hire and fire us, we writers are well read enough to know where hubris leads . . .

And with that in mind, I'd like to introduce you to one of the bravest men I've met in the TV business . . .

## Meet Terence Winter

Long before I met him, Terence Winter had already risked everything once to reinvent himself. He'd pulled himself up from a working-class background, gone to law school, and practiced corporate law for a couple of years in New York. He could have been set up for life.

Instead, he walked away from it to move to Los Angeles to reinvent himself as a TV writer.

And it took him years to get anywhere. Finally, he was admitted into one of those trainee programs for talented beginners—this was the one at Warner Bros. That led to his first job on a short-lived show called *The Great Defender*, and when that was cancelled, he moved on to that series' showrunners' next gig, which is where I met him.

At our first meeting, those showrunners raved about Terry, and as soon as I met him I understood why. He was probably the funniest person I'd ever met, and his writing was even better. My partner and I worked closely that season with Terry, and I don't think I've ever had as much fun in a writers' room.

And then we were cancelled, and Terry was kind of adrift. He was a huge talent, but that talent wasn't finding its outlet. I hired him to write a *Diagnosis Murder* episode and recommended him to a friend of mine who was running *The New Adventures of Flipper* who gave him a staff job. Terry kicked around on marginal dramas and even more marginal sitcoms.

Terry was lost. Even the industry couldn't really figure out which box they could fit him into. And then he saw the pilot for *The Sopranos*.

(And if you think it's a coincidence that both of my stories of reinvention center on that show, it's not. Because *The Sopranos* was the series that reinvented dramatic television . . .)

Terry knew this show was where he had to be. He'd grown up around guys like these characters; he knew the voice. But by the time he saw the pilot, the show was already staffed up for the first season. There were no jobs.

So Terry set out to make sure that when one opened up, it would go to him. Fortunately, one of the writers hired was Frank Renzulli, whom Terry had met on *The Great Defenders*. And he spent the next year sending him script drafts, talking through the stories with him. It was, he's said, like he was part of the writing room even though he was nowhere near it. And when a position opened up in the second season, Terry got it.

Because he'd spent a year reinventing himself as the only person for the job.

If you follow credits, you know that after this, Terence Winter never had to reinvent his career again. His work on *The Sopranos* led to the chance to create and run first *Boardwalk Empire* and then *Vinyl*, and his screenplay for *The Wolf of Wall Street* was nominated for an Oscar.

But none of that could have happened if he hadn't had the strength at two points in his life to stand up and say:

I will decide who I am going to be.

Showrunner **WILLIAM RABKIN** has written and/or produced more than 300 hours of dramatic television, including a dozen pilots and movies in Germany and China. He has consulted for TV writers, directors, producers, and executives in China, Brazil, Sweden, Spain, and Germany. Rabkin teaches television and screenwriting at Long Island University's MFA in Television Writing and Producing, and UC Riverside-Palm Desert's Low Residency MFA in Creative Writing and Writing for the Performing Arts. He is the author of seven novels and two books on writing for television, *Successful Television Writing* (with Lee Goldberg) and *Writing the Pilot*.

William Rabkin

Photo by Carrie Rabkin

# ART VS. COMMERCE
## The Cage Match in My Brain Continues
▶ By Shalom Auslander

*ART—idealistic, insistent, committed—and COMMERCE—serious, adult, responsible—battle in my mind every day, and the day I was asked to contribute an essay to this volume on art and commerce in the film and TV industry was no exception.*

Illustration by Orli Auslander

ART: No. No way. I'm not doing it.

COMMERCE: Why not? It's business. It'll take two minutes.

ART: First of all, it never takes two minutes. Second of all, why? I have a hundred other projects I'm in the middle of, projects that matter to me, on a personal level. What could possibly be the reason for doing this?

COMMERCE: It could be good for your career.

ART: Good for my career?

COMMERCE: Yes. You become an "authority." Other people ask you to contribute to their books: "How to Write a TV Show in Six Minutes," "Showrunning for Dummies," "So You Want to Write a Novel"—that kind of thing. People think you know what you're doing, you get to plug your books and shows—that's good for your career. The problem with you, Art, is that you're naïve.

ART: How am I naïve?

COMMERCE: Look, someone sits in their room, and they feel something. They feel it deeply, truly, and they want to express it, share it with the world. That is beautiful—and human. I believe all humans have this need to create, to express, to share. But just as not all that is shared deserves to be called Art, not all Art deserves to be shared. The idea that these personal opinions and feelings and expressions should come before the realities of the medium—and in the case of television and film, these are extremely expensive mediums— is naïve.

ART: To pronounce Art naïve is to prove that you, Commerce, are myopic. Art has always depended to some degree on Commerce, and Commerce has always depended on Art—whether it was Rembrandt's struggle with his patrons or Shakespeare's indebtedness to his. But Commerce is arrogant. I would suggest that the problem facing TV and film is an excess of Commerce and the resulting lack of Art. There's no personal expression, no single point of view. There are only formulas filmed more elaborately than they were before, tropes trotted out unchanged but for the technology used to present them, clichés recast for the moment in time but fundamentally the same as ever. My young children can tell within the first fifteen minutes of any film—by the time the "hero" has "saved the cat!"—exactly how it is going to end. The film industry applauds itself more than any other because nobody else will. What is there to applaud? To admire? Art demands courage, daring, risk. The people who point fingers at artists for living in "ivory towers" have obviously never been in an ivory tower. I will tell you this: The walls are covered with blood, the floor with tears. It is hard work, harder than any board meeting or budget session or marketing luncheon. Naïve? Artists challenge themselves. They look into abysses that others won't. They dare to show what they find to the world, because they know something about darkness: You can't bomb it away. You can't throw money at it to leave. You can only shed light on it. The irony of the situation is this: Art is the one thing that can save film and TV, and Commerce treats Art as a danger, as something to be controlled and contained and feared. The crucified is the savior.

DON'T CALL ME 'NAIVE'!

Illustration by Orli Auslander

COMMERCE: You speak of your children, though. There are mouths to feed, schools to pay for. What do you suggest is the answer to that?

ART: There are practical considerations, no doubt. I know a man who worked as a corporate attorney for many years. He had a very big house. Cable railings up the wazoo. It was a Corporate Attorney's House. And when he realized that the life he wanted to lead was a writer's life, he sold it. He bought a Writer's House. No pool. No cable rails. The people who do good work in any industry—publishing, art, film—make a decision: The work is more important than the Tesla. The infinity pool isn't worth writing *Iron Man 17*. And here's another irony: The more defiant they are about their art, the more likely it is that Commerce will eventually come calling. Artists, remember this: All you have is your voice. Don't give it away. Don't change it. If you start to let Commerce into the discussion of Art, then whatever was once Art—whatever was You—will be turned into Commerce. And Commerce isn't unique. It isn't special. It's average. All Commerce sounds alike. And so the minute you acquiesce to Commerce, your Art dies, and your chances for Commerce die with it.

COMMERCE: But Teslas are awesome. Infinity pools are fun. Why shouldn't you be able to enjoy these things? You have an ability that others do not. Why not profit from it? Some people can build houses. Some people can argue the intricacies of law. Some people can repair a failing heart. Is it such a crime for these people to be rewarded financially? I think a cardiologist deserves an infinity pool. I know you'll shout "Materialism!" but it's more than that. It's security, stability, safety. We're lucky to be able to have it. Most of the world doesn't. Why shouldn't we enjoy it? Here's an irony for *you*: Those who don't have these things want them, and those who get them feel guilty for having them.

ART: I think that brings up an important point: Art is difficult. An infinity pool doesn't interfere with the cardiologist's work. A Tesla won't make a lawyer argue his client's case less insistently. But Art has a perilous relationship with these rewards. Art must be careful. Materialism isn't designed to extinguish the need for self-expression, but it often does. Sit around your *Iron Man 17* infinity pool long enough, and you might not want to think about life and death and existence and the poor and love and the human heart. It's not a small decision. It's a life choice. The Olympic runner must feel restricted when her friends at dinner eat all that they want while she can only have the salad. But that's what she does so that she can run the way she wishes. Here's what I do so that I can write: I don't watch TV. I don't go online. I don't have a Twitter account, or a Facebook account, or whatever account is the account to have. I haven't read a newspaper—or a news site—in fifteen years. I don't read books, except by dead people. I want a clear mind. I want to hear my voice, not the voice of marketers and trends and popularity. I could read Vonnegut and Beckett day and night, but then I begin to sound like them. And as much as I love them, I don't want to sound like them. So I don't read them, not when I'm writing. I don't drink the night before I write. I walk. A lot. In the cold, in the heat. Walking is thinking. It's frustrating. It's difficult. I fail, over and over. People think I'm weird. "I never see you without that laptop!" I'm not great fun at parties. I can't discuss the latest movies. I don't know the names of the celebrities they are mentioning. I sit alone—in my office, in coffee shops—and people think I'm lucky. "How nice it would be to write." It would nice to be an Olympic runner, too.

COMMERCE: Ditchdiggers.

ART: Yes, I know, Commerce. "It's better than digging ditches." Can we all just agree that ditchdiggers have difficult jobs and move on? But Art is its own difficulty, one that the world has always failed to understand. Honesty is hard. Vulnerability is terrifying. Art is admission, confession—and no soothing voice comes from the other side of the wall declaring absolution. It's intense self-examination, with a mountain of self-reproach, in the hopes of a sliver of self-knowledge and a fleeting moment of self-acceptance. That's what Art is, and that's more important than ditches, however physically difficult digging one may be.

COMMERCE: I think we agree more than we disagree. Commerce actually needs unique voices. Smart Commerce should buy unique voices, should encourage unique voices. You're right—Commerce is desperate for unique voices. But there aren't that many. And we still have to produce Something—some film, some book, some TV series—and minus Voice and Art, we have to come up with it ourselves. So we get The Theme Stated on page 7 and The Catalyst on page 15, and The Love Interest soon after that, and yes, I think Commerce would agree that most of that is well-constructed garbage. But that is the fault of the Artists, then, isn't it?

ART: Fantastic. The butcher blames the cow for being dead. But I agree with this: Art is difficult to make, and Artists should be more committed to it—to what it takes to make it, and to protect it after that. And Commerce would do well to remember this: When Art leads, we have better films and more anxious money-men. When Commerce leads, we have comfortable businessmen and shitty films. I vote for anxious moneymen.

COMMERCE: So, then, why is Auslander writing this essay?

ART: It could be good for his career.

COMMERCE: So he's a whore.

ART: It'll take two minutes . . .

---

**SHALOM AUSLANDER** is an internationally acclaimed writer of fiction, nonfiction, TV, stage, and film. His short story collection *Beware of God* was published to unanimous critical acclaim, his memoir *Foreskin's Lament* was an international bestseller, and his novel *Hope: A Tragedy*, which he is currently adapting for the stage, was a finalist for the 2013 James Thurber Award. In 2014, he created, wrote, and produced the series *Happyish* for Showtime, starring Kathryn Hahn, Steve Coogan, Bradley Whitford, and Ellen Barkin, which was "one of the most talked about and controversial" shows of the year. A longtime contributor to NPR's *This American Life*, he has published fiction and essays in *The New Yorker*, *The New York Times*, *Esquire*, and *GQ*, among many others.

Shalom Auslander

Photo by Franco Vogt

# EVERYTHING I NEED TO KNOW ABOUT A CAREER IN HOLLYWOOD . . .

## I Learned From Writing Scripts

▶ By Rosanne Welch

When you study story structure from any of the many books published by the likes of Jule Selbo or Syd Field or Robert McKee, you learn much more than writing. You learn lessons in life.

Oddly enough, I had never heard of any of those books on how to write for television before I began writing for television—a job I enjoyed for nearly twenty years. It was only in the aftermath that I found those books in planning curriculum for my students, and then I realized that a study of the steps of story structure is actually a study of how to live, survive, and thrive when life throws the inevitable third act twist at you.

As a television writer with credits on *Touched by an Angel*, *Beverly Hills 90210*, and *Picket Fences* and currently a professor of screenwriting, I have a unique perspective on the act of climbing one impossible career track and then starting over and climbing an entirely new path that still involves all my main loves in life—writing, mentoring, and storytelling. In fact, a few years ago, I was the keynote speaker for a conference (held in Hawaii so I said, yes!), and one of my speeches was about moving from the role of co-producer to earning my PhD and being published in a new field. I also remember the oddity of being interviewed by a college dean who wanted to know why I was interested in a full-time professorship. He thought since I had already "climbed one mountain" there was no need to climb another. I had to explain that having achieved my PhD, I wanted to take this new career as far as I could—just as I had with my last career. It never seemed odd to me. But then writers enjoy dabbling in the lives of all the characters they create—doctors, lawyers, Indian chiefs—so wanting the full experience of a new career seemed perfectly normal.

As a Sicilian-American kid growing up in Cleveland in the 1970s, I dreamed of writing for television. I spent my summer vacation days wallowing, watching old black-and-white movie reruns, but by night I would soak in new, innovative sit-coms such as *All in the Family* and *Maude*. I fell in love with television. Everyone said you had to "know someone" in the business to land a job, so I moved from Cleveland to California to meet someone I could know!

When my college sweetheart asked me the classic, "Will you marry me?" I countered with, "Will you move to California?" At that crucial juncture in my life, his yes was almost more important than mine. So the day after our wedding, we packed up a rented Hertz-Penske truck with all our family's hand-me-down furniture and drove off to pursue careers in television writing and computers (my new husband's major).

For the first year in Los Angeles, I paid the rent by teaching at a Catholic school. But in the evenings, I took classes in writing for television. And I was advised during those evening classes that "to be in the business you need to be *in* the business." So I tossed off the teaching career (a mite too casually) and became a writer's secretary. It turned out writers were interested in having former high school English teachers as their assistants, because we could correct their spelling errors before the executive producer read their scripts. And we were also great at research. And at getting coffee, arranging their wives' anniversary weekends at the spa, and babysitting their toddlers who would come to the office "to see how Daddy makes television." None of these tasks was in my job description, but they all fell under the heading of "favors we offer our bosses in hopes that they will reciprocate with the favor of reading our spec scripts and recommending us to their agents."

You know the old trope about how overnight sensations take ten years? Well, ten years later, I finally landed an agent who came to me by way of some writ-er-producers I worked for reading my writing samples and showing them to their agent. I finally "knew someone" and became a freelance writer, and those freelance episodes led me to the staff of *Touched by an Angel*. After a slew of shows that offered to buy one of my scripts but were then cancelled before the contracts could be signed, *Touched* felt as comfortable to me as a high school history class—especially since I'd attended and then taught at Catholic high schools in Cleveland and California.

I'm not referring to the spiritual content of a show, by the way—two traveling angels who step into shattered lives and help characters rebuild. I'm talking about that comfort you feel when you've walked the halls of a place from freshman (staff writer) to senior year (co-producer), and you come to know every nook and cranny of the writers' conference room.

That kind of comfort can be rare for television writers, as shows have a tendency to come and go with great regularity. So landing on what became a nine-year institution (though I only spent seven seasons there) was both a blessing and a bit of a curse. Traveling from show to show is a hectic, nomadic lifestyle—a throwback to the myth of the carnie setting up and tearing down tents in a day. But in settling in on one show, what can happen is that producers—future possible employers—begin to pigeonhole you as only being able to write that one kind of show. And that can hurt you when the steady show finally comes to a close, as they all do eventually.

The second blessing/curse aspect of being a writer is that by virtue of your artistic sensitivity, you notice things other folks might miss—things like realizing that where you are on any given day is no indicator of where you will be in a day or two. You realize that both your television show and, in fact, your whole career are constantly hanging in the balance, affected by factors that you have no control over. Often, Emmy-winning shows are canceled due to no fault of your own; such was my experience on *Picket Fences*.

And that sensitivity makes you aware, if you're fortunate, of the luck of the draw your talent has earned for you—and of the fragility of that luck.

That epiphany came to me one day while walking down a hallway at the *Touched* offices on Ventura Boulevard. I was suddenly awash with the realization that it wouldn't last forever—that I wouldn't be walking down that same hallway ten, five, or even two years from that moment. I likened it to the feeling you get as a senior in high school when every event is "the last time I will ever take a bow on this stage" or "the last time I will ever make out with a cute boy in this hallway." A friend of mine who is an actress had the same epiphany one day sitting in the makeup chair as a supporting cast member on a new pilot. She willed herself to sit back, relax, and soak it all in, because there was no guarantee that the show would become a hit and therefore a permanent experience. (It didn't last past the fifth episode, and her life of auditioning more than performing returned to normal.)

Eventually, my time at *Touched* ended, and that's when I learned that writing for television had taught me more about living than I knew. It's why audiences continue to watch television shows and movies—whether on large multiplex screens or small ones that sit in the palms of their hands. We need the lessons of story structure, the lessons of life. Characters always want something they don't have. They try valiantly to achieve that want. They are often denied that want and need to undergo more training and research to finally achieve it. But in the third act twist, they often learn that they didn't need those ruby slippers after all. They discover that they always had the power to go home—they only had to learn it for themselves.

The effect of pigeonholing rippled across the entire staff of the show, which meant that where I once had nine possible future bosses and colleagues on nine future shows, the possibility of being hired by any nine of them dried up as most of them didn't find future television work either. In film, writers can often make a living by hiring themselves out as rewriters on other people's scripts. While they may never see their name in the credits, they can continue to earn money as writers. In television, though, we write spec pilots for which we aren't paid in hopes of having the spec purchased and produced—and unless you're already a hit producer with three shows on the air, this is akin to buying weekly lottery tickets in hopes of hitting it big. I did that for a few years, as did my friends.

I lived off the tidy pile of savings I had accrued as a writer/co-producer, because one does make a nice series of paychecks while on staff. What other job gives you a weekly paycheck *and* a lump sum of cash for every script you complete? One of the first lessons new writers need to learn is how to save and invest. I often tell my students this—and by way of example, I explain that my son was able to continue in private school because of the savings I invested in the early days of my career.

But when the specs stop selling, and even stop earning you meetings with development executives who *might* staff you on other shows . . .

And when the staffing meetings dry up because other producers never watched your show and think that must be the only genre you can write . . .

When you pitch a women's network a show about a US female journalist assigned to the Rome Bureau where she'll meet interesting and exciting people, and the female executive tells you they define their female characters by the men in their lives . . .

When you find out that even your agent has fallen for the pigeonholing . . . that he didn't send your material to a new show about four gay men living in San Francisco because he didn't think you'd want to write for that kind of show after *Touched* . . .

You begin to see the writing on the wall. How many clues does a detective need to gather before the resolution in Act 4 explains it all so cleanly and concisely?

By the way . . .

I did finally get a meeting with the producers of the San Francisco-based show, but they met with me only to say that they loved what they read but had already offered the job to someone else. They promised that if she fell through . . .

But no one walks away from a full-time writing staff job. I thanked them, knowing I had just lost the chance to rewrite my reputation in a town that lives by branding you as soon as they can.

Here's something I learned from this experience. No one understands the breadth of what you have to offer but you. All the screenwriting books will tell you that the most classic, longest-lasting stories teach us things. Our own stories teach us things, too—and themes become clearer as the story goes on.

A trusted advisor in my career suggested that I write a spec pilot set in a place like the Hamptons, with a 17-year-old female lead having an affair with her father's best friend and business partner. That's when I finally balked.

To me, television had been the place where I learned life lessons from all my favorite friends, regulars on such shows as *The Monkees* and *MacGyver* and *The Mary Tyler Moore Show*. *The Monkees* taught me to support my friends who live a life of creativity. *MacGyver* taught me that science was cool. *The Mary Tyler Moore Show* taught me to stand up for myself in the workplace. What was the life lesson I would put into the world with the story of a teenage girl and her relationship with her father's business partner?

It wasn't a life lesson I wanted to teach. So I didn't. And my trusted advisor and I parted ways.

As when a character faces her darkest days, sometimes you need to reassess. What do I want? What do I need? What talents do I possess that I can polish to attain these new—or newly redefined—goals? I had unexpectedly wandered into the third act of my own story.

I came to realize that I love to write, no matter the medium. I had published essays in newspapers and magazines while writing for television. Heck, I started out as the editor of my high school newspaper and yearbook, and I went on to write freelance pieces for local and national newspapers. During my first year on staff,

I compiled an *Encyclopedia of Women in Aviation and Space*, reading biographies of famous female pilots in between meetings and while taking network notes. I researched, sold, and produced a documentary for ABC NEWS/NIGHTLINE in my second summer hiatus from *Touched* merely because the subject matter was so compelling—and because it involved a visit to the White House, something this grandchild of Sicilian immigrants found deeply compelling!

On the set of ABC NEWS/NIGHTLINE to film the opening segment of *Boys to Men: Bill Clinton and the Boys Nation Class of 1963*, a documentary Welch researched, wrote, and produced as a freelancer

Photo by Daniel H. Forer

I also knew that I loved to teach but wouldn't want to return to high school since it wouldn't allow me to teach television writing. A return to college was in the cards for me—to train and gain the knowledge I required for this third (or was it fourth?) career.

I often tell people that my 40th birthday present to myself was a PhD, rather than a Porsche—and it has been the present that gained far more in value than a trophy car ever could. Since then, I've had the pleasure of giving notes to students writing specs for all of my favorite television shows. I've had the chance to write essays and book chapters—and whole books—about shows I love and the influence they've wielded in the world.

Do I miss being on a television staff? Sure. I have my down days. I was at a party a while back with several parents from my son's school, and I made a comment dismissing the life I was leading, dismissing myself. One of the other moms told me to reassess. Her husband had come to Los Angeles in a similar way (truck full of stuff—no connections) and had never sold any writing to Hollywood. She reminded me I had a page on IMDb, a stack of recordings of episodes that I'd written and helped produce, and I still had my house.

And she's right. I have all of those things. And more importantly, I have the opportunity to teach my students how to dream. The creativity I thought I'd miss in the writers' room I find every day in the classroom with my students.

Most stories culminate in a *crisis*, where a lead character makes a dramatic decision—followed by the *climax*, where the protagonist lives with the consequences of that decision. Most stories, though, don't end when the credits roll. They live on after the finale. Remember that, and you'll do just fine in your second—or third—or fourth act!

---

**DR. ROSANNE WELCH** teaches in the Master of Fine Arts in Screenwriting program at California State University Fullerton and in the Stephens College MFA in Screenwriting program. Her credits as a television writer/producer include *Beverly Hills 90210*, *Touched by an Angel*, and *ABC NEWS/NIGHTLINE*. Her research focuses on bringing attention to the work of screenwriters (authorship studies) and involves television programs such as *Doctor Who* and *The Monkees*, and films like *The Thin Man*, *Adam's Rib*, and *A Star is Born*. Welch's publications include *Torchwood Declassified: Investigating Mainstream Cult Television*, *Doctor Who and Race: An Anthology*, *Women in American History and Culture*, as well as articles in the *Journal of Screenwriting* and *The Los Angeles Times*.

Dr. Rosanne Welch

Photo by Douglas E. Welch

# STARTING OVER IN AMERICA
## From Writing to Directing and Back Again
▶ An Interview With Kirsten Sheridan

Kirsten Sheridan has directed three feature films: *Disco Pigs* (2001), *August Rush* (2007), and *Dollhouse* (2012). She co-wrote the Oscar-nominated screenplay *In America* (2002) with her sister, Naomi Sheridan, and her father, Jim Sheridan. In 2013, she moved with her family to Los Angeles to pursue a career in US television and features.

Kirsten Sheridan

Photo by Anthony Woods

After several moves from Ireland to the States and back again, Sheridan is accustomed to picking up and starting anew. She explains her most recent decision to move back to the United States, why she's choosing to stick with screenwriting over directing for now, and why she opened her acting studio in Ireland after *August Rush*. She also addresses the dynamics of working with and getting feedback from her father, the complicated business of casting films, and balancing family and career.

**You were an early bloomer, writing the script for *In America*. How old were you when you wrote that?**
I started as a teenager, but then we came back to it years later—maybe ten years later.

**Writer or director? Which do you identify with more?**
These days I think of myself more as a writer. I've recently chosen that I'm not going to direct stuff just because the time pressure is too great in directing. You can raise a family as a writer, you know? And I think it's just really challenging to

raise a family and direct. It has to be really worth it. I'm waiting for the story that's really worth it.

Kirsten is currently in development on her film *Amy Winehouse*, which she wrote and is scheduled to direct as well.

**Do you miss directing when you're not doing it?**
I feel like the whole basis of the story and also the tone of a story is dictated so early on, in the script, that really, I feel I write like a director. I tend to write visually. But I spent a lot of years in independent film, and I suppose when you're writing, you can dream—and when you're directing, you have to compromise and sacrifice every five minutes, you know? So the only real thing I enjoy about directing is the bond in working with the actors.

**And writing alone in a room—that can be a whole different strain sometimes. Or are you someone who craves that?**
Well, I do enjoy the more hermit-like distance of being a writer. I actually tend to write more in cafés. If I was in the house 24/7 it might get a little bit more isolated, you know? So I write after the kids go to school. It's basically nine until two-thirty every day.

**Every day?**
Usually, yes. At least when I have to turn something in. I spend a huge amount of time researching first—and then I start writing. Because my kids are in school all day, it means I have to be totally focused between those hours. I guess it probably helps to see other people working, too.

But I do enjoy working with people. I started an acting school in Ireland with some other film directors about four years ago now. And we started this new way of teaching with an amazing acting coach, Gerry Grennell, a guy who has this incredible kind of out-there philosophy in terms of acting. So for about a three-year period, I worked with actors almost every single day. It was amazing. So really I feel like it fed that part of my life. I didn't need to direct a film. I was getting a lot from working with these actors on a daily basis. It's a totally different animal to being on set in a pressurized, time-sensitive environment.

**So you started the school when? After *August Rush*?**
Right. I think what happened, I didn't realize that you probably have to jump on another film pretty quickly. You'd be smart to have your next film financed and ready as soon as your first one is out. But I didn't work that quickly, and everything I was trying to do after *August Rush*, it was smaller and European—and maybe I should have thought about jumping straight into an American project. I tried for quite a while, though, with my films in Ireland. But in the indie world, you can end up feeling like a horrible salesperson. You're all trying to get the same actors! I mean, the reality is, you've got a 0.1 percent chance, and so unless you've written something that speaks to them 100 percent and makes perfect sense for their career at that exact time, you have no hope in hell. So it's like, you write a script for a year for a 0.1 percent chance. I just couldn't do it after a while.

**What's fascinating to me about that is that *August Rush* was enormous. You were coming off this huge and beautiful movie.**
Well, it was pretty big in the sense that it was a $30 million budget, and we made back about $60 million, so it was a financial success. But it was a lot less of a critical success. Plus, I think at that time, with all the mega-movies, to have a $30 million movie was really in the middle ground. It wasn't edgy Sundance, and it wasn't Marvel comics Universal, so that's a very tricky middle ground, I think.

**So in a situation like that, is your father offering advice?**
Not so much. It's not even that he wouldn't offer advice—it's just that he finances his movies a certain way, or else he got offered a few in the last decade—you know, straight offers. So his experiences of getting a movie set up are quite different to mine.

And again, people would ask me at every film festival I would go to, do you think your dad can get a script to this actor and that actor? And then you're asking your own family to do what you hate doing yourself, getting through agents and hoping the top ten people will read, and it's just really cringey and embarrassing to have to work that way.

So I'm really not asking my dad to put in a phone call to another agent, you know? And besides, who says those ten actors are the top ten? Sales agents. But that doesn't mean anything really. You end up financing a film based on some bullshit numbers that make no sense. You don't have the freedom to just find the right actor. That's a huge reason why I want to work in TV.

**How did it affect you, growing up with a father with that status—especially when you were young? What was that like?**

He'd done theater for twenty years, and then once he got into the film business, he was successful almost overnight. It's just such a tough road, the theater. So that was a big shift for us as a family, because we also got money overnight. But I was still pretty young and kind of consumed with my own life in school, so his status didn't even hit me until around the Oscar time. I just kind of kept my head down and kept a low profile. Ireland is good that way.

## By the way . . .

Jim Sheridan was nominated for multiple Oscars for *My Left Foot* (1990) and *In the Name of the Father* (1993).

**Did your mother work when you were growing up?**

Yeah, she was a teacher for years when I was in grade school. And then when we moved back to Ireland and *My Left Foot* took off, she stopped working. But she was a teacher for years, which was pretty important for everyone actually, because she really knew how to deal with kids.

**How does your mother feel about your career?**

She's proud of all of her kids no matter what. My little sister's a teacher, and my older sister's a writer. My mom is the one in the family who's surrounded by writers, and I think she's also the one who's well able to clear the decks. If you're telling her a story, she'll be able to pick holes in it. She'll be like, hang on a second, now wait a second, go back, something's wrong there!

**Does she do any of her own writing?**

No. That's a good thing, in a way. She's very much in the real world. She's never wanted to be a writer—and I think if she had, that would have been really hard for her actually, to live that life alongside her husband. But it's funny, everyone in my family is either a teacher or a writer.

"I used to write screenplays in the way that I *thought* they should be written … and that puts you at a huge disadvantage, because you're writing a generic version of someone else's writing, who's writing a generic version of someone else's writing. So I think I've realized that it can take years to discover what you're about, what your truth is, and then apply it to your writing. It never stops."

**Writing with your father on *In America*, what was that like?**

My dad has such a particular point of view when it comes to writing. But then you also have to find your own truth. I would disagree with him a lot, nowadays too actually—and that's at times a thorn as well. But it's funny, because I used to write screenplays in the way that I *thought* they should be written. Growing up watching movies, you think things should happen a certain way, and then at some point, you realize that you're actually just taking a generic approach. And that puts you at a huge disadvantage, because you're writing a generic version of someone else's writing, who's writing a generic version of someone else's writing. So I think I've realized that it can take years to discover what you're about, what your truth is, and then apply it to your writing. It never stops.

**You say it puts you at a disadvantage—a disadvantage in the sense that your writing is less interesting to producers or backers because it's less authentic to you?**

That, and actually, really being clear and passionate about what you want to say, that's a big part of maturing as a writer. For me, I think that only crystalized when I moved back to America. Because when I was in Ireland, for whatever reason, I was very much an ostrich in the sand in terms of the world. I would never watch the news—it would just depress me, the feeling of helplessness. But I think since being here in America, I've started paying attention a bit more to things I want to speak up about. I'm letting those things feed my writing.

# The Writing Process

What does Sheridan's writing process look like? She says she tends to be attracted to real-life stories, because there are natural boundaries to work within. She researches for months before she writes, generally resulting in about 100 pages of notes. She gathers everything she can find about the subject or character or world, and then she writes full lines, images, and scene ideas. Once she starts writing pages, she can easily write ten pages a day, typically leading to two or three drafts before she turns in the script. With a commissioned script, she said, there's a danger in writing too many drafts—because that tends to mean that nobody had a clear idea of what the project was in the beginning. But this can also happen with her personal projects. As she said, some projects she'll put away and return to five years later and then realize it's about something completely different, so she goes down a different route with it.

**So let's talk about the actual day-to-day of screenwriting for a living. You write while the kids are in school, and then what? You pick them up and do the afterschool, dinner, bedtime routine? Are you able to write so intensely and then just put your story aside? Are you able to limit living in the world of your story to that five-hour period during the day?**

Yes, because I have no choice! When I pick up the kids from school, I'm honestly just bombarded with thoughts and questions. Sometimes my daughter's getting old enough now where she'll be able to talk to me about writing, and that's kind of fun. But other than that, you're just bombarded. I mean, like any writer, something will come to you at midnight, or smack bang while you're making dinner, but you have a family!

**Do you have friends in the industry? I'm curious if your industry relationships turn into friendships or vice versa.**

Both really. I think that's pretty much the case for everyone in the industry now. But being a working mom, it's mostly just work and children, work and family, that's it. Which is why not only do I not have time to go to those DGA and WGA things, I don't ever go anywhere. But I'm fine with that at the moment. I don't particularly feel like I need the social life I used to have. Even when I was in my 20s, I still had kids then, but I definitely had more of a social life. I think you just learn to prioritize when you get older—or you have to and you make your peace with it.

**And sometimes prioritizing means making a fresh start, packing up and moving to LA?**

Right, it does—or figuring out what you want to be doing and how you can build your life around it. But like I say, it's a winding road, but you find your voice eventually, if you're lucky. I mean, I still like the stories that I got interested in years ago, but I think, especially as a woman, you have to have a really, really clear voice. You certainly know what a Quentin Tarantino film is, you know what his personality is like through his films. And now I think I probably even know what a Kathryn Bigelow movie is. And that was huge, by the way. I think people don't talk about that enough—being the first female director to win. I think that was just unbelievably enormous, a huge moment really.

**She's telling stories that we don't typically see from a female director, but they're very clearly the stories she wants to tell.**

I think you have to write from a place of passion, something you're driven to write. This is what people see in your writing. For me, the things that really hit me after moving here was kids and guns and prescription drugs. Those two things just blew my mind. To think that there are 4-year-olds on Prozac blew my mind. So I started looking into it, probably because I knew that if anyone ever told me my kid needed Prozac, I'd have to leave the country. And the idea that my kids have to do lockdown drills because of a potential shooter—that is also mind-blowing to me. That is the biggest downside to living here. So it stemmed from a very personal reaction to a very real thing. And I guess the older I get, the more I think if I'm going to say something then I better say it loud and fast. Rather than searching for your voice, it's like, what are you actually passionate about? Then you'll find the rest. It will follow.

**So is this what you're writing about now? A piece about Prozac?**

I got a commission to write something about a mother and daughter, and I was able to take that idea and pitch it back to them focusing on prescription drugs—abuse in kids under the age of 10 in America. So in this case, I've been lucky to take their idea and match it with mine.

**You pitch a story back to them to match your interests—that takes a certain amount of confidence in owning your story, believing that your version of the story is better than the original, do you think? How did you develop that level of confidence?**

That's interesting, actually. I read a talk recently with Sheryl Sandberg, and she was saying that when she was in college with Mark Zuckerberg, people would say, how do you think you did on that test? And she was like, oh, you know, I'm not sure, I didn't study enough. And then they'd ask him, and he'd go, oh, I aced it, I just totally aced it. So it is a certain amount of self-confidence that we need to hold onto—this sense of, hang on a second, I'm not leaving the table, I'm here to stay. I think that's really important. And from my own point of view, you have to be even more aggressive with that as a woman. And yet being overtly aggressive is never fun, so it's quite a tough balance. I guess for me, it's really only recently that I got so passionate about things that it doesn't matter whether I feel I'm ready—this story has to be told, so let's get on with it. And then you're not worrying about self-image. You're just saying, let's do this.

**It's not a matter of promoting yourself—it's more about promoting this project.**
Yeah, exactly.

**So someone who wants to be a screenwriter, what advice do you have in terms of respecting your passion as a writer, owning your voice and story?**
What's become so clear to me is how strong of a voice you need to have. You really need to have something to say. And if you don't have something to say about a particular subject, then don't do it. Find the one thing that you're wildly passionate about, and work on that project. For women and minorities especially. And for women, not only is the playing field not level—10 percent of women get X amount, all of those horrendous statistics—but also the *content* of what gets made isn't level. The hero's journey is inherently a male journey. And it's been that way for thirty, fifty years, however long. So I think young women today, they need to take ownership of that and counter it in some ways. Write a new narrative for the heroine's journey.

# LIFE LESSONS IN WRITING FOR YOUNG AUDIENCES

## Wisdom From the Head Writer for *Sesame Street*

▸ An Interview With Lou Berger

Lou Berger joined the staff of the Children's Television Workshop to write for the *Sesame Street* series in 1988. He became head writer in 1998. Over the two decades that he was with the series, Lou received ten Emmy awards. He wrote the prime-time special *Sesame Street Stays Up Late*, an international New Year's Eve show; and co-writing with Judy Freudberg, he wrote the primetime special *The Street We Live On*, which was nom-

Lou Berger

Photo by Lily Field Berger

inated for a primetime Emmy for Outstanding Children's Program. Lou also received an Emmy song nomination for his work as lyricist on "The Street I Live On."

Lou was one of the creators of PBS's *Between the Lions*, he was one of two writers to launch PBS's *Reading Rainbow*, and he was head writer for Nickelodeon's *Pinwheel*. He is an alumnus of NYC's High School of Performing Arts, Hofstra University (he received a scholarship in acting), and Hunter College where he got his graduate degree in playwriting. He has received two John Golden Awards for playwriting, and in 1979, he was the recipient of a National Endowment for the Arts grant for playwriting.

Lou has taught as a guest professor for graduate playwriting at Hunter College, and he's been a seminar guest artist at NYU's Tisch School and Harvard University's School of Education to discuss writing for *Sesame Street*.

**Twenty years on *Sesame Street*. It's a unique situation for a screenwriter—to be with the same show for that many years.**

It was a crazy and wonderful time. I was very lucky to be there for what I call the Golden Age. It was a great group of people.

> "The fun of *Sesame Street* always was that if you wrote a show, you were invited to be on the set for the shoot with the Muppets and the characters. My first year was basically a combination of terror and joy, and then the terror got less and less, and the joy became more prevalent."

**I'd like to talk about your path to *Sesame Street*. What was your experience like at the High School of Performing Arts?**

It changed my life. I grew up in Brooklyn, and I was failing everything in junior high except English. But I would do comedy sketches for the talent show with my friends, the "Take It or Leave It Players," we called ourselves, and my guidance counselor suggested I go audition for the school. And I get there and all of a sudden I'm with these creative and talented people—music, theater, and dance majors. It was a new world to me. I was terrified the first year, but I suddenly had a whole vocabulary of theater and acting and reading plays and improvisation and being with the more offbeat kids. It was a great experience for me.

**Do you think it opened up your future in a way?**

Yes! It just was the right place for me to be. I also don't think I would have graduated from Erasmus Hall High School. And I'm serious about that. I would have been lost in a school with 8,000 kids. At Performing Arts, there were only 600 kids in the whole school, 120 kids in drama. So I had math teachers who would come into my homeroom to sit and tutor me because they wanted to get me through.

**One-on-one support.**

Right, and then the other thing I had later—many years later—was one-on-one time with a mentor. I was very fortunate because my mentor is a wonderful writer-director, Robert Benton. I worked in his office over the years.

Robert Benton wrote and directed *Kramer vs. Kramer* (1979), starring Dustin Hoffman and Meryl Streep. The film won five Oscars, including Best Director and Best Screenplay Based on Material from Another Medium.

**Robert Benton of *Kramer vs. Kramer*? That's incredible. When did you work for him?**

It was incredible. This was before I went to graduate school. My girlfriend at the time, now my wife, she was babysitting his son, and she helped make the introduction. She knew I wanted to be a writer, of course. But he's been a huge, kind influence in my life. He's somebody I can give my work to, so whenever I work on something, I'll send it over to get his feedback.

**What kind of work were you doing for him at the time?**

I was just typing. He was working, and I was typing. But he was one of the first people I would tell anecdotes to about my dad. And he said, "You should write a play," which ended up becoming the play that got me attention in graduate school.

**So you worked for him and then went to grad school. What was the play called?**

It was a play called *Show on the Road*. I went to graduate school at the University of Wisconsin, Madison, and their PBS station was WHA. They were looking to produce an original play, and I was there at just the right time. Somebody saw this little play that I'd written and said, "Would you like to rewrite it for television?" And I was taught to always say *yes*, so I did, and through the Communications department, the play was picked up nationally and won all sorts of awards. It was thrilling, because by the time it aired in 1978, I was back in New York and it was on Channel 13 right after Neil Simon's *The Good Doctor*.

**This was a play about your father?**

It was autobiographical, about me and my father when he used to drive me to the High School of Performing Arts, how private and embarrassed the son was by his father's endless curiosity about everything he was doing. It really was a very loving relationship. The producer cast me as my father. After my dad watched the teleplay, he was very touched. He said, "The only problem I have with this play is that I remember the son being more obnoxious."

I think of it every now and then. Sometimes you work on a project, and it's like catching the right wave—everything seems aligned. When I came back to New York, people had seen it, which helped break down the door to writing for television.

**Did you need an agent to get your first writing job?**
I finally got an agent, but I was very lucky. Because of the teleplay, I actually got a few phone calls, and one of them was from somebody at Children's Television Workshop who knew of a new network called Nickelodeon, and I got a job writing for a show called *Hocus Focus*, followed by the series *Pinwheel*, and I became the head writer for that. And then after that, I wrote for *Reading Rainbow*, and then *Sesame Street*.

**Did you know *Sesame Street* very well before you started working there?**
I'd watched the show when it first came on in 1969. And then I started watching again when my son was born in 1979, and I got there finally about a decade later. But when I watched it with my son, I remember thinking it would be the most wonderful show to write for, because it worked on two levels—it was warm, and it was funny.

**What was the setup in the beginning? What was a typical day for a staff writer?**
It was the most extraordinary place to be. It was what you hear idealistically about how you'd like to work. I joined a staff of twenty writers plus a wonderful head writer, Norman Stiles, and there were great people working there then—people like Jon Stone who was one of the creators; Jeff Moss, the brilliant writer-composer; the great producer Dulcy Singer; producer-director Lisa Simon; producer-animation coordinator Arlene Sherman; and the talented cast and Muppeteers. Great people!

The way *Sesame Street* worked was you were assigned a show and you were responsible for the whole hour, which meant that you wrote a street story, a Muppet insert, like a Bert and Ernie sketch or a Grover sketch, a few songs—you were responsible for that hour. And you would meet with Norman and kick ideas back and forth, and if he liked it, he'd say, give it a shot. Or you would just do it without talking to him at first. There was an enormous amount of freedom. And I was working with people I'd admired for years.

**Were you nervous your first year?**

I really felt the pressure of wanting to do well, but at the same time, the group was so much fun to work with. So my first year was basically a combination of terror and joy, and then the terror got less and less, and the joy became more prevalent. The fun of *Sesame Street* always was that if you wrote a show, you were invited to be on the set for the shoot with the Muppets and the characters.

**What was the expected timeline for writing one episode?**

You wrote as many over the season as you could, and it used to take me about three weeks to a month to do a show. It was a demanding show to write, and you would get rewrites all the time. Nobody ever handed in a show to *Sesame Street* and they would say, "Thank you, that's it." You would always get very interesting rewrite ideas.

**From Norman?**

From Norman, and then you would get notes later from production people— like, "What you want us to do is impossible. Is there another way to do that?"

**Did you have an office at the time?**

No, not in the beginning. My office was at home. Most days when I was a staff writer, I would get up in the morning, go out for coffee, and come back to the house and write my show. I had to have a feeling that I had a real job, so I had to be very strict about it. I like writing in the mornings. And then I would go into the city for meetings—1 Lincoln Plaza, across the street from Lincoln Center. I really looked forward to the meetings, because you spend a lot of time in your head as a writer, and it's good to go out and meet with other people who are doing it.

**How did it work when you wrote the songs? Did you write the lyrics and collaborate with a composer?**

Well, I would write the lyrics first in my house. There was a small group of terrific composers at *Sesame Street*, people like Chris Cerf and Stephen Lawrence, and they would match the lyrics to the composer that they felt was right for it. So if I was working with Stephen on a song, I'd go to his apartment where he had a studio, and he'd play the music for me, and then we'd go back and forth. When I was head writer, I had a piano in my office—I had an office as head writer—so the music director would come in and mess around and play music. I loved that part of it, working with the composers and the musicians.

**The collaborative nature of it?**

I was always that way. As head writer, I liked to have meetings in the office one-on-one with writers. I wasn't a big one for emails. We used to have somebody in the music department—he was about twenty feet from my office, and he would email me, and I'd never answer him. And when he'd say, "Why won't you answer my emails?" I'd say, "Why don't you just come in and talk? It's an old-fashioned thing, but we'll get stuff done." There's something about sitting in an office writing a show like *Sesame Street*, or other shows—sitting at a table, sometimes what's not being said is important, facial expressions and rhythm. Most of the time writers wanted to come and see me in my office.

**Did you outline the shows first? As a group? As individual writers?**

I had writers who liked to outline. There were a handful of writers who would ask if they could do an outline first, and the answer was always, "Of course, whatever makes you comfortable." And we'd look at the outline together and talk it through. But other writers really wanted to go to draft first. They wanted the freedom to write.

I'm the sort that it was hard for me to outline, because once I outlined, I lost interest. I wanted the freedom of writing it first and not talking it through. One of the things I used to talk about as head writer was scenic routes—that sometimes you're writing, and all of a sudden you go off someplace you didn't expect, and my feeling was, don't get nervous about that! It's a scenic route. You can always get back to the main highway, but there might be something there, and you can't know unless you're writing.

**Being a head writer for so long, what would you say makes for a writer that you want to keep on staff or move up, as compared to a writer that isn't working as well?**

Well, all writers aren't created equal. On any staff, there's always going to be people who are just more gifted, for whatever reason, and at *Sesame Street* we had a handful of extraordinarily gifted writers. Besides the talent and humor, which is very hard to define, all of the great writers I've worked with share one thing—when they write a script, they're invested in it moment to moment. There are no gratuitous moments, not even in a Bert and Ernie scene. There are some writers who basically give you an outline even in their draft, and you don't quite believe that the scene is really unfolding.

**As compared to the great writers?**

Who moment to moment invest in it with energy and a sense of listening to the characters. And they always surprise you. It always goes in a direction that's a little bit different, because it's not just an exercise. The people I want to work with, they're constantly questioning, constantly looking at the script. One of the great writers at *Sesame Street*, who passed away recently and was one of my great friends, was Judy Freudberg. Judy was great at that. We'd all be talking, and then suddenly, she would stop and say, "Hold on, hold on. This moment here, I don't believe the way it's happening. It's too easy." And sometimes you couldn't define what it was, but then you'd talk it through, and she'd be right. It's a moment-to-moment investment of energy in the writing.

**What about the way a writer interacts with you or with other staff? Did some work better or worse than others?**

It's interesting, but it's very important that a group of writers can sit in a room together. There's something in the chemistry—again, something hard to define. And you're looking for people who aren't afraid to rewrite. You have to be able to take notes and not argue about them too much. But what Norman wanted—and I did too—was a shared sensibility in terms of comedy. It was the idea that *Sesame Street* was a community, and we wanted a writing staff that could work together and rewrite, rewrite, rewrite if they were asked.

**Did you rewrite each other, or just your own episodes?**

You rewrote your own episodes, but at meetings, we used to sometimes say, "Is anybody working on a script that's having a problem? Do you want to throw it out to the writers?" And everybody felt very good about that.

> "Target where it is that you think you'd most love to work, and figure out how to get there. Do you want to work on a television show? For a movie producer who produces films you love? Okay, then do that thing where you say, 'Do I know anybody who knows somebody who can get somebody to read it?' I don't know any more practical advice than that."

**So it was a good working group.**

It was. And also there was shared credit. *Sesame Street* had a credit roll of all the writers. There was no individual show credit. Now, if you wanted to submit something for a Writers Guild Award, then you could submit an individual show. But even when we were nominated for Emmys, it was a group award, because we were all credited for the whole show.

**Why did you decide to leave the show when you did?**

Well, by 2008, the show had changed. It went from 100 shows a season when I came on as staff writer, down to sixty-five, then down to fifty, and finally they cut it to twenty-six shows in the end. One of the great things about *Sesame Street* was that you always felt good about writing for a rich curriculum—you really were teaching. And with 100 shows, that curriculum book, it used to be huge. It used to be a curriculum-based show.

**With fewer shows, was there a sense that each show was more precious?**

Yes, when we got down to so few shows, with the original producers gone, there was an attitude then of not taking risks. It's a philosophical thing, but I believe very strongly that when you're studying writing or acting or music, whatever, one of the things that a good professor teaches you is not to be afraid to fall on your face. You can't be scared to go down one of the scenic routes, because it's on that route that you might come up with something that's never been done before. It may not work, but it might.

So it was time for me to leave. What was very hard was that I left behind some extraordinarily wonderful writer friends. But I wanted to do other writing—writing books and working on some theater pieces. It was time.

**Any final advice for aspiring writers?**

You always feel a little uncertain giving anybody advice, but if I had to say, there are two things—one is to first do the work. Have something to show people. It's not enough to just come in and say, "This is what I want to do." I've had people come meet me at *Sesame Street*, and they'd say, "I know I can do this." And you ask them to show you something, but they don't really have anything to show. So do the writing, do the work. That's number one.

The other thing is really the most practical, because it works—and it's the six degrees of separation. Target where it is that you think you'd most love to work, and figure out how to get there. Do you want to work on a television show? For a movie producer who produces films you love? Okay, then do that thing where you say, "Do I know anybody who knows somebody who can get somebody to read it?" I don't know any more practical advice than that. We tend to know people who know people, but that takes a bit of detective work.

**What about the idea that it might be perceived as rude to ask for help, or to ask people to introduce you to someone?**

I don't agree with that. You have to choose the people who will take you seriously. Listen, when I was head writer, my assistant would come in and say so-and-so is on the phone again asking about a writing job, or we got another letter from so-and-so—and I remember taking those people very seriously. We had so few jobs, and we weren't auditioning, so if I looked at the résumé and saw an interesting person on paper, or if somebody said to me, you have to meet this person, then I would meet them—and if they'd done the work, if they had something good to show, then I would ask my assistant keep this one on file. Because things do open up.

People can be more receptive than you might think. You should never feel like you're bothering anybody, unless you really are bothering them. But you should know when you are. So make that call to somebody if you think you have something worthwhile to show. That's not a bad thing.

**Did you call Robert Benton initially?**

I made the phone call, and I thought I'd be bothering him, and I must have stuttered through the whole thing. But he said, "No, send me a script. Send me something." And I had something to send him. And this was the amazing thing. He invited me to his home, poured me a glass of wine, and he said, "Now I'm going to tell you what I think of your work. I think you're very talented, but do you mind if I take it apart for you?" And we then spent the rest of the night dismantling what I wrote. It was one of the great lessons I ever had.

**I can imagine! So what are you working on now?**

I have two plays, both musicals. I was telling my wife Lily this the other day—when I was 9 years old, I had an extraordinary teacher, Mrs. Kosakowski. And Mrs. Kosakowski would walk around the classroom and put her finger on you making prophetic declarations, and she said to me, "You're a writer. Go to the back of the classroom and write a play." Then she'd say to another kid, "You're an inventor. Invent something." This was after the first few months of getting to know the kids. So I wrote a play when I was 9, *Boo-Boo the Happy–Sad Clown* (a tragi-comedy!), and it was put on for the whole school. And I remember realizing, wow, I like doing this. And now it's what I'm doing every day. I'm going back to writing plays that I hope are for kids and their parents.

## Full Circle

Lou wrote as a child—he wrote for children, and now he's writing with his children.

**What are the next steps in terms of putting up your shows?**

Well, for one of them, a musical, my son Spencer is writing the music. He happens to be a brilliant composer. He has his own band, which he writes the songs for and is the lead singer. When Spencer was 9, he sang in the children's chorus at the Metropolitan Opera. He's written astonishingly beautiful melodies for the musical.

**Is this the first time you've collaborated with your son?**

Yes, and it's been a joy. There is lots of bouncing around of ideas, and we both, fortunately, feel that we can say exactly what's on our mind.

**So it has really come full circle. Your play that got you attention in the beginning was about you and your father, and now you're working with your son.**

Isn't it something? And also, I still seek feedback from my daughter Elizabeth, who's a remarkably gifted writer-producer for television and film, as well as a produced playwright. When she was little, she'd sometimes sit next to me while I was writing *Sesame Street*, and as I wrote a scene, I'd read it to her. I remember her once telling me, "I don't think Big Bird would say that." I asked her, "What would Big Bird say?" and we went back and forth and arrived at a compromise. I'm still getting helpful notes! I'm very lucky—my kids and my wife are very perceptive and insightful audiences.

**Is your routine the same? Do you still get a cup of coffee and come back home to write?**

Exactly the same. I haven't changed since I was 9. It's unfortunate in many ways!

**Are you sending your work to Robert Benton now?**

I sent him my last book *Dream Dog*, published by Random House. And happily, he loved it.

# INDEX

**Anna Weinstein** is the Series Editor for PERFORM. A writer and editor with over fifteen years of experience in educational publishing, she received her MFA in Writing for the Performing Arts from the University of California at Riverside–Palm Desert and her BA in Communication Studies/Performance from the University of North Carolina at Chapel Hill. She teaches introductory and advanced screenwriting at Auburn University, and she is a frequent contributor to *Film International*, where she publishes interviews with award-winning female directors in her series "Diva Directors Around the Globe."